Rancho Cooking

Mexican and Californian Recipes

Jacqueline Higuera McMahan

SASQUATCH BOOKS
SEATTLE

Printed in the United States of America
Distributed in Canada by Raincoast Books, Ltd.
07 06 05 04 03 02 01   5 4 3 2 1

Cover and interior color photographs: Caroline Kopp
Cover and interior design: Karen Schober
Composition: Justine Matthies
Black and white interior photographs: Courtesy of Jacqueline Higuera McMahan
Copy editor: Susan Derecskey
Proofreader: Sigrid Asmus
Indexer: Miriam Bulmer

Library of Congress Cataloging in Publication Data
McMahan, Jacqueline Higuera
        Rancho cooking : Mexican and Californian recipes / by Jacqueline Higuera McMahan.
               p.   cm.
        Includes bibliographical references and index.
        ISBN 1-57061-242-0
        1. Cookery, Mexican. 2. Cookery, American—California style. I. Title.

TX716.M4 M395 2001
641.5972—dc21   00-052259

Sasquatch Books
615 Second Avenue
Seattle, Washington 98104
(206) 467-4300
www.SasquatchBooks.com
books@SasquatchBooks.com

Rancho
Cooking

a

contents

recipe list

Acknowledgments

I owe the deepest gratitude to the Higuera and Chavarria cooks, whose oral history of recipes evolved into my kitchen. Were it not for my family's love of the table, these recipes could not have survived. My gratitude also extends to my husband, Robert McMahan, who has come to love rancho food as much as or even more than almost anyone. It is great to love someone whose persistence is a match for your own. And to my sons, Ian and O'Reilly McMahan, who were weaned on chiles and who have never flinched. To Tracy McMahan, freshly married into this family and already up to Red Enchilada breakfasts. To Jeff Chavarria (The Asador) and his wife, Gretchen, for continuing the quest for the perfect barbecue. To my brother, Alan, for keeping the palilli tradition alive. To my late father, Bill, who single-handedly saved the Spanish oregano. To my cousin, Debbie Santos Drummond, for her love of history, her loan of old photographs, and her lucid memory of the dove story. To Uncle William Chavarria for his stories and who, at eighty-eight, is an impeccable Spanish gentleman. To all of the Santa Barbara *descendientes*—Miguel Acosta, Isabel Robles Cordero, Elizabeth Erro Hvolboll, and Arnold and Colleen Robles, who have given me their family recipes and their hospitality. To the late Father Maynard Geigor, once the venerable scholar of Mission Santa Barbara, who first inspired me over twenty years ago when he unlocked a cabinet containing the precious letters of the de la Guerra family. To Jim Norris, the erudite historian who saved me. To Patricia Hinds, for finding me the best pure masa and chiles in Santa Barbara. To Kendra Racouillat, for Chocolate Sundays and helping test recipes. To Mary Stec for finding late squash blossoms in October and giving me other exotic ingredients while helping test recipes. To the incomparable Caroline Kopp, for trying so diligently to capture the vision of rancho food and succeeding so well, with the assistance of Mary Stec and her impromptu food styling. To my agent, Martha Casselman, for her talent and sensitivity to the rancho lore, and to my editor, Jennie McDonald, whose steadfast belief and friendship kept my nose to the *molcajete*. To Gary Luke at Sasquatch, for being at Sasquatch, along with Justine Matthies and Karen Schober for their attention to detail. To the cooks who have inspired me—Marion Cunningham, Rick Bayless, Zarela Martinez, Beth Hensperger, and Cheryl and Bill Jamison, and lastly, to my mother, Marie, and my grandmother, Della, who instilled a passion for cooking, for making the kitchen the best room in the house, for savoring one's food, and for never, never standing up while eating.

El Principio: The Beginning

AN ISLAND CALLED CALIFORNIA

Across the Bay from Yerba Buena, as San Francisco was still called in the nineteenth century, they gathered at the long table in the rancho's dining room. Supper was the usual cups of chocolate and *biscochuelos*. Dusk had snuffed out the last rays of light penetrating the deep window and someone had already lit the candles in the iron chandelier high above the table. They heard the flutter of wings. A white dove circled above them and then suddenly flew through the flames of the candles, extinguishing them in her passage. No one spoke as the bird disappeared in the darkness. In a heart-beat, the dove returned to fly back through the candles, restoring the flames, then disappearing for the last time.

They all knew, my family, that the dove was an omen. Something was coming; they should not be afraid. They had always been respectful of omens. The year was 1846, just before the U.S. Government took over California from Mexico, Spain having lost its dominion over California in 1821. It was three years before the Gold Rush but the lush land and natural harbors were already calling a siren song to foreigners. My family and other Californios could not have known that the pastoral life they had come to love was soon to be changed forever. They were fifty years behind in their attire, not having been exposed to any major center of civilization, and they were naive in their assumption about their isolation. But the Californios had accomplished one thing: They made California look like paradise to the rest of the world.

California was once as isolated as the imaginary island from which it took its name. No one came here before almost dying from hardship and near starvation. And most did—except the Spaniards who accompanied Captain Juan Bautista de Anza on the expedition from Mexico. My great-great-great grandfather, Ignacio Higuera, passed the test of survival along with his fellow *soldados de cuera* and citizen colonists. They saw their survival as a sign that they were meant to be here. With remarkable opti-mism they overlooked the way they had to live—by campfire with spare rations of boiled *carne seca* and *frijoles*. It was to pass, this discomfort.

For a while, they were left to themselves with only Franciscan padres and native Indians within the island of California. They planted olive trees, fig trees, orange trees, pomegranates, and vineyards all in the image of mother Spain, to whom they clung tenaciously like adopted children. Their allowance was a fraction of what was needed to develop California. Nevertheless, after serving for years as a soldier, a man might be granted thousands of acres of the most beautiful land—far more beautiful to their eyes than the Sinaloa or Sonoran desert they had left in Mexico.

When José Loreto Higuera, Ignacio's son, rode through the valley of Santa Clara, he knew he wanted his rancho to be along the *contra costa*, or eastern shore, of San Francisco Bay, where oaks provided shade and lupine was as thick as an oriental car-pet. The mustard grew so tall a horseman could tie the grasses above his horse's head.

After thirty-five years of service, José was granted almost four thousand acres, considered modest by land-grant standards but lavish to him. His grant, one of the last Spanish grants, was issued in 1821, just before Mexico not only declared independence from Spain but also renounced the ownership of California.

José Loreto's land grant stretched from the southeastern shores of the Bay, and up over the low-lying Diablo mountains. Grizzly bears tramped through the area on their way to the marshy shore, where they dug for their favorite food, the juicy roots of young tules. Rancho Los Tularcitos, named because of its proximity to this marshland, was the unofficial mecca for grizzlies during the early years.

Upon entering the rancho domain, you passed the sycamore tree that was part of the old boundary line and then rode your horse down the long sweep of the olive grove that became known as The Lane. As soon as you rode out of the shady Lane, the bright sunlight forced the undulating hills upon you. The rancho pushed against the protection of the velvety rise of foothills at its back. During the rainy months, small streams ran through the hills all the way to the inland sea. Near the main adobe, Calera Creek often rose up the banks of the *arroyo*, once the site of the rancho's own gristmill. The millstones still lie buried within the river banks.

Adobe walls, ancient ruins by the twentieth century, enclosed the living area of the rancho—the adobe home, numerous adobe outbuildings, the vineyard, the orchard, the kitchen garden, the water tower, and corrals. In some spots, as much as thirteen feet of prickly pear cactus backed up to the wall. Trespassers, such as bears, were discouraged if not by the wall then by the threat of the cactus, which also served as the world's only edible fencing.

As if that weren't enough to deter intruders, the foundation of the main adobe house was sunk three feet below ground, affording more protection during onslaughts from bandits or Indians. The original rectangular adobe, large enough to house all of José Loreto's eighteen children, was built in 1829, and it was from then until well after the Gold Rush that bands of dissident Indians raided ranchos. José's father, Ignacio Higuera, had been violently assassinated by Indians when he, in his role as majordomo, accompanied Mission San José's padre to a remote village to administer to sick Indians. The fear of an Indian attack was realized on a night in 1850, when a whole carriage of visitors was slaughtered in The Lane.

Understandably, ranchos had some fortress qualities—for good reason. The high adobe walls, the deep windows with thick shutters, and the cactus fence gave the illusion of security. In reality, the rancheros spent more time thinking of how to be hospitable.

They preferred to be sitting in the arbor rather than within protected walls. As Rancho Los Tularcitos grew old and near its end, certain features seemed never to change. The mile-long Lane remained, like a regal dowager. The gnarled pear trees along the creek, the cactus fencing, almost indestructible, and the century-old fig tree, whose arched branches had dug in and rooted, throwing up a thicket of little fig trees until an eighty-foot bower created a perfect place for children to hide from bears and ghosts.

The old fig, one of the first fruits brought to California, was near the adobe ranch house; it was one of the first trees you came upon, and it was the last to die, within a few months of the rancho being lost by the Higueras. The fig, part of the Spanish past, was almost as holy as the olive. The things the Californios loved the most—the olive, the fig, and the chile—persisted longest in their survival.

THE MISSIONS

From 1776 to 1821, while the continent of Europe was changing, a few hundred Spanish soldiers, colonists, and Franciscan priests set about the transformation of California. The chain of twenty-one missions they eventually established were the last outposts of the Spanish Empire. They epitomized what could be wrought upon a wilderness when the sword and the cross came together. Half of the known world belonged to the Spanish Crown, and Spain wanted to extend its roots into California, an uncivilized place. Twenty-four years before the first mission was established, a map printed in England still showed California as an island. While this remote island was seen as barbaric, Spain moved in. The missions were the beachhead.

All twenty-one missions, begun with San Diego in 1769 at a starvation level, were thriving by the end of the eighteenth century. Many of the padres, often educated men, were botanical experts who cleverly sent for root cuttings that were environmentally suited for California's climate—a duplicate of the known familiar climate of the Iberian peninsula. If a mission did not resemble a factory, it resembled a far-flung rancho or a small city. It wasn't until the early nineteenth century that there were many land-grant ranchos; and all life revolved around the mission and the *presidio*. Each mission had its claim to fame, depending on its setting and the personality of the padre in charge. San Gabriel became known for its fine wine, San José for Indian music, San Fernando for cattle raising and the lucrative hide and tallow trade, and San Francisco for its rebellious converts.

In a sense, the missions' very success helped bring about their demise. Their prime locations near harbors were coveted, their rich land desired, their industry and even their precious religious relics were seen as valuable collectibles. Then, secularization, begun by Mexico in 1831, sealed the fate of the missions. They were no longer needed nor wanted.

THE CALIFORNIOS

The Californios, the soldiers and colonists remaining in California, met the same fate as the missions. They came, they established the Spanish Empire's last outpost, and they were tantalized with offerings of land that seemed to be endless. And then the roles they played were no longer necessary. The era they belonged to existed in romantic memories, the tales of the storytellers. Their ranchos, like the missions, were on the richest coastal land, the land eventually desired by the *extranjeros*.

The isolation of the Californios lasted just long enough to allow certain quirks to develop. They had their own colloquialisms, their own style of dance, their own Spanish titles of don and doña, and their own style of food.

The spoken tongue was Spanish and was considered by those speaking it to be the language of God. English, only spoken by foreigners, seemed rough to the ear and was deemed the idiom of birds. The Californios were suspicious of foreigners, who accepted their hospitality and then took the whole bowl of silver coins left for guests to use discriminately as needed. Foreigners took advantage of their hospitality. Historians of the day noted how lazy the Californios were for not building roads and bridges, an obvious lack of Yankee industry. More important to the Californios was the ritual of life. The huge gap between the Californio gracious pace of life and the incoming foreigners' way of life was widening.

The movement of the settlers into the West came upon California like the fog that still sneaks into the alleyways of San Francisco, penetrating every space. Trails were cut. Ships found better routes to the Pacific Coast. Gold was struck in the placid hills. The Californios did not have the luxury of time to adapt to the lifestyle preferred by New Englanders and other foreigners. Word quickly spread around the world that streets in California were paved in gold. Gold had never impressed the Californios, who had been known to use gold nuggets the size of footballs as doorstops.

Rancho Los Tularcitos was inhabited by the Higuera family and their *descendientes* for almost 130 years. By the onset of the twentieth century, the original land grant was reduced to a fifteen-acre plot hanging by the thread of The Lane of olive trees.

The family still gathered its forces at the communal table, like the old dons they professed to be, feeding off the tales as much as the food they came to be known for. Each storyteller put in his own *cuchara*, or spoon, and the tales spun like a web encircling them. Each cook became famous in her or his own way: Grandmama for her chileña pie; Mama for her red enchiladas and thick rancho frijoles and pies; Aunt Nicolassa for her exquisite pastries; Aunt Emma for her flour tortillas; the renowned *asadors* for their barbecues.

A story can be told in two ways: The way it happened or the way it is remembered. The first way is favored by written tradition and the second by long oral tradition. The storytellers were here first and could relate the meaning of the dove. Within this volume, as you might have guessed, the storyteller has the favored spot at the table and what we cannot tell you, we will feed you.

¡Buen Provecho!

Authentic California Rancho Cuisine

To understand California's rancho cuisine, one needs to take into consideration both Mexico and Spain as they were in those early years. Historically, the Spaniards were great borrowers. They had even borrowed from their Moorish invaders. When the Spaniards conquered Mexico in 1519, they either had to borrow Indian foods or starve to death. They adopted four prime Mexican ingredients: tomatoes, chiles, corn, and chocolate.

The story of Mexican cuisine is that of the Aztec and other Indian foods embellished by the Spanish conquerors and then given Spanish names. More than two hundred years went by and this blend of foods was carried north into Spanish territories. The *soldados de cuera*, sent to colonize California, were given meager rations and told that they were "dining with the King." In the end, the Spanish King turned out to be a cheapskate, providing only bare essentials.

Many plants familiar from Spain were grown by the Californios, thanks to the botanical knowledge of the Spanish padres, who recognized the similarity between the California coast and much of Spain. But the settlers also hungered for the things they had learned to love in Mexico: the tomatoes, chiles, squash, pumpkins, and corn. The blend of Spanish and Mexican merged into Californian. In time, the Californios, particularly the rancheros, thought of their style—and themselves—as a separate one.

CALIFORNIO FAVORITES

Barbecuing came into its own on the ranchos; it was the only way of cooking for celebrations or feasts. Its perfection became the calling of a new breed, the *asador*.

Olive oil was used lavishly for cooking, anointing vegetables and marinating meats to be barbecued. On the ranchos, olive oil was preferred over lard except when making tortillas and tamales.

Fresh herbs such as sweet basil, Italian parsley, cilantro, bay leaves, mint, oregano, and wild marjoram (called Spanish oregano by the Californios) were greatly appreciated. All the ranchos and missions had herb gardens. Black pepper, cumin, and red chile were favorite seasonings.

Flour tortillas were favored over corn tortillas probably because most of the Californios had come up from Sinaloa and Sonora where wheat, which had been introduced into Mexico by the Spaniards in the sixteenth century, had been favored over corn as a crop.

Often in this book, I use a combination of English and Spanish in a recipe title, such as Red Enchilada. It is a good example of how the culture and the cuisine are a blend. The recipes here are representative of our rancho family who, luckily for us, very much enjoyed eating and cooking. Recipes were preserved in my family by word of mouth and use. As long as a dish is cooked, it won't be lost. Many other recipes were given to me by *descendientes* from other rancho families. At times, I have taken liberties with old recipes, for example reducing the prodigious amounts of extra virgin olive oil favored by Grandmama and other cooks of the past. I have relied on modern conveniences like the food processor and many other pieces of equipment to ease labor in the kitchen. In all recipes, I have drawn for inspiration on both my rancho foundation and the four and a half years my husband and I lived in Mexico. My passion for the chipotle chile is just a small example of my love of Mexican cuisine and my appreciation for how it reawakened my interest in rancho cuisine.

In the end, the cooking I prefer can be gathered into a traveling enchilada. Where it came from and where it ended up is not as important as how it tastes.

—*Jacqueline Higuera McMahan*

chiles

THE HEART OF THE CUISINE

chiles are in our

blood, my grandmother told me when I was very small. I pictured rivers of dark chile flowing in our veins. Within the family fold, a love of chiles was expected. When I tasted a particularly hot sarsa and didn't flinch, I saw my grandfather looking at me in a proud way. I was only five. This bond with chiles goes back a long way. All the way to the Valley of Mexico.

The Spanish colonists who came up the trail from Mexico to help settle California brought red chiles and tortillas, which had become most favored ingredients along with the chocolate rations.

The Spaniards entered the Valley of Mexico in 1521 and took to chiles as though they had been born eating them. The Aztecs succumbed to the conquerors who in turn succumbed to the foods of the conquered. One of the greatest exchanges of the world's ingredients took place. Chiles captivated the Spaniards more than any other New World ingredient. They soon spread the gospel around the world as sailing ships went far away with chiles and their seeds as precious cargo.

More than 250 years after the Conquest of Mexico, when the descendants of the conquistadors went forth to colonize California, they had chiles in their saddlebags. You could follow their path northward into California, Arizona, and New Mexico by the chile plants left in their wake. My great-great-great grandfather followed that trail, along with the Anza party, and so we blame him for our life-long affair with chiles.

My earliest food memory is of the pungent smell of my grandmother's kitchen. Chile was so thick in the air you could taste it by just taking a breath.

When I smell chile being puréed or cooked, a hunger comes over me as soon as the primal scent hits my nostrils. I don't remember a time when I didn't smell chile. It was in all the kitchens where I grew up. Every house I live in will eventually absorb the fragrance of chiles into its walls. I have heard that bakers' kitchens are imbued with yeast spores, but mine has chile spores, of this I am sure. My sons have told me that the scent of burning chiles is the smell of home.

Distinguishing the Types of Dried Red Chiles

Cooking with chiles is easier than you may think, requiring simple steps that you can intersperse with other chores. This listing of chiles is not meant to be exhaustive but just of the chiles frequently used in the recipes in this book. Get to know what chiles are available in your area. I send for many of my favorite chiles through mail-order sources, and during chile season, normally from August to October, I have fresh green and red chiles shipped by two-day air from farms in New Mexico. You identify chiles as much by color, shape, and size as by name. Often you cannot depend upon the names given. Chiles are frequently given whimsical names in different places.

California Chile: A brownish-red dried chile with a shiny skin. (This chile is known as the Anaheim when fresh and green.) It was called *chile colorado* (red chile) by the early settlers and mission fathers of California. The mild California chile, raised commercially on a huge scale and most often oven-dried, is a distant relative of the red chile brought up from Mexico. I use the California chile only with the New Mexican, guajillo, and ancho chiles, to add a needed flavor boost. These are often found in supermarkets, in cellophane packets.

New Mexican Chile: A type of chile grown in New Mexico, similar in shape to the California chile but with more flavor and heat. If you order from a chile farm in New Mexico, you will be asked if you want the 6-4 (mild), the Big Jim (large, thicker, and very mild), Barker (hot), or the Sandía (very, very hot). Just know that what New Mexicans describe as mild may not be what you describe as mild. Also, chile heat varies depending on the weather, the rain, and the mound of dirt where the chiles were grown. I like to use the dried Barker chile tamed with a couple of ancho chiles for Red Chile Sauce. Standard, commercial New Mexican chiles are found in supermarkets in cellophane packets, but they are never as good as the ones shipped from chile farms or those we purchase in specialty stores that carry mainly chile products.

Ancho Chile: A large, heart-shape chile with a deep brownish-red color and a wrinkled appearance. It is the dried version of the poblano (often called the pasilla in California), mild and sweetish, often compared to raisins because of its fruitiness. Occasionally ancho is picante hot. Because of its thick flesh, the ancho gives an incomparable richness and body to sauces. In Mexico—and in my kitchen—it is the favorite chile. These are often found in supermarkets in cellophane packets.

Pasilla Negro or Pasilla Chile: A long, slender, and almost black Mexican chile. The pasilla gives the characteristic black ochre color to traditional mole poblano. These chiles are sometimes called just pasillas or just negros, so look more for their long, narrow shape. These are found in Mexican grocery stores but rarely in supermarkets. Mail-order houses such as Pendery's of Texas (see page 223) are a reliable source.

Mulato Chile: This chile is the same shape as the ancho but darker brown and less wrinkly. It is difficult to tell the two apart unless they are side by side. It is always required in classic mole recipes. Search for the mulato chile in Mexican grocery stores or mercados.

Guajillo Chile: A smooth, shiny, light red chile with the same shape as the California or New Mexican chile but shorter. It is usually hot with nutty overtones. I like to use a couple of the guajillos in my sauces to add depth of flavor. These are available by mail order or in Mexican stores.

Chipotle Chile: The smoked version of the ripe (red) jalapeño. The jalapeño's thick flesh is difficult to air-dry, making it perfect to dry by smoking over low field fires or in pits. A couple of California ranches are now smoke-drying their own chipotles (see page 223). Depending on the type of fuel used for the smoking process, the chipotle's flavor will vary. Chipotle chiles become more than a chile, they become a mysterious spice when added to foods. The chipotle is probably my favorite small chile. It is available dried in Mexican stores, by mail order, and from local farmers' markets. You can also buy chipotles reconstituted in adobo sauce in small cans. I am never without a can of chipotles en adobo for emergencies. Herdez is a good brand.

Distinguishing the Types of Fresh Green Chiles

The listing below does not include the full variety of fresh chiles now available in many places, particularly those with large Hispanic populations, but includes those chiles favored in rancho cooking. They are generally available in supermarkets.

Long Green Chiles or Anaheims: A type of long green chile grown by the early Californios and harvested in the summer for some dishes like rellenos. They really preferred to let the chile turn red so they could dry it and use it in sauces. Much of the green chile's flavor lies beneath the skin, so when you char it over a flame the flavor is enhanced by the caramelization. Steam the charred chile under a wet paper towel for ten minutes and then slip off the skin.

New Mexican Green Chile: Many types exist, in all gradations of heat. These chiles look similar to the Anaheim but have considerably more flavor and fire. The Barker and the Sandía, when fresh, are very hot. When dried and used for making Red Chile Sauce, their heat can be tempered with milder chiles like the ancho. All fresh New Mexican chiles need to be sent for by mail order (see page 223).

Poblano Chile: The heart-shaped, favorite chile of Mexico. The poblano is thicker walled than the Anaheim green chile, with a rich flavor, making it the perfect chile for stuffing. This is also the chile typically used for *rajas,* strips of chile sautéed with onion and cheese and used for garnishing grilled meats. Char poblanos over a flame or on the little asador grill that is made to fit over a stove burner. Steam the charred chiles under wet paper towels for ten minutes to loosen the skins. Rub off the skins with the paper towel.

Jalapeño, Serrano, and Güero Chiles: The typical salsa chiles. The serrano is as big as your little finger and a bit hotter than the jalapeño. I love to char the jalapeño just for the burnt flavor. When using the serrano, I never bother to seed it; I just slice and mince. To easily remove a jalapeño chile from its seed core, just stand it on its tip. Use a sharp paring knife to cut down the sides of the chile, from stem to tip. You should end up with just the seed core clinging to the stem. Cut the chile flesh into strips and then mince. One of our favorite salsas now is made of blackened plum tomatoes, charred jalapeños, a charred onion, a couple of cloves of garlic, a fistful of cilantro, and salt. Purée in a food processor and you will have a wickedly good and simple salsa. The güero is a pale lime-green chile usually found in supermarkets. It's very hot, and comparable with the jalapeño, but thinner-walled. It's about the same size as the jalapeño and can be used in place of it.

red chile sauce

✕✕✕

The foundation of many of the Spanish California and rancho dishes was the sauce made from red chiles that were allowed to ripen on the vine and then picked in the autumn months. The red chiles would be strung out on poles to dry in the sun and then carried into adobe sheds at night when the damp fogs drifted in from San Francisco Bay. Red Chile Sauce was the pride of the kitchen and used for the famous Red Enchiladas. This sauce distinguishes itself by the toasted flour roux used to deepen the flavors and the tiny bit of vinegar used to sweeten the chile.

I have found that steaming dried chiles, as opposed to soaking them in boiling water, preserves more of the chile flavor.

  18 dried California or New Mexican chiles or a combination of both
  2 ancho chiles
  3 cloves garlic
  2½ cups water
  3 tablespoons pure olive oil
  3 tablespoons all-purpose flour
  1½ teaspoons dried oregano
  1 tablespoon apple cider vinegar
  1 teaspoon salt
  Pinch of sugar (optional)
  ½ to 1 cup water or mild chicken broth, to thin sauce

RINSE THE CHILES under cold running water. Use scissors to cut off the stems and cut the chiles in half. Shake out the seeds onto a paper towel. Put the seeds in your garden for the birds. Place the chiles and garlic in the top half of a steamer over simmering water. Steam for 25 minutes.

REMOVE THE CHILES from heat. Place one-third of the chiles in a blender with ½ cup water, and purée until smooth. Pour the purée into a wire strainer nested over a large bowl. Continue puréeing the rest of the chiles, the garlic, and more water, in batches. Push all of the chile purée through the strainer using a spatula or wooden spoon. Be sure to scrape off the chile purée clinging to the bottom of the strainer. Pour 1 cup water into the blender and turn it on to help clean the blades. Pour this chile water through the strainer to catch the last bit of goodness. You should have about 3½ cups chile purée. The exact yield depends on the size of the dried chiles and water needed to purée.

HEAT THE OLIVE OIL in a deep skillet over medium heat and add the flour, toasting lightly until nut brown. Whisk in the chile purée and add the oregano, vinegar, and salt. Simmer the sauce for 20 minutes to blend the flavors. Taste, and if the sauce seems a bit sharp add a pinch of sugar. If the sauce seems thick, add water or broth, and simmer again for about 5 minutes. Use immediately or store in the refrigerator, covered, for up to 5 days. Also, the sauce can be frozen for up to 6 months. If you have a small amount of sauce left, you can freeze it and use it to add flavor to other dishes such as stews.

Makes 3 to 4 cups

quick red chile sauce

✕✕✕

Many of the old-timers who related their recipes to me repeatedly mentioned Las Palmas red chile in a can. They relied on it to such a degree that I couldn't ignore it. By the time the quick sauce is doctored up, it is quite good. One of my favorite rancho cooks, Mike Acosta, relies on his palate as the final judge. If in the end the sauce is still lacking, he adds brown sugar to bring up the flavor.

- 1 tablespoon olive oil
- 4 cloves garlic, minced
- 2 teaspoons dried oregano
- ½ teaspoon ground cumin
- 1 can (28 ounces) red chile purée, preferably Las Palmas brand
- 2 tablespoons masa harina
- 1 cup water
- 1 to 2 tablespoons red chile powder (preferably Dixon)
- 1 tablespoon brown sugar (optional)

HEAT THE OLIVE OIL over medium heat and add the garlic. Sauté for 1 minute but do not burn. Add the oregano, cumin, and red chile purée. Bring to a simmer and cook for 10 minutes. Blend the masa harina flour with ½ cup water to make a paste, then whisk in the rest of the water. Add to the red chile and simmer for 5 minutes. Season the sauce to taste with the red chile powder. Add enough brown sugar to bring up the flavor, if necessary.

Makes about 4 cups

classic red enchiladas

✕✕✕

The enchilada was a raft on the chile river running between Mexico, California, and the Southwest. It took on different qualities depending on where it made landfall. In California, this traveling enchilada became our very own red enchilada, ultimately symbolizing the fusion of Mexico and Spanish California.

The recipe is probably as old as the trail between the two countries but even that could be endlessly argued in our family, since along with a love of food went a love of debate about food. Until one of my aunts added hamburger in 1950, no one tampered with the Red Enchilada. It was a law unto itself.

Red Enchiladas were served for any grand event but in particular barbecues where long pans of Red Enchiladas awaited the eaters, who expected them to be there. Everyone in the kitchen knew about hiding a few enchiladas for breakfast, another family ritual. They were topped with eggs sizzled in olive oil and served with big cups of coffee laced with Pet milk.

Try to make the enchiladas the day before you need them. The sauce will soak into the tortillas and make the enchiladas even better.

3 tablespoons olive oil

5 onions, chopped

Salt and pepper

1 tablespoon dried oregano

3 cups Red Chile Sauce (page 7)

10 flour tortillas, homemade or the thinnest you can find

6 cups (1½ pounds) grated medium-sharp Cheddar cheese

1 cup pitted black olives or home-cured olives (see page 71)

OIL 2 LONG RECTANGULAR BAKING DISHES to hold 5 huge enchiladas each.

HEAT THE OIL IN A LARGE SKILLET. Add the onions and sauté slowly over low heat, stirring frequently, until softened, about 20 minutes. Season to taste with salt, pepper, and oregano.

SPOON 1 CUP OF THE SAUCE onto a wide dinner plate; dip both sides of a tortilla in the sauce. Place ½ cup grated cheese, 2 olives, and ⅓ cup sautéed onions down the middle of the tortilla. Fold each side of the tortilla over the filling. Place the enchilada, folded side down, in the baking dish. Repeat with the remaining tortillas, adding more sauce to the plate as needed. Pour ½ cup more sauce over the enchiladas. Sprinkle the remaining cheese in a strip down the middle. Decorate with any remaining olives. Cover the pans and refrigerate until ready to bake.

PREHEAT THE OVEN to 350°F. Bake the enchiladas for 18 minutes. As soon as they puff up they are ready.

Makes 10 huge enchiladas (hide one for breakfast)

VARIATION: Some Santa Barbara *descendientes* gave me recipes calling for 4 chopped hard-boiled eggs to be added to the onion-cheese-olive enchilada filling. This version is popular during Lent.

rancho chilaquiles

✕✕✕

Nothing was wasted in the rancho kitchen. Stale tortillas were made into delicious chilaquiles, another favorite breakfast dish. Since I always have a package of corn tortillas in the refrigerator, I inevitably end up with stale ones for chilaquiles or homemade tostada chips. Stale tortillas, which are drier than fresh, absorb less oil during frying.

Accompany this spicy breakfast, brunch, or lunch dish with refried beans, fruit, and café con leche.

  ¼ cup pure olive oil or canola oil
  12 stale corn tortillas, cut into eighths
  1½ cups chopped mild onions
  2 cloves garlic, minced
  1 teaspoon dried oregano
  ½ teaspoon ground cumin
  2 cups Red Chile Sauce (page 7) or Quick Red Chile Sauce (page 8)
  1 cup pitted black olives or home-cured olives (see page 71)
  2 cups grated sharp Cheddar cheese
  ½ cup crumbled queso fresco or cotija cheese

HEAT THE OIL IN A 10-INCH SKILLET over medium-high heat and fry the tortilla wedges, a handful at a time, until they are crisp around the edges. They do not have to be completely crisp. Remove to a paper towel and blot. Continue frying the rest.

POUR OUT ALL BUT A GLAZE OF OIL in the skillet and sauté the onions until they soften, about 8 minutes. Stir in the garlic, oregano, and cumin. Add all of the tortilla strips. Pour the Red Chile Sauce over the top and add the olives and the grated Cheddar. Simmer, uncovered, for about 10 minutes, or until the tortilla strips soften and the cheese melts. Don't stir too much or the tortillas will break up. Before serving, sprinkle the crumbled queso fresco over the top.

Serves 4

ojos de buey
[ox eyes or eggs in chile]

xxx

Carretas, or carts pulled by oxen, were the major form of California travel besides riding horseback until the mid-1800s when the first real carriage appeared. The Californios fondly named this dish of eggs poached in Red Chile Sauce after their beloved oxen. If you asked what was for breakfast, the reply of "ox eyes" was meant as a *chiste*, or joke, at the expense of the unsuspecting guest. Ojos de Buey is the earlier version of Huevos Rancheros (page 128) but even spicier.

Serve the eggs with *frijoles* or breakfast potatoes.

    2 tablespoons pure olive oil or lard
    6 corn tortillas
    2 cups Red Chile Sauce (page 7)
    8 eggs
    ¾ cup halved pitted black olives
    Sprigs of fresh herbs, such as chives, parsley, or oregano, minced

HEAT THE OIL IN A SKILLET over medium-high heat and fry the tortillas, turning once, until softened. Drain on paper towels, blotting any excess oil.

OIL A 13 X 9-INCH CASSEROLE DISH and spread ½ cup of the sauce over the bottom. Pat in the softened tortillas. Spread ½ cup of the sauce over the tortillas. One at a time, break an egg into a cup and then slip the egg on top of the sauce. Continue with each egg. Pour the remaining cup of sauce around the eggs and the edge of the casserole.

PREHEAT THE OVEN TO 350°F. Place the casserole in the oven and bake for about 10 minutes, depending on how cooked you want your eggs. You may need to cook them 2 to 5 minutes longer. Remove from the oven and garnish with olives and minced chives, parsley, or oregano.

4 servings

stacked enchilada pie

✕✕✕

Sometimes a recipe will chase, elude, and then find you. This enchilada pie, which followed me from Santa Barbara to San Diego, is one of those. Isabel Robles gave me her rendition and then I found Isabel Salcido's version in Jim Peyton's extraordinary book, *La Cocina de la Frontera*. The union of both recipes into the one below was a favorite of my tasters while working on this book. Serve this with frijoles.

The flavor of the enchilada pie improves greatly if it is made the day before it is to be served, as this allows time for the sauce to soak into the tortillas.

¼ cup corn oil or canola oil
10 stale corn tortillas
1 cup minced mild onions
2½ cups Red Chile Sauce (page 7) or Quick Red Chile Sauce (page 8)
1 cup halved pitted black olives
3 cups grated medium-sharp Cheddar cheese

Garnishes
½ cup Red Chile Sauce (page 7) or Quick Red Chile Sauce (page 8), hot
¼ cup *crema mexicana*
½ cup crumbled queso fresco or cotija cheese
1 cup washed and crisped romaine leaves, cut into ribbons
2 teaspoons olive oil
Pinch of salt
2 teaspoons wine vinegar
1 avocado, peeled and sliced (optional)

HEAT THE OIL IN A SMALL SKILLET over medium heat and fry the tortillas about 1 minute on each side. Drain on paper towels. Sauté the onions over medium heat for 3 minutes, just long enough to remove the raw flavor.

DIP A FRIED TORTILLA, using tongs or your fingers, into the sauce. Lay it on an oven-proof platter or in a shallow casserole. Sprinkle on some onions, olives, and grated cheese. Keep dipping, stacking, and layering ingredients until you have used all the tortillas. Press the stack from the top middle so everything sticks together. Pour any remaining sauce around the base of the stack.

PREHEAT THE OVEN to 350°F. Bake for 15 minutes.

JUST BEFORE SERVING, drizzle hot Red Chile Sauce decoratively over the sides, drizzle crema over the top, and sprinkle on the crumbled queso fresco. Toss the romaine with the olive oil, salt, and vinegar. Arrange romaine ribbons around the base of the stack with a little on top. Garnish with avocado slices if you like. Serve immediately by cutting the stack into 4 wedges.

Serves 4 for lunch or dinner or 6 with side dishes

NOTE: Crema mexicana is thinner and sweeter than sour cream. It is sold in plastic jars, usually in the cheese section of supermarkets. The Cacique brand is the best.

enchiladas de pollo

×××

Raisins, almonds, and sherry were considered luxurious refinements in old Californio dishes. These ingredients, used to transform ordinary fare into feast dishes, were brought to Mexico by the Spaniards and then carried into California and the Southwest. Plain boiled chicken and a little minced onion were used as a filling for everyday enchiladas.

- 1 chicken (3 pounds), disjointed, or 2 whole chicken breasts, split and skin removed
- 5 cups water or chicken stock
- 1 cup salsa or Sarsa (page 45)
- 2 dried California or New Mexican chiles, washed and cut into pieces
- 2 cloves garlic
- 1 teaspoon dried oregano
- 2 bay leaves
- 1 teaspoon salt
- 1/4 cup minced cilantro
- 1/2 cup black raisins
- 1/4 cup sherry or claret
- 2 tablespoons light canola or olive oil
- 12 corn tortillas or 8 flour tortillas
- 1/4 cup slivered almonds, toasted
- 2 cups grated Monterey Jack cheese
- 2 cups Red Chile Sauce (page 7) or Quick Red Chile Sauce (page 8)

POACH THE CHICKEN in the water in a 3-quart pot, simmering over low heat for 10 minutes. Skim any foam off the top. Next add the salsa, chiles, garlic, oregano, bay leaves, salt, and cilantro. Continue to cook for about 25 minutes more, making sure the chicken is submerged. Turn off the heat and let the chicken steep in the broth for 30 minutes.

REMOVE THE CHICKEN from the broth and reserve the broth for soups and stews. When cool enough to handle, pull the meat off the bones. Cut into chunks and pull into shreds with your fingers. You should have about 3 cups shredded chicken. Moisten with some of the broth.

SOAK THE RAISINS in the sherry to plump.

HEAT 2 TEASPOONS OF THE OIL in a skillet over medium heat, and heat each tortilla to make it more pliable and to seal the surface. Keep adding oil to the skillet, 1 teaspoon at a time, as needed. Set aside the tortillas while you prepare the filling.

COMBINE THE SHREDDED CHICKEN, plumped raisins, almonds, and 1½ cups of the cheese.

DIP EACH TORTILLA IN THE SAUCE to coat completely. (I like to add some of the salsa broth to the sauce for extra flavor.) Place some filling down the middle of each tortilla and roll it up. Place in a greased baking dish (you will need two dishes). Sprinkle with the ½ cup reserved cheese.

PREHEAT THE OVEN TO 350°F. Bake for 12 minutes.

Serves 6

tostones

In eighteenth-century Mexico and California, a *tostón* was a silver doubloon worth fifty cents. It was natural for the Californios of that period to name round slices of potato in chile sauce after the silver coins. They probably had more potatoes than silver! I was inspired by an updated version served at Pasqual's, our favorite café in Santa Fe, to add cheese and green onions to the rancho tostones.

    4 russet potatoes, scrubbed
    1 tablespoon canola or olive oil
Red Chile Gravy
    2 tablespoons canola or pure olive oil
    2 tablespoons flour
    1 clove garlic, finely minced
    ½ teaspoon ground cumin
    1 teaspoon dried oregano
    ½ cup excellent red chile powder (see page 223)

1½ cups cold water

2 cups light chicken broth

1 teaspoon vinegar

1 teaspoon salt

Garnish (optional)

1½ cups grated Monterey Jack cheese

3 green onions, minced

PREHEAT THE OVEN to 350°F.

BAKE THE POTATOES for at least 45 minutes. Allow them to cool so you can easily peel and cut them into ¼-inch slices. Heat the oil in a 10-inch cast-iron skillet over medium heat. Brown the slices of potatoes, turning frequently. Meanwhile, prepare the gravy.

HEAT THE ADDITIONAL 2 TABLESPOONS OIL in another skillet and blend in the flour. Cook until the flour is golden to make a roux, then stir in the garlic. Cook for just 1 minute. Add the cumin and oregano. Remove skillet from the heat.

COMBINE THE CHILE POWDER and water in a medium bowl, whisking until well blended. Add the chicken broth. Whisk this chile mixture into the flour roux. Place the skillet back over medium heat, and whisk the sauce to keep it smooth. Add the vinegar and salt and simmer for at least 15 minutes until the gravy thickens.

TO SERVE THE TOSTONES, arrange the potatoes in a shallow casserole or in 6 individual bowls and drizzle the gravy over the top. Garnish with the cheese and minced green onions, if desired.

Serves 6

adobado
[chile-soaked pork or spareribs]

———————— ✕✕✕ ————————

Meats were often marinated in a red chile sauce as a flavorful tenderizer. Versions of adobado appear from California to New Mexico.

12 dried California or New Mexican chiles

5 dried ancho chiles

2 to 3 cups water to purée chiles

2 tablespoons canned chipotles en adobo

4 cloves garlic

1 tablespoon dried oregano

1 teaspoon crushed cumin seeds

2 tablespoons honey

2 tablespoons apple cider vinegar

1 teaspoon salt

3 pounds whole boneless pork loin, 2 tenderloins, or 4 pounds spareribs

1 bottle beer (14 ounces)

1 onion, sliced

CUT THE CHILES IN HALF and shake out most of the seeds. Cut off the stems. Rinse any dust off and place the chiles in a steamer insert over simmering water. Steam for 20 minutes.

PURÉE THE CHILES in 3 batches, placing one third of the chiles at a time in a blender jar (a food processor does not work well for this task). Add about ¾ cup water to each batch and purée. Add the chipotles, garlic, oregano, cumin, honey, vinegar, and salt to the last batch. You should have about 1 quart.

DRY THE LOIN (or spareribs if you are using them) with paper towels. Place in a non-reactive bowl and rub in 1 cup of the chile sauce, reserving the remaining sauce. Marinate overnight in the refrigerator.

PREHEAT THE OVEN to 350°F. Remove the meat from the refrigerator at least 30 minutes before cooking. Place the meat in an oiled Dutch oven and pour the beer on it. Place slices of onion on top. Cover and bake for 1½ hours.

IF YOU ARE COOKING SPARERIBS, remove them from the oven and finish them on a medium-hot grill. Brush with chile and cook for about 20 minutes more. If you are cooking a loin or 2 tenderloins, spread ½ cup additional chile sauce over the top and bake for 30 minutes more. When done, remove the meat to a platter to cool a little before slicing. The pork adobado is also delicious the next day to fill burritos.

Serves 8 with side dishes

rancho fideo

———————— xxx ————————

My grandmother was very picky about fideo, the wirelike strands of pasta that are sold in coils. We had to search for the tiniest strands to make her happy. Regular vermicelli, a substitute used by some cooks, was not acceptable to her, the most persnickety cook I've ever known but also one of the best.

Fideo gives the most flavor when toasted. Traditionally, fideo was fried in oil until golden, but I have found that oven-toasting works even better and doesn't require oil.

12 ounces fideo coils (see page 223)

6 cups water

1 teaspoon salt

1½ cups Red Chile Sauce (page 7) or Red Chile Gravy (page 14)

1 tablespoon olive oil

½ cup grated dry Monterey Jack or Parmesan cheese

PREHEAT THE OVEN to 350°F.

BREAK UP THE FIDEO COILS and place them on baking sheets. Toast until the fideo turns golden, 8 to 10 minutes. Do not allow the fideo to get dark brown. Immediately remove from the oven.

BRING THE WATER TO A BOIL in a 3-quart saucepan over medium heat. Add salt and toasted fideos. Cook until just tender, about 8 minutes. Drain.

WHILE THE FIDEOS ARE COOKING, heat the chile sauce. Toss the fideos with the olive oil and the warmed sauce. Sprinkle with cheese and serve.

Serves 4 to 6 as a side dish

pollo mole ranchero
[chicken mole, rancho style]

✕✕✕

The chicken mole that was cooked on the California ranchos was not as complex as the mole poblanos of Mexico. Rancho cooks did not have a great variety of dried chiles available nor all of the various nuts and seeds. Still, the simpler rancho mole makes a velvety and delicious stew that is less labor intensive than Mexican mole. Serve it with rice, beans, and plenty of tortillas to sop up the mole sauce.

1 chicken, 3½ pounds, disjointed, gizzards and liver reserved for another use

5 cups water

1 cup salsa, homemade or bottled

2 cloves peeled garlic

2 bay leaves

1 teaspoon salt

8 dried California or New Mexican chiles

4 ancho chiles

3 cloves unpeeled garlic

1 tomato

¼ cup almonds, toasted

¼ cup raisins steeped in ¼ cup sherry

2 tablespoons pure olive oil

1 tablet Mexican chocolate (2 ounces), chopped

Salt and freshly ground black pepper

1 to 2 chipotle chiles

PLACE THE CHICKEN and water in a large 4-quart pot and bring to a simmer over medium-low heat. Cook for 10 minutes, skimming off any surface foam. Add the salsa, peeled garlic, bay leaves, and salt and simmer for 25 minutes. Cool the chicken in the broth for 15 minutes. Pour the broth through a mesh strainer, pressing broth from the solids. Remember to scrape off the bottom of the strainer.

CUT OFF THE STEMS of the chiles and cut the chiles in half, shaking out most of the seeds. Soak in hot water for 20 minutes or steam for 25 minutes.

CHAR THE UNPEELED GARLIC and tomato in a dry skillet over medium heat until softened, about 15 minutes.

PLACE THE SOFTENED CHILES and 1 cup of the reserved broth in a blender jar. Purée, adding more broth if necessary. Pour out half of the chile purée and add the garlic, charred tomato with its skin, toasted almonds, and raisins. Add 1 cup more of reserved salsa broth, and purée to a smooth sauce. Add more liquid if necessary to achieve a sauce consistency.

HEAT 2 TABLESPOONS OF OIL in a deep pot over medium-low heat. (Mole sauce tends to splatter.) Add the chile purée and the chocolate, whisking constantly. Add more broth if the mole becomes too thick. Add salt and pepper to taste. Add whole chipotle chiles. Simmer for 20 minutes more to meld the flavors. The mole should not taste chocolatey but rather a little sweet and smoky.

STIR IN THE COOKED CHICKEN, enveloping it with the mole sauce. Simmer for at least 20 minutes so the flavors penetrate the chicken.

Serves 6

NOTE: Pollo Mole Ranchero can also used as a filling for enchiladas and tamales.

THE LEGACY OF ollas

The olla, or clay stewpot, reigned supreme in the rancho kitchen. There was not a day without stew or frijoles simmering in an olla. Foreigners, that is, anybody not a Californio, often complained about being constantly served *olla podrida*, a Spanish stew containing chicken, beef, chickpeas, and whatever else was available. The protest of too much stew was never heard in our kitchen

The Higuera family, as seen against the lush backdrop of the garden and orchards of Rancho Los Tularcitos.

where there was a Chile Colorado one day and a rich guisado of chicken or oxtails the next.

A good cook could transform a minimum of ingredients into a stew to feed many mouths. With culinary magic, the sum was always greater than the humble parts. Perhaps that is why Santa Teresa, the unofficial patron saint of Spanish cooking, said that "God walks among the stewpots." According to my grandmother, a good cook could stretch a pot of stew just by adding another scrap of meat, some potatoes, and a little help from Santa Teresa.

In the bygone days of the California ranchos, it was not unheard of to seat fifteen hungry people at the table for a midday meal. Adding to the mouths to feed was the unexpected visitor, two or three hours away from the comforts of his own table. In fact, the gauge of a good stew was how far down the road a guest was when the aroma reached him and his horse. A radius line could be drawn from the pot to encircle the kitchen. A simmering olla, at its most succulent moment, drew in the eaters as if they were coming to Mecca. *"Más vale llegar a tiempo que ser invitado"* (it's better to show up at the right time than to be invited) is an old California proverb. At mealtimes, there was hardly ever a vacant place at the rancho tables; however, an unexpected guest was always made to feel that the olla was bottomless. Which is why God made frijoles.

Stews and Battles

The fact that stew played a major role in the minor, little-known Battle of Santa Clara was not unusual, and we were made to understand that if not for the Higueras' way with stew, the hapless rancheros could not have continued even their short-lived rebellion nor fed their captive. Our family always seemed to be able to focus on food even in the face of battle!

This particular story began with the arrival of U.S. troops for fact-finding as a preliminary to the takeover of California. Officers confiscated the best horses of the rancheros, often their favorite steeds, while on so-called cattle-buying raids. The Californios had already experienced the turnover of California from Spain to Mexico in 1821. There had been no earth-shattering differences between the landlords, so the U.S. domination in 1846 did not overly concern the rancheros in northern California until their prime horses were taken. They were ready to fight for their honor.

José Loreto Higuera, my great-great-grandfather, and his ranchero paisanos were not about to ignore the insult. Ranchos were considered inviolable, and the Americans had crossed a sacred boundary. Virtually weaponless and small in number, the rancheros rallied by riding from rancho to rancho in support of one another. They hid out on Rancho Los Tularcitos with a captured U.S. officer caught cattle buying. The cruelest thing they did was to make the poor man ride with them through the cold rain and fog while they displayed their legendary horsemanship. Lieutenant Bartlett, effete Easterner that he was, was hard-pressed to ride with his swashbuckling captors during his three-week captivity. Ultimately the rancheros, armed only with fine horsemanship and a few sorry guns and knives strapped to willow poles, went off to face the Americans and lose honorably in the short Battle of Santa Clara. Some concessions were later granted to the rancheros, especially concerning their horses.

The Higueras were not only proud that they had fought for their honor but that their rancho was used as one of the headquarters for the dissidents, and that they had hospitably cared for Lieutenant Bartlett. He admitted what fine hosts they were after he spent his last days in captivity tied to a sycamore tree while being spoonfed *aguardiente* (Spanish brandy) and the best stew he had ever eaten. Before they allowed him to return to San Francisco he had to submit to a fiesta held in his honor.

chile colorado

✕✕✕

This stew, also known as carne con chile, was cooked more frequently than any other, even olla podrida. It used the two most plentiful ingredients of the rancho kitchen, beef and red chiles. The key to success was to deeply brown the beef, thus achieving the caramelization needed for the richest broth. A broth such as this helped warm Lieutenant Barlett after the long rides his captors so relished.

3½ pounds beef roast, chuck, rump, or shoulder clod

1 tablespoon pure olive oil

2 medium onions, chopped

1 tablespoon minced garlic

2 teaspoons salt

4 cups beef stock or water

2 cups Red Chile Sauce (page 7)

1 tablespoon cumin seeds, toasted and crushed

1 tablespoon dried oregano

1 to 2 tablespoons New Mexican chile powder (optional)

3 tablespoons masa harina flour

¼ cup water

1 cup black olives, for garnish

¼ cup minced cilantro, for garnish

Tortillas, for dunking

CUT THE MEAT into 2-inch chunks and dry well with paper towels. Heat the oil in a heavy pot with a lid over medium heat, and brown the meat on all sides in small batches. Remove the meat chunks as they brown.

USING THE SAME POT, sauté the onions until soft and golden, about 10 minutes. Blend the garlic and salt together and stir into the onions. Add the browned meat and the collected juices. Add the beef stock. Cover and simmer over medium heat for 1½ hours.

DRAIN OFF ALL BUT 1 CUP of broth from the pot. Use this extra broth to make a *sopa* the next day. To the remaining broth and meat in the pot, add the Red Chile Sauce, cumin, oregano, and chile powder if you want the stew to be really picante. Simmer on low heat for 1 hour more. The chile will penetrate the meat. Taste for seasoning and add more salt or spices, if needed.

BLEND THE MASA HARINA into the water and blend into the stew to thicken it. Simmer for 5 minutes. Just before serving, add the olives and cilantro. Serve in big bowls accompanied by plenty of tortillas for dunking.

Serves 6 to 8

guisado de carne
[beef stew]

✕✕✕

A guisado was distinguished from ordinary beef stew by the greater range of spices and herbs used. This was not a plain stew. Rancho cooks loved their dry spice rubs, which were liberally applied to meats whether they were being prepared for guisados, roasting, or barbecues. To enrich a guisado even more, the cook added caldo, or broth, instead of plain water.

2½ pounds beef round, cut into 1½-inch cubes

1 teaspoon crushed cumin

2 teaspoons dried oregano

2 teaspoons paprika

1 teaspoon freshly ground black pepper

2 teaspoons sea salt

3 tablespoons olive oil

1½ cups sliced onions

4 cloves garlic, minced

2 tablespoons wine vinegar

2 bay leaves

2 tomatoes, peeled, seeded, and diced

2 long green chiles, diced (do not char)

3 cups beef broth or water

Salt and freshly ground black pepper

2 russet potatoes, peeled and quartered (optional)

Bread or tortillas, for dunking

DRY THE MEAT CUBES with paper towels. Combine the cumin, oregano, paprika, pepper, and sea salt to make a dry rub. Rub onto the meat and let it sit for 20 minutes.

HEAT 1 TABLESPOON OF THE OLIVE OIL in a large heavy skillet over medium-high heat and brown the meat in batches. Transfer the meat to a plate.

ADD THE REMAINING 2 tablespoons olive oil to the skillet and sauté the onions until softened and golden, about 10 minutes. Add the garlic and cook briefly. Add the browned meat, all the juices, the vinegar, bay leaves, tomatoes, green chiles, and broth. Simmer over low heat for 1½ hours, or until the meat is tender.

SEASON WITH SALT AND PEPPER if needed. Add the potato, if you like, near the end of the cooking time when the meat is already tender. Cover the pot and cook the guisado until potatoes are tender, about 20 minutes. Serve immediately in bowls, accompanied by bread or tortillas for dunking.

Serves 6

guisado de gallina

—✕✕✕—

Many of the rancho recipes exemplify the fusion of Mexican and Spanish ingredients. The recipe for Guisado de Gallina portrays more of the European connection. The Spaniards introduced chickens to the New World along with the use of wine, sugar, cinnamon, cloves, raisins, and olives. Practically everything brought from Spain is collected in this guisado. Serve this guisado with steamed rice or noodles.

I chicken (3½ pounds), disjointed and with the breast cut into 4 pieces
3 tablespoons olive oil
I teaspoon sea salt
I teaspoon freshly ground black pepper
2 teaspoons dried oregano or thyme
4 cloves garlic, minced
I onion, chopped
3 tomatoes
I cup red wine
2 tablespoons sugar
2 cinnamon sticks
¼ teaspoon ground cinnamon
¼ teaspoon ground cloves
¼ to ½ teaspoon cayenne pepper
½ cup black raisins
½ cup olives
Freshly ground black pepper

DRY THE CHICKEN WELL with paper towels. Use poultry shears or a sharp paring knife to cut off excess fat and skin, leaving a small amount of skin for flavor. Make a seasoning paste of 2 tablespoons of the oil, the sea salt, pepper, oregano, and garlic. Rub over the surfaces of the chicken pieces, reserving the back and neck for making broth.

BROWN THE CHICKEN PIECES in a heavy 3-quart stewpot over medium heat. The olive oil used in the rub should provide enough oil for sautéing but add 1 or 2 teaspoons more if the chicken sticks. Brown the chicken pieces on both sides, then remove.

ADD A LITTLE MORE OLIVE OIL and sauté the onion over very low heat until soft and translucent, about 8 minutes. Meanwhile, either broil the tomatoes to loosen the skins or hold them over a flame. Remove the skins, flick out the seeds, and chop. Add the tomatoes to the onions and continue to sauté for another 2 minutes more.

ADD THE RED WINE, sugar, cinnamon sticks, ground cinnamon, cloves, cayenne, raisins, and olives. Put the browned chicken back into the stewpot. Simmer for 30 minutes, turning the chicken pieces in the sauce occasionally. Add pepper to taste. For a thicker sauce, remove a cup of the cooking liquid and cook it down in a small open skillet for about 10 minutes.

ARRANGE THE CHICKEN on a platter, pour over the wine glaze, and serve.

Serves 4

oxtail stew

✕✕✕

Oxtail stew, popular for family dinners, produces one of the richest broths you'll ever taste. Grandmama called it "the family stew," so no one got picky about what they were eating, especially the kids. Some of us never knew for years what made up "the family stew." We just knew that it was good. When I served it to my then seven-year-old twin sons for the first time, they wanted to know why the bones were shaped like propellers. I prefer to make the stew the day before I serve it, so any congealed fat can be easily lifted off after chilling.

5 pounds meaty oxtails, cut into small sections
½ cup flour
1 teaspoon salt
½ teaspoon freshly ground black pepper
1 teaspoon paprika, preferably smoky Spanish paprika
2 teaspoons dried oregano
2 tablespoons olive oil, or more as needed
¼ cup brandy
2 medium onions, chopped
2 cloves garlic, minced
2 bay leaves
2 cups red wine, or as needed

1 cup beef or chicken broth, or as needed
2 tablespoons tomato paste
1 long piece of orange zest
3 carrots, peeled and thickly sliced
Rice or noodles, for serving
Bread, for dunking

DRY THE OXTAILS with paper towels. Combine the flour, salt, pepper, paprika, and oregano on a piece of wax paper. Dust the oxtails with the seasoned flour, rubbing it in to make it adhere well. Pat off the excess. Heat 1 tablespoon of the oil in an oven-proof stewpot over medium-high heat and brown the oxtails in batches, removing the meat as it browns. Add more oil as needed. Drain off any excess oil and place all the oxtails back into the pot. Heat the brandy in a small saucepan, ignite it, and pour the flaming brandy over the oxtails. Add the onions, garlic, bay leaves, wine, broth, tomato paste, and orange zest. Simmer on top of the stove over low heat for 30 minutes, skimming off foam.

PREHEAT THE OVEN to 325°F. Cover the pot and place it in the oven for 3 to 4 hours, checking periodically to make sure the liquid has not evaporated. Add a little more wine, broth, or water if necessary. The oxtails should be meltingly tender and practically fall off the bone.

COOL THE STEW DOWN and then place the pot in the refrigerator overnight. Lift off the congealed fat on the surface, leaving every scrap of the precious jellied caramelized juices. Before serving, heat the stew, again adding more liquid if needed. Add the carrots. Simmer for 20 minutes. Serve with rice or noodles. Accompany with bread for dunking.

Serves 4 to 6

pork stew with purslane

✕✕✕

Purslane, called *verdolaga* in Spanish, was a much appreciated green among the Californios and now its mildly tart flavor and nutritional value are being acclaimed by many chefs. It resembles watercress but with thicker stems and leaves. The flavor is slightly acidic, balancing well with meat, potatoes, and white cheese. When cooked in stews, this tart green becomes sweeter.

Purslane loves damp, freshly tilled soil, where it crawls like a weed among the other plants of your garden. Sometimes I have found it during the summer months in farmers' markets. Last year, it appeared among the herbs in my own garden. I have no idea where it came from!

2½ pounds boneless country-style pork spareribs

I teaspoon sea salt

3 cloves garlic, minced

I teaspoon freshly ground black pepper

2 tablespoons olive oil

5 cups water

2 bay leaves

I tablespoon red chile powder

¼ pound chorizo or spicy sausage, cooked and crumbled

I teaspoon dried oregano

6 quartered new potatoes or Red Bliss potatoes

2 cups purslane with some stems

Tortillas or bread, for dunking

CUT THE PORK into 2-inch pieces. Trim off excess fat. Dry the meat with paper towels. Mix a paste of the salt, garlic, and pepper. Rub onto the meat. Heat the olive oil in a heavy saucepan over medium heat and brown the pork in 2 batches. Return the pork to the saucepan and add the water and bay leaves. Simmer until tender, 45 minutes to 1 hour. Lift out the meat, cool, and refrigerate. Refrigerate the broth separately for several hours or overnight. Lift off the congealed fat and discard.

PUT THE PORK and broth back into the saucepan. Add the chile powder, chorizo, oregano, and potatoes. Simmer for 10 minutes.

USE A SHARP KNIFE to slice off the more tender stems of purslane with the leaves, as you would do with watercress (the thicker stems are woody and tough). Rinse in cold water to rid the leaves of clinging dust. (Since purslane grows on top of the ground as a creeper, it doesn't have much earth clinging to it.) Steam for 5 minutes.

Drain, cool, and chop it roughly. Add to the rest of the stew and simmer for 15 minutes more or until potatoes are tender. Serve in bowls accompanied by tortillas or chunks of crusty bread.

Serves 6

braised pot roast with beer

⋊⋉⋊

Braising with beer was a happy discovery I made while living in Mexico and attempting to cook beef that we swore had fed on maguey cactus and wandered a thousand miles. The beer works as a natural tenderizer for tougher meats.

   4 pounds beef roast, such as chuck or rump roast
   2 tablespoons olive oil
   2 onions, chopped
   1 can beer (12 ounces)
   4 cloves garlic, minced
   Salt and freshly ground black pepper

PREHEAT THE OVEN to 350°F.

TRIM EXCESSIVE FAT off the meat. Dry well with paper towels. Heat the oil in a heavy pot with a lid over medium-high heat and brown to a deep mahogany on both sides. Add the onions to one side of the roast and brown them also. Pour in the beer. Press the minced garlic on top of the roast. Sprinkle the top of the roast with salt and pepper. Cover tightly.

BAKE UNTIL VERY TENDER, about 2½ hours. Check after 1½ hours to see if more liquid is needed. Add water if necessary. Defat the broth if you wish to serve it with the roast. Slice and serve.

Serves 6 to 8

NOTE: The braised meat is also delicious when shredded for burritos.

VARIATION: Green Chile Stew. Cook the meat as described and let it cool for 10 to 15 minutes. Cut the meat into large chunks and put it back into the pot with the braising juices. Add 2 cups water, ¼ cup red chile powder, 2 cans (4 ounces each) drained and chopped green chiles, and 2 peeled and quartered russet potatoes. Cover and bake for 30 to 45 minutes more.

red chile, pork, and cactus stew

✕✕✕

Most of the ranchos grew prickly pear cactus around the family's abode to keep out grizzly bears, coyotes, and other unwelcome visitors. The prickly pear cactus, also called *nopal,* was prized not only as a fence but also as a delicious vegetable that is still highly appreciated today by Latinos in California, Arizona, and New Mexico. In Mexico, the *ensalada de nopalitos,* or cactus salad, remains a classic among many of the regional cuisines. When spring comes, you can find nopal paddles, despined and ready to cook, in Mexican supermarkets and some farmers' markets. Choose the paddles that are thin and bright green. Mike Dominguez Acosta, whose recipe is given below, says that only the tongue-shaped paddles should be used since they have the best flavor.

Mike once agreed to make his red chile, pork, and cactus stew for a fiesta we were hosting. It was a dry year in Santa Barbara and he worried that the young cactus wouldn't be mature enough in time for his stew. The fiesta was seven weeks away. I had to check in with Mike every day for the last month to get an update on the number of tongue-shaped cactus paddles in his yard. Instead of watching paint dry, we were watching the cactus grow!

2 cactus paddles, cleaned and despined (see page 33)

4 quarts water, for blanching cactus

1 tablespoon salt

½ onion

1 clove garlic

Several sprigs of cilantro

2½ pounds pork, finely diced, cut from chops or the loin

3 cloves garlic, minced

1 large can (1 pound, 12 ounces) red chile purée, preferably Las Palmas brand

3 teaspoons dried oregano

2 teaspoons cumin seed, toasted

Salt

2 tablespoons masa harina

¼ cup water

¼ cup minced cilantro

Tortillas, for serving

IF YOU BUY YOUR CACTUS PADDLES already cleaned, rub them with wadded-up paper towels to be sure the paddles are free of spines. Cut the paddles into ½ x 2-inch strips.

BRING THE WATER, salt, onion, 1 clove garlic, and cilantro sprigs to a boil in a large pot over medium-high heat and drop in the cactus strips. Blanch the cactus, uncovered, until crisp-tender, about 4 minutes. Then, using a slotted spoon, place the cactus in a bowl of cold water with a handful of ice cubes. Leave undisturbed for 5 minutes. Drain the cactus in a colander and set aside.

PLACE THE MEAT IN A POT and add 3 cups water. Simmer, covered, until the water is just about gone and some of the fat is released, about 45 minutes to 1 hour. Tilt the pot and drain off the fat.

ADD THE 3 CLOVES GARLIC, red chile purée, oregano, cumin, and salt to the taste. Simmer, covered, for about 30 minutes. Add the precooked cactus paddle strips and simmer, covered, for 15 minutes more.

BLEND THE MASA HARINA with the water to make a paste. Whisk into the stew to thicken. Simmer for 5 minutes, adding the minced cilantro at the very end. Serve the cactus stew in bowls, accompanied by tortillas.

Serves 6 to 8

Cleaning Cactus Paddles

Clean and prepare the cactus paddles outside, over newspapers. Use tongs to hold a cactus paddle. Be mindful that the spines are sharp. Use a sharp paring knife to slice off the nodes (where the spines are). Keep a damp paper towel nearby to wipe the spines off, making sure that the spines are on the towel and not remaining on your knife. Trim around the edge of the paddle where the spines grow closely together. Do not peel the whole cactus paddle, as this would release too much of the juices. Just remove the nodes and spines on both sides. Trim off the blunt end where the paddle was cut from the plant. Finally, place the wiped cactus paddle on a clean board and cut into ½ x 2-inch strips.

rancho pozole

——————— ✕✕✕ ———————

Rancho cooks elaborated upon the leaner mission pozole, which was often just fri-joles and pozole kernels, by adding braised pork, chicken, and, of course, red chile sauce. In days past, the cooks added half a pig's head, especially if the pozole was to be served as a feast dish. As with all stews, the idea was to allow the ingredients to flavor each other. The pozole kernels give an earthy corn essence to the pot and the braised meat greatly seasons the pozole. We like to serve an array of crisp condiments for people to add to their bowls at serving time.

    2 cups frozen pozole *(nixtamal)* or canned hominy
    8 cups water
    2 pounds pork, butt end of loin
    6 cups chicken broth
    4 chicken legs with thighs attached (about 2½ pounds)
    2 cups chopped onions
    1 tablespoon dried oregano
    1 teaspoon crushed cumin seeds
    1 teaspoon salt, or as needed
    2 teaspoons minced garlic
    2 cups Red Chile Sauce (page 7) or canned sauce
    2 bay leaves
    1 cup water
    4 fresh Anaheim, New Mexican, or poblano chiles, charred, peeled, and chopped,
        or 1 can (7 ounces) green chiles
    1 teaspoon freshly ground black pepper

Condiments

    Minced cilantro
    Shredded iceberg lettuce
    Chopped white onion
    Sliced radishes
    Lime wedges
    Black olives
    Dried oregano

IF USING FROZEN POZOLE, thaw what you need and rinse in a colander. Place in a pot and cover with the 8 cups of water. Do not add salt. Cover and simmer the pot over low heat until the kernels "flower" or burst, about 1½ hours. The kernels should still have a certain firmness to the bite. If using canned hominy, open the cans and drain.

CUT THE PORK into small cubes. Place in a heavy-bottomed cooking pot with 1 cup of the broth. Simmer over medium heat until the broth reduces and the pork starts to brown in its own juices and fat, about 15 minutes. Remove skin from the chicken legs. Add the onions and chicken and sprinkle with oregano, cumin, salt, and garlic. Add the remaining broth, the chile sauce, bay leaves, the cooked pozole kernels, and 1 more cup of water. Simmer for 1 hour, partially covered. Stir in the chiles and cook for 30 minutes more. Season with more salt and freshly ground pepper.

SERVE YOUR GUESTS bowls of pozole and let them garnish to their liking with cilantro, lettuce, onion, radishes, limes, olives, and dried oregano.

Serves 6 to 8

Pozole

Pozole, otherwise known as hominy, is made by a process that not only increases the corn's nutritional value but also loosens the hulls from the swollen corn kernels. The kernels of field corn are soaked in calcium hydrate, a lime treatment (lime as in limestone, not the fruit), which firms them up, making them even chewier. This soaked corn, known in Mexico as *nixtamal*, is dried and ground to make the masa for tortillas and tamales, a major source of calcium.

pozole de frijoles y trigo
[beans and wheat berry stew]

———————— ✕✕✕ ————————

Beans and wheat, early products of the mission gardens and ranchos, were simmered together to make a nourishing stew. During the research for this book, I often spoke with *descendientes*, and certain dishes were invariably mentioned. Beans and wheat berries were always fondly recalled and often poignantly wished for at the moment of recollection. Serve this pozole as a nourishing lunch or *almuerzo*.

   1 pound dried pink beans
   8 cups water
   ½ cup wheat berries
   1 tablespoon salt
   2 tablespoons bacon grease or pure olive oil

WASH THE BEANS in a sieve and pick over for stones. Cover with the water and bring to a simmer over medium heat. Cook, covered, for 1½ hours over low heat. When the beans are tender, rinse the wheat berries in a sieve, and add to the beans. Add salt. Simmer until both the beans and wheat berries are quite tender, about 45 minutes. Add more liquid, such as boiling water, if necessary.

HEAT THE BACON GREASE or oil in a heavy skillet over medium-high heat and ladle in 1 cup of beans and berries. Simmer and mash the concoction until it becomes thicker. Add more of the bean liquor from the pot. Simmer and keep adding beans and kernels. Cook until the pozole is thick.

Serves 8

NOTE: Wheat berries are available at health food stores.

estofado de aves
[dove or squab stew]

⟩⟨⟩⟨

On Rancho Los Tularcitos, when the population of wild doves and pigeons grew so overpowering that they were taking too much of the fruit or olives, the uncles had a remedy. They waited until dusk, when the birds flew in to nest for the night, and shot into the eucalyptus trees at the end of The Lane. If they returned with enough doves, at least a dozen, a wine stew was prepared. The doves on the rancho feasted mainly on the olives in The Lane and this was thought to give them extra savor. Farm-raised squab, which make a delicious broth, can be substituted here.

    3 teaspoons sea salt
    2 cloves garlic, minced
    2 teaspoons dried oregano
    2 teaspoons dried basil
    12 doves, pigeons, or squabs
    2 tablespoons olive oil
    ½ cup chopped onions
    Freshly ground black pepper
    2 cups dry red wine
    1 cup chicken broth or water
    Bread, for dunking

MASH THE SEA SALT, garlic, oregano, and basil together into a seasoning paste. Rub over all the surfaces of the birds. Heat the oil in a stewpot over medium heat and sauté the onion for 8 minutes. Push to the side of the pot and brown the birds in batches until golden brown on all sides. Sprinkle with pepper during the frying.

POUR THE WINE and broth over all and simmer, covered, until tender, 45 minutes to 1 hour. Domesticated squab do not have to be simmered as long since they are more tender. Check from time to time to make sure that the birds are not sticking and liquid has not evaporated. Add more wine or water if necessary, but not too much; the broth should be thick and velvety.

SERVE EACH PERSON a bowl with a bird, halved with poultry shears, and the broth. The broth was and is as much appreciated as anything, so have plenty of crusty bread for dunking.

Serves 6

THE asador
AND THE GLORY OF THE BARBECUE

every generation in the Higuera family witnessed the birth of an *asador*, a master barbecuer. The calling was handed down like fine silver spurs. Each time the ageless ritual of grilling and roasting meat was reenacted under the big sky, the asador was king of the land. The art of barbecue, harkening back to the cattle-rich land-grant days, is deeply entrenched in the culinary

*Grandpa (right), the archetypal asador, shares the camaraderie
of the pit with a crony and one of the rancho boys.*

history of California. The Mexican-born sons and grandsons of the conquistadors cooked over campfires as they made their way north from outposts in Sinaloa and Sonora to the outposts of California and the Southwest. The campfire and the *parilla*, or grill, belonged to the domain of the soldier, the *vaquero*, or cowboy, and the ranchero. They, in time, preferred the taste of food cooked outdoors. The style, having evolved in a male-dominated world, remained firmly entrenched among the men, far away from kitchens.

For as long as anyone could remember, my grandfather held the honored position of asador on Rancho Los Tularcitos, When he was in his seventies, he relinquished his honored position to his youngest son, Jack. The rank of asador has little to do with seniority and more to do with whether or not you are blessed with the passion. Years later, when it was time, Jack "handed over the fork" to his son, Jeff Chavarria, who now presides. Jeff's son, Joaquin, has the signs of an asador-in-the-making, but for now he stands in his father's broad shadow.

Barbecue Day

The day before a barbecue, the rancho began to awaken from the slumber of quiet weekdays. There was a hum in the air. A barbecue was coming. Grandmama and Grandpa came from their house in San José, with their five children in tow, to help with last-minute preparations. Grandmama spent hours in the kitchen with Aunt Nick, Aunt Emma, and Aunt Dora making flour tortillas, red enchiladas, and frijoles. The century-old adobe resounded with happy voices with the anticipation of a barbecue making it seem like the night before Christmas.

The bachelor uncles retold the same ghost stories just before bedtime, assuring that the children couldn't sleep peacefully for hours. On each bed, with their mattresses of sheep's wool, three children huddled together. Having fallen under the spell of the house and the storytellers, they heard the prowling spirits, the talking coyotes, and went to the deep window in the middle of the night to look for the flickering lights in the foothills.

On Sunday morning, the tired children awakened to the sounds of their mothers and aunts cooking. As soon as the older children appeared, they were fed and given little jobs like putting the watermelons to chill in Calera Creek. Someone was sent to collect palm fronds for a makeshift broom to sweep the pathways before guests arrived. There was no expanse of lawn, only packed dirt courtyards, which were kept as smooth as tile. The arbor, overgrown with mission grapes, was arranged with chairs for the ladies, who kept out of the sun. Pots and cans of geraniums were lined up by the long tables.

Grandpa surveyed the preparation of the fires late in the morning, arranging all the accoutrements of his trade. Long-handled forks, knives, marinades, and red wine for the asador. If there had been a recent storm, men were sent out to search the creek beds for tree roots to stoke the fires. Fruit-tree wood and walnut wood were stacked near the barbecue. A coffee can filled with water stood nearby, ready for emergency action. A rag tied on the end of a walnut branch was doused in the water and dribbled over leaping flames before they could char the meat.

I remember the barbecue taking a very long time, so long that the scent of meat juices dripping onto embers was unbearable and drew an ever-present audience. Grandpa cut off little tidbits of the crusty edges of meat or sausage and wrapped them in tortillas stolen from the kitchen, as an offering to the ever hungry. Most asadors cook little sides of sausages or mountain oysters to pacify the onlookers. A good asador keeps the fiesta coming within his arena.

I waited until I knew it was the right time for our little ritual, and then I would go stand quietly by Grandpa's side. And he, just as quietly, would take a piece of crusty bread, which he always had hidden, and dab at the juices of the grilling meat. To accompany the black-flecked, smoky, oregano-tasting bread were snippets of meat he cut off with his pocket knife.

Around midday, after everyone had wandered up and down The Lane, taken walks, and checked on ripening fruit in the orchards, the barbecued meats and all the trimmings were carried to the tables, which were covered with white table-cloths. The food was endless, with pans and pans of red enchiladas, sarsa, corn on the cob, salads, frijoles, barbecued meats, and delicate flour tortillas wrapped in embroidered dishtowels. Aunt Emma, one of my grandfather's sisters, was legendary for her tortillas. After spending hours before the wood stove, making the thinnest, most delicate tortillas, she never allowed them to be placed on the table where they might mingle with Other Tortillas. If you wanted one of Aunt Emma's tortillas, you had to go where she sat with them possessively on her lap. She awarded one tortilla at a time to each eater. She was furious when a visiting gentleman went back for seconds and asked for "Two, this time."

Eating went on for hours so that the food could be savored and discussed. In fact, favored guests were those who noticed little details. Just before it got too dark to find your way down the pathways, glasses were raised for the tenth time to the asador, the cooks, the friends, and the rancho. I remember my own little glass of port, water, and sugar and how I loved to clink everyone else's glass; I still do.

Salute, salute, salute.

At the end of the day, one voice began singing the plaintive, lovely "Adios, adios, amores," the song which ended all Old California gatherings. Finally everyone at the table was singing.

carne asada

On California ranchos, carne asada referred to grilled meats whereas in Mexico, carne asada is a particularly thin cut of steak sliced with the grain. Our asador followed the time-honored ritual of rubbing the meats hours in advance with a dry marinade of minced herbs, salt, black pepper, garlic, olive oil, and vinegar or wine. The marinade flavors the meat marvelously and helps create a delicious crust when grilled.

- 4 pounds flank steak, tri-tip, or 5 pounds butterflied lamb
- 8 garlic cloves
- 1 tablespoon sea salt
- ¼ cup minced parsley
- 3 tablespoons dried oregano
- 1 to 2 teaspoons crushed red pepper

2 teaspoons freshly ground black pepper

1/4 cup fresh rosemary needles (optional)

2 tablespoons to 1/2 cup red wine vinegar, depending on amount of meat

2 tablespoons to 1/4 cup fruity olive oil, depending on amount of meat

Red Chile Sarsa (page 46) or Sarsa (page 45), for serving

AT LEAST 3 HOURS BEFORE BARBECUING, trim off any excess fat from the meat to prevent flare-ups. Prepare the dry marinade by placing the garlic, salt, parsley, oregano, red pepper, and black pepper on a board and mincing into a rough paste. You can also do this in a food processor. If you are cooking lamb, add the rosemary needles.

RUB THE SEASONING PASTE over all the surfaces of the meat. Place the meat in bowls or crocks and sprinkle with wine vinegar and olive oil. If you are preparing only 2 pounds or less of meat, use the smaller amount of vinegar and olive oil. Refrigerate the meat while marinating anywhere from 2 hours to overnight.

AT LEAST I HOUR BEFORE BARBECUE TIME, start the fire with crumpled newspapers, small bits of kindling like dry branches, grapevine cuttings, or good hardwood charcoal. Do not use liquid starter. Place your choice of wood over the embers of the kindling. We often use almond wood because of its steady heat. Do not use a resinous wood like pine. Allow the fire to burn down to white, glowing embers.

REMOVE THE MEAT from the refrigerator at least 30 minutes before barbecuing. Do not barbecue ice-cold meat. Place the meat over the hotter part of the fire first to sear and seal in the juices. Then raise the grate or remove the meat to spread out the coals. Return the meat to the medium-hot grill. Brush on more marinade halfway through cooking (for judging cooking times, see page 63). Do not drizzle marinade onto the embers; the oil will cause flare-ups. Turn the meat about every 8 minutes. Drizzle water on any flare-up with a soaking wet rag. A plant mister is cute but sprays over too much area.

AFTER REMOVING CARNE ASADA from the grill, allow it to rest 10 minutes, then cut into thin slices against the grain and place on a platter. Accompany with salsas such as Red Chile Sarsa and/or fresh tomato Sarsa, which is my favorite.

Serves 10 to 12 with side dishes

sarsa

The word *sarsa* belongs to the old vernacular favored by Californios when referring to their favorite things. Salsa and sarsa are sort of the same thing but sarsa is meant to be chunkier and calls for milder green chiles. Add a jalapeño or two if you want a more picante sarsa. Finally, everything is anointed with wine vinegar and olive oil.

Sarsa is typically eaten on top of frijoles or wrapped in a tortilla, but barbecued meats were never served without it.

4 large tomatoes
4 green Anaheim chiles
1 sweet red onion diced
1 garlic clove, minced
1 to 2 teaspoons salt
1 tablespoon wine vinegar
2 teaspoons fruity olive oil
¼ cup finely snipped cilantro
1 sprig of oregano

CHAR THE TOMATOES over a gas flame or on a grill. Char the chiles until blackened in the same way. Place the chiles under a damp cloth or paper towels to steam for 10 minutes. Meanwhile, pull off the tomato skins, cut the tomatoes in half, and remove the seeds. Dice the tomatoes. Use a paper towel to rub off the blackened skins from the chiles. Slit the chiles open and pull out the seeds, reserving some of them. Dice the chiles and add to the tomatoes. Add the onion, garlic, salt, vinegar, olive oil, and cilantro. Add enough reserved chile seeds to lend authority to the sarsa. Immerse the oregano sprig in the sarsa and set in a cool place until the barbecue is ready.

Makes about 5 cups

NOTE: Fresh sarsa keeps for a day, but if you happen to have some left over, simmer it in a saucepan for 5 minutes and serve over Huevos Rancheros (page 128). To make the sarsa spicier, add 2 to 4 teaspoons chile powder.

red chile sarsa

xxx

Isabel Robles, a *descendiente* with whom I recently shared a lively Californio meal, spoke hungrily of this robust sarsa that her mother always served at barbecues. My family had never made this sarsa—which goes to show that there was some diversity among the early ranchero families. Food preferences and style varied according to how much time family members had spent in Mexico, Spain, or even South America.

12 dried red chiles, such as California or New Mexican
Water, for puréeing
2 green onions, minced
2 cloves garlic, minced
2 tablespoons olive oil
1 teaspoon dried oregano
1½ teaspoons salt
Freshly ground black pepper
1 cup black or green olives
1 to 2 teaspoons reserved chile seeds

WIPE CHILE SURFACES CLEAN, as they are usually dusty. Place in a heavy, dry skillet over medium heat to toast, pressing them down with a spatula as they soften. Turn after 1 minute to soften the other side. Do not burn the chiles, or they will become bitter. Remove the chiles from the skillet, cut in half, and shake out most of the seeds, reserving them. Place the chiles in a bowl and cover with boiling water. Soak for 15 minutes.

LIFT OUT ONE THIRD OF THE CHILES and place in a blender jar, adding ¼ cup water to help purée them. Add more water if necessary. Purée the chiles and pour into a strainer set over a bowl. Continue to purée the chiles, adding water to help, and pour into the strainer. Press the purée through the strainer with a wide spoon. Scrape all the chile residue off the bottom of the strainer. Discard the chile skins.

STIR THE GREEN ONIONS, garlic, olive oil, oregano, salt, pepper, and olives into the chile purée. (It was believed that you had to use olives with pits, the way they were cured on the ranchos, for the added flavor.) Store in the refrigerator for 2 hours to let the flavors blend. Sprinkle the reserved chile seeds on top just before serving.

Makes about 3 cups

Salsa

In earlier times, sarsa or salsa was served as a condiment with barbecued, grilled, and roasted meats, just as chimichurri sauce is used in Argentina. Then someone discovered how good it was as a topping for plain rice or beans. Sarsa was an ever-present condiment on rancho tables. It wasn't until the twentieth century that salsa was turned into a snack food in which to dip chips.

salsa verde

Salsa verde, a close relative of Argentina's chimichurri sauce, now so popular, was introduced by the great number of South Americans who made their way to California in the nineteenth century. We find it necessary to make huge quantities of this salsa for our barbecues because people seem to have an insatiable appetite for it.

2 cloves garlic, minced
3 tablespoons minced fresh oregano or 1 tablespoon dried oregano
¼ cup minced Italian parsley
1 teaspoon freshly ground black pepper
1 teaspoon sea salt
½ cup fruity olive oil
3 tablespoons red wine vinegar

CHOP THE GARLIC, oregano, and parsley together. Stir in the pepper, salt, olive oil, and red wine vinegar. Make several hours before the barbecue and serve with the grilled meats. It is good brushed on meats just before removing them from the grill.

Makes 1¼ cups

chimichurri sauce

✕✕✕

The *chef de la parilla* of the Mansión de San Angel, one of our favorite restaurants in Mexico City, shared this salsa with me more than thirty years ago. It is slightly different from our Salsa Verde (page 47). The chef kept Chimichurri Sauce bottled, ready and waiting for barbecued meats, because people always kept asking for more.

I cup minced cilantro
I cup minced Italian parsley
¼ cup dried oregano, or less
½ cup white wine vinegar
¼ cup water
I tablespoon minced garlic
I teaspoon crushed red pepper
I tablespoon crushed peppercorns
I tablespoon crushed whole cloves
2 tablespoons to ¼ cup olive oil
I teaspoon sea salt

COMBINE THE CILANTRO, parsley, oregano, vinegar, water, and garlic in a large glass jar. Wash a square of cheesecloth and tie up the red pepper, peppercorns, and cloves. Immerse in the herbs. Marinate for 2 days. Remove the cheesecloth of spices. Season the sauce with a little olive oil and sea salt. Enjoy with grilled sausages, steaks, or with Pollo Adobe (page 49).

Makes about 2 cups

pollo adobe

✕✕✕

For large barbecues, butterflied chickens were weighted down with cast-iron pans filled with adobe bricks and grilled. It looks quite silly and sounds even sillier, but once you taste the chicken, you won't laugh. It helps to make 2 chickens (remember to double the seasoning rub) because they are so good the next day.

I whole chicken (2½ to 3 pounds)
I lemon
2 teaspoons sea salt
I teaspoon freshly ground black pepper
2 garlic cloves, minced
I to 2 teaspoons crushed red pepper
2 tablespoons minced cilantro
I tablespoon olive oil

USING SHEARS, cut out the backbone of the chicken. Remove and discard excess fat. Place the chicken, skin side up, on a work surface and, using both hands, press down hard on the breastbone until you hear it crack. This step allows the chicken to completely flatten out under the weight.

PUT THE CHICKEN IN A GLASS DISH and squeeze the lemon over the bird. Combine the salt, black pepper, garlic, red pepper, cilantro, and olive oil to make a paste. Rub over all surfaces, even under the skin. Let marinate for 1 hour or up to 24 hours, refrigerated. Be sure to remove the chicken at least 30 minutes before grilling so it isn't ice cold. Make slits in the breast skin and tuck the chicken legs into the pockets, to make a more compact package.

PREHEAT THE GRILL to medium heat.

PLACE THE CHICKEN ON THE GRILL, skin side down. Wrap a 12-inch cast-iron pan with foil. Oil the foil and then place the pan on top of the chicken. Place a heavy brick in the pan. Grill for 15 minutes. Turn the chicken, replace the pan and brick, and grill 20 minutes more, until deep brown but still juicy. Eat with your fingers.

Serves 2

joe's dunked bread

This recipe is from the legendary barbecuer, Joe Guidetti, who lives on a ranch in San Luis Obispo County. In his day, he presided over barbecues for governors and regular people alike. He always served this bread alongside barbecued tri-tip, beans, and salsa.

This recipe doubles and triples ad infinitum for big barbecues.

> 8 tablespoons (1 stick) salted butter
> ½ cup beer, or more as needed (preferably Bohemia)
> 4 to 6 cloves garlic, smashed
> 1 loaf French bread, cut in half lengthwise

PLACE THE BUTTER, beer, and garlic in a large roasting pan that can be placed at one end of the grill. Heat until the butter melts and starts to bubble a little. Add a little more beer if too much liquid evaporates. Cut 1-inch-deep slashes along the length of each piece of bread. Dip each piece into the butter-beer mixture, dunking all of the slashes. When ready to serve the barbecue, heat the bread at the end of the grill where the fire is low until it turns slightly golden around the edges. When the smell of this bread grilling drifts out in the breeze, it is ready.

Serves 8

butterflied lamb in pomegranate juice

Lamb was a favorite meat for barbecuing on the ranchos. In fact, no one can recall lamb ever being cooked in an indoor oven. The pomegranate juice acts as a tenderizer and gives a tart, fruity pungency to the meat. The more tender, mild-tasting lamb now available does not require as long a marinating time as was needed in the past. The fresh herbs tossed on the dying embers of the fire release herbal oils into the smoke to further flavor the meat.

Serve the lamb with Vegetables on the Grill (page 54) and rice or Eggplant Enchiladas (page 55).

I butterflied leg of lamb (about 4 pounds)

2 cloves garlic, cut into slivers

4 tablespoons finely minced fresh rosemary (see Notes)

I tablespoon finely minced garlic

I teaspoon sea salt, or as needed

2 tablespoons olive oil

2 cups pomegranate juice, natural and unsweetened (see Notes)

Freshly ground black pepper

2 long branches (10 inches) of rosemary

TRIM OFF ANY EXCESS FAT. Cut slits in the meat and stuff in the slivers of garlic. Combine the minced rosemary, garlic, salt, and olive oil to make a paste. Rub over all of the surfaces of the meat. Place the meat in a shallow glass dish and add pomegranate juice to cover. Marinate for 2 hours in the refrigerator, turning once. Bring the meat to room temperature before grilling.

ABOUT 45 MINUTES BEFORE GRILLING TIME, build a fire. When the coals are covered with grayish ash, place the grill rack 5 to 6 inches above the heat, or use a gas grill.

SEASON THE MEAT with more salt and pepper.

PLACE THE MEAT ON THE GRILL. For rare meat, cook for 20 minutes per side; for medium rare, 25 minutes per side. The exact timing will depend upon the heat of the fire and the thickness of the meat. The softer the meat feels in the middle when you push your finger into it, the more rare it is. The firmer the meat, the more well done.

DURING THE LAST 10 MINUTES of grilling, place the branches of rosemary on the coals. Turn the meat once so both sides benefit from the herbal smoke. Brush with the pomegranate marinade.

REMOVE FROM THE GRILL and let the meat rest for 10 minutes. Slice and serve.

Serves 10

NOTES: For cooking we prefer Tuscan rosemary, which grows in an upright bush, rather than the creeping rosemary, which can be bitter. Unsweetened pomegranate juice is usually available at health food stores.

homemade chorizo

xxxx

It was very common for chorizo and eggs to be served the morning of a big barbecue. The asador and his men stayed up nursing the fires for at least eight hours to heat the boulders lining the deep pits. It was still chilly at six in the morning when they came into the warm kitchen looking for something good to eat. Most likely, they needed hearty food to counteract the brandy they had used for fuel during the night while they were working. While waiting for breakfast, they consumed large cups of "white coffee"—rich dark coffee heavily laced with Pet milk and sugar.

This recipe was frequently doubled.

2 pounds boneless pork with some fat

4 cloves garlic, minced

3 teaspoons dried oregano

I teaspoon freshly ground black pepper

2 teaspoons cumin seed, crushed very fine

I tablespoon sea salt

4 to 6 tablespoons powdered red chile, preferably New Mexican, Californian, or mixed, or powdered red chile and puréed chipotle en adobo

I to 2 teaspoons chile seeds, reserved from whole chiles (optional)

¼ cup paprika

½ cup red wine vinegar or cider vinegar

2 tablespoons port wine

CUT THE PORK INTO SMALL PIECES and grind them in a food processor with short pulses so as not to purée them. (My grandmother and mother both had meat grinders that someone had to crank by hand. We usually took turns because huge quantities of chorizo were prepared.) Transfer to a bowl.

COMBINE THE GARLIC, oregano, pepper, cumin, salt, chile powder (if you like spiciness, use the larger amount of chile), chile seeds, paprika, vinegar, and port for a traditional touch.

ADD THE SPICE MIXTURE to ground pork, working it in with your hands until it is well colored. As María Torres Yzábal says in her traditional Sonoran recipe, "Add enough paprika that your hands are stained red." Otherwise, the chorizo will cook up grayish. Do a quick taste test by frying a little patty of chorizo to see if the seasonings are to your taste. Remember that the flavors will intensify as the chorizo stands. Let the chorizo mellow in a covered glass bowl in the refrigerator for at least 24 hours. It freezes well, in small packages.

Makes 2 pounds chorizo

NOTE: You can use already ground unseasoned pork, which supermarkets have available, in a pinch. It is not quite the same but it is very good. This way you can quickly make up a homemade batch of chorizo, which is much better than store-bought.

rancho breakfast of chorizo and eggs

✕✕✕

This was a favorite breakfast, right up there next to *palillis* (the cousins to sopaipillas). The smell of chorizo cooking, drifting out on a cool morning, made everyone hungry who said they were not hungry. Our favorite lunch as kids was chorizo and scrambled eggs between two pieces of toasted Wonder bread.

This recipe was frequently tripled or quadrupled the morning of a pit barbecue, which took even more hungry helpers.

    I pound Homemade Chorizo (page 52)
    8 eggs
    I tablespoon water
    Warm tortillas or toasted bread, for serving

FRY THE CHORIZO in a large skillet over medium-high heat. (I now use one that is nonstick.) Drain off the fat and blot the chorizo. While the chorizo is cooking, beat the eggs and water until frothy. Pour the eggs on top of the chorizo and let them set for a minute over medium heat. Stir the eggs and chorizo until done but still moist. Serve with warm tortillas or chunks of toasted bread.

Serves 4

vegetables on the grill

✕✕✕

Often when Grandpa was barbecuing lamb, he also grilled garden vegetables like bell peppers, Spanish onions, chiles, zucchini, corn, eggplant, and tomatoes. You don't have to grill all of them on the same occasion, a few will do. The grill should be rubbed with oil so the skins of the vegetables don't stick. Thick pieces of country bread are delicious when brushed with the basil-garlic oil and eaten with pieces of grilled vegetables for an open sandwich. Teleme or Italian fontina cheese can also be layered on pieces of grilled vegetables placed on herby grilled bread.

2 red onions, cut into 1-inch-thick slices

2 green or red bell peppers, halved from stem to bottom

3 green Anaheim or New Mexican chiles

3 poblano chiles

4 medium tomatoes

4 small zucchini, halved lengthwise

6 ears of corn, broken in half

I eggplant, trimmed and sliced ¼ inch thick

Basil-Garlic Oil

½ cup basil leaves

2 cloves garlic

¾ cup fruity olive oil

I teaspoon salt

I tablespoon sherry vinegar or balsamic vinegar

Table Condiments

Cruet of sherry vinegar or balsamic vinegar

Cruet of extra virgin olive oil

Sea salt

Pepper mill

Freshly grated Parmesan cheese

WASH AND DRY ALL THE VEGETABLES, and cut as directed.

TO MAKE THE BASIL-GARLIC OIL, place the basil, garlic, olive oil, salt, and vinegar in a food processor and purée to a liquid.

BUILD A FIRE if it's not already started. Use a paper towel to rub about 1 tablespoon of oil onto the grill rack to keep the vegetables from sticking.

BRUSH THE VEGETABLES very lightly with the Basil-Garlic Oil. Spread on the rack and grill over whitened coals. Brush more heavily with the seasoned oil after turning. The corn needs about 12 minutes to cook. The bell pepper halves require about 5 minutes per side, as do the Anaheim chiles and poblano chiles. The peppers should not completely collapse but have a little crispness remaining. The onions and eggplant will take about 4 minutes per side. The zucchini halves and the tomatoes will cook the most quickly, about 3 to 4 minutes per side. Remove the vegetables as they are done.

ARRANGE THE GRILLED VEGETABLES on a large platter. Serve with a little dish of Basil-Garlic Oil, some vinegar, olive oil, sea salt, a pepper mill, and some freshly grated Parmesan cheese. Each person can dress his or her own grilled vegetables. Don't forget the grilled bread.

Serves 8

eggplant enchiladas

✕✕✕

I fling tradition to the wind by using eggplant leftover from grilling for enchilada filling. I often grill extra eggplant because the charred herbal flavor gives so much to these enchiladas. Grandmama would never have done this since she only made Red Enchiladas (page 9), but she always forgave every culinary transgression as long as it tasted good. Besides, I divide my loyalty by taking inspiration from the caramelized onions that permeate the rancho cooking style. These enchiladas play the old Red Enchilada song with a few new instruments. They are best when made the day before they are needed.

Eggplant Filling
    I medium eggplant, cut crosswise into ½-inch slices
    ¼ cup Basil-Garlic Oil (page 54)
    I tablespoon olive oil
    2 onions, chopped
    3 teaspoons dried oregano
    ½ teaspoon salt

Red Chile Sauce
    10 California or mild New Mexican dried chiles or a combination
    Water, for puréeing
    I clove garlic mashed with I teaspoon salt
    2 tablespoons olive oil
    2 tablespoons flour
    I teaspoon dried oregano
    I tablespoon vinegar

Assembly

    3 tablespoons pure olive oil

    12 corn tortillas

    2½ cups grated medium-sharp Cheddar cheese

    ½ cup crumbled queso fresco

BRUSH THE EGGPLANT SLICES with Basil-Garlic Oil and grill or broil for 8 to 10 minutes, turning once. Set aside to cool.

HEAT THE OLIVE OIL IN A LARGE SKILLET over medium-low heat and sauté the onion gently for 15 minutes. Cut the cooled eggplant into ½-inch cubes and stir into the onions. Season with oregano and salt. Cook for 3 minutes more. Set aside.

TO MAKE THE RED CHILE SAUCE, remove the stems from the chiles and cut them in half lengthwise, shaking out the seeds. Steam the chiles over simmering water for 25 minutes. Use tongs to lift the chiles into a blender in batches. Add ¾ cup water to each batch to help in puréeing. Add the garlic and salt. Heat the olive oil in a saucepan over medium heat, add the flour, and toast until golden. Add the oregano. Whisk in the chile purée until completely blended with the roux. Add the vinegar. Simmer the sauce, covered, for 15 minutes. Add more water if necessary.

HEAT 1 TABLESPOON OIL at a time in a skillet over medium heat to fry the tortillas, until softened, turning once. Stack tortillas on a paper towel.

PREHEAT THE OVEN to 350°F.

TO MAKE THE ENCHILADAS, dip a softened tortilla into the warm sauce and place on a flat plate. Place 3 tablespoons Cheddar cheese and about 2 tablespoons eggplant mixture down the center. Fold over the sides of the tortilla and place, seam down, in a long, greased baking dish. Continue with the rest of the tortillas. You will need 2 baking dishes. Drizzle on more sauce and sprinkle with more Cheddar cheese.

BAKE FOR 12 TO 15 MINUTES. Before serving, sprinkle queso fresco over enchiladas.

Makes 12 enchiladas

The Grandest Barbecue of All: The Pit Barbecue

The anticipation of barbecue day meant no detail was too much trouble. The smallest child was given a job that made him feel important, even if all he did was carry a baby armload of kindling. When all the jobs were done at the end of the day, the children were rounded up by either Grandpa or his brothers. The reward was a story. The word got out to come to the long table in the rancho kitchen or, if it was not yet dusk, to the grape arbor. Grandpa was famous among all the children, not for his barbecuing but because he could peel an apple in one long unbroken strip. Always fair, Grandpa gave the peel to a different child each time. The best part was being the one to get an apple peel as long as a snake. You could slowly nibble on it, making it last, and watch the envious looks of your cousins while the story unfolded. We all hoped for the Plum Bear story, our favorite.

The Plum Bear of Rancho Los Tularcitos

On the rancho, grizzly bears were considered the outlaws of the animal world. They lived in the nearby foothills, too close for anyone's comfort, especially since it was easy for them to pay a call at the back door or saunter down the main street of the pueblo, looking for snacks. When they were hungry, almost nothing stopped them from plundering. Grizzlies were frightening and scary, but no one had been eye to eye with one until the Plum Bear came along.

A plum tree right next to the kitchen adobe was so heavy with fruit its boughs were hanging near the ground, where the bear could have picked all the plums he wanted. But no, our bear climbed the tree, not an easy task for a bear. The Plum Bear decided that he wanted the plums on the end of the bough on top of the roof. Anyone who knew anything about fruit knew that the ripest ones were at the top. Our bear was a fruit expert, and his only choice was to climb the tree and climb onto the roof of the adobe so he could get the best plum. The roof of the old adobe was not made to support bears.

Some women were busy cooking when the bear fell through the roof. His descent into the adobe must have surprised him as much as it surprised the women making tortillas. They ran screaming out of the little house, leaving it to the perplexed bear.

Horses were always kept ready, with riatas coiled at the saddle bow. Upon hearing the screams of the women, several men jumped on their waiting steeds and surrounded the Plum Bear, who had made his way out of the house. He was swiftly lassoed and tied up to a nearby sycamore tree, the best kind of tree for securing bears.

Whenever I heard this story as a child, I felt immensely sorry for the bear who had only sought the perfect plum at the top of the tree. I wondered then—and still do—if he got the plum. Excited over capturing a grizzly, the men sent messengers to neighboring ranchos to announce the staging of a bear and bull fight to be followed, of course, by a barbecue. The cruel practice of these events ended in the 1860s. I still feel sorry for the Plum Bear who lost to the bull as did many other grizzlies, before and after, who roamed the Diablo foothills near the rancho.

Even though the bear and bull fights were discontinued, when a beef was slaughtered, the head was reserved for a barbecue. The following directions can be used for any pit barbecue. Even whole prepared turkeys can be cooked using this ancient technique. In different rural areas of the country, from California to Texas, pit barbecues are still enjoyed.

The Pit

Days before a barbecue, a pit was dug in a large open area. Only the men tending the fires and the asador were permitted on the ledge around the pit. The cooked meat was more easily lifted out of the pit from the ledge.

The boys searched for smooth stones from the creek bed. Once they had a generous pile assembled, the stones were placed in a deep layer at the bottom of the pit. The fires were built on top of the stones and stoked until they became red hot.

Whether several beef roasts were to be cooked or a bull's head, the fire was started the night before the barbecue, about twelve hours before serving time. For five hours during the night, hard wood was added continuously to the fire. The feeding of the fire, usually nursed along by a comradely group of men, was one of the most important aspects of the ritual. The group sustained itself into the long, cool hours of the morning with endless stories and the asador's provisions, usually an assortment of libations. The wives and mothers got up early and with them came the smell of freshly made coffee, chorizo and eggs, tortillas, or Grandmama's potato pan rolls—a macho breakfast since the barbecue was part of the rites of machismo.

The Bull's Head Barbecue
and Other Pit Barbecued Meats

To make the great effort of preparing a pit barbecue worthwhile, choose large roasts, weighing ten to twenty pounds each. You can only err in leaving the meat too long in the pit so that it overcooks and becomes mushy.

In the early morning hours (5 a.m.), the bull's head was thoroughly washed down with buckets of cold water or a garden hose. The hair was left decorously on the head, and bouquets of mint, oregano, and rosemary were stuffed into the ears and mouth. There always was and still is one little boy who takes on this job with relish.

Gunnysacking was wrapped around the head, with wire to bind it tightly, to make it easier to lift it in and out of the pit. Next wine was poured over the gunnysacking. Between 6 and 8 a.m., coals were raked to the sides of the pit, and banana leaves were arranged on the hot stones. On the rancho, crisscrossed palm or banana leaves were arranged over the hot stones to keep the burlap from scorching. Next a 3 x 2-foot piece of chicken wire was placed on top of the leaves.

The wrapped bull's head and any other wrapped packages of meat were placed on the wire with more layers of palm or banana leaves. A large sheet of tin was positioned over the leaves to keep the dirt from falling onto the meat. Helpers quickly shoveled a layer of earth over the pit. The asador stood back and watched for steam, a sign that the pit was not completely sealed. Any visible vent was quickly covered with a shovelful of dirt. In olden times, after the last shovelful, the asador marked a cross in the earth and spilled on a glass of red wine for a blessing.

Eight hours later, it was announced to the gathering that the pit was to be unearthed. Everyone gathered for the ceremony. The dirt was carefully shoveled to one side, the sheet of tin removed, and the leaves peeled away. The wrapped bull's head and other bundles of meat were lifted out onto a heavy board. The mesmerized onlookers watched as deft hands removed the baling wire and gunnysacking to reveal the contents. The eyes of the bull were tokens given to the chief asador along with the cheeks, which were a delicacy. Today, this custom is gladly ignored.

The asador's men lifted the meat onto a board garnished with oregano and rosemary. Sharp knives and forks clicked in unison as they sliced up the roast, the tongue, a favorite of the rancheros, and pulled the meat off the head with a fork. The other pit-cooked meats were shredded and served with sarsa, red chile sarsa, and chimichurri sauce. Freshly made flour tortillas were offered so everyone could wrap up a burrito.

jeff chavarria's smoked, herb-crusted pit beef

✕✕✕

When you do a pit barbecue, season your meat at least a day in advance. You can use this recipe to cook either in the traditional earthen pit or in an improvised pit, that is, a kettle grill. My cousin, Jeff Chavarria, who now holds the title of asador, doesn't go more than a few days without barbecuing even if it's snowing in Lake Tahoe, where he lives. He devised this method to flavor the meat more intensely.

Serve the meat with tortillas, thick rancho beans, and sarsa.

First Day

>   1 center-cut chuck roast (10 to 12 pounds)
>   1 head garlic, separated and peeled
>   1 tablespoon kosher salt
>   1½ tablespoons freshly ground black pepper

Second Day

>   ½ cup chopped fresh basil
>   ½ cup chopped fresh oregano
>   ½ cup chopped fresh rosemary
>   ¼ cup minced garlic
>   1 tablespoon grated lime zest
>   2 Anaheim chiles, minced, including seeds and skins
>   1 tablespoon kosher salt
>   1 tablespoon freshly ground black pepper
>   3 tablespoons New Mexican ground red chile (optional)
>   Several branches of fresh rosemary
>   About ½ cup dry red wine

ON THE FIRST DAY, prepare a wood and charcoal fire in a kettle grill with a cover. Let it burn down to barely smoldering. Push the fire to the edges of the barbecue.

PREPARE THE MEAT. Using a small sharp knife, make slits all over the meat and insert a garlic clove into each slit. Rub salt and pepper over the roast. Place the meat on the grill, put the cover on, and smoke the meat for 2 hours, turning several times. The temperature should be no more than 250°F since you are just initially smoking the meat. Remove the meat after 2 hours and let it cool. Wrap it in foil, then refrigerate overnight.

ON THE SECOND DAY, prepare a fire in the grill at least 3 hours before serving time. Let the coals burn down to the gray-ash stage.

COMBINE THE BASIL, oregano, rosemary, garlic, lime zest, chiles, salt, pepper, and ground chile. Rub this herbal mix on all sides of the chilled, smoked roast.

LAY OUT A LENGTH OF CHEESECLOTH cut long enough to encase the roast. Place the roast on the cheesecloth and begin rolling it up, adding rosemary sprigs as you go. Douse the cheesecloth with red wine until it is heavily soaked. Wrap the meat in a long piece of heavy-duty aluminum foil, then seal tightly.

PLACE THE MEAT ON THE GRILL RACK in a barbecue, cover the grill, and cook for 3 hours, adding more coals as needed. Check the internal temperature of the meat with an instant-read thermometer. The meat is done when it registers 160 to 165°F. If you like rare meat, remove it at 145 to 155°F. If you cook roast in an earthen pit, it will require 7 to 8 hours, and of course you will be unable to check the meat's temperature during cooking.

LET THE MEAT REST for 15 minutes before carving.

Serves 16 to 18

jeff's chile ribs

Just as I have tweaked old recipes and updated them, my cousin Jeff Chavarria has revised old barbecue techniques, having experimented with different woods and different methods of smoking. We now use a greater variety of herbs and spices than the cooks and asadors of the past.

Spice Rub
> 2 tablespoons kosher salt
> ¼ cup brown sugar
> 2 tablespoons ground cumin
> 2 tablespoons chile powder, preferably ancho
> 1 tablespoon freshly ground black pepper, or less if desired
> 1 teaspoon cayenne pepper, or less if desired
> ¼ cup sweet smoked Spanish paprika (see Notes)

Ribs
> 10 pounds baby back pork ribs

Whiskey Glaze
> ¼ cup honey
> ½ cup whiskey

TO MAKE THE SPICE RUB, combine the salt, brown sugar, cumin, chile powder, pepper, cayenne, and paprika in a bowl and blend well. Pat the ribs dry with paper towels, then rub in the spice mixture. Place the ribs in a long pan, cover tightly, and refrigerate overnight.

TO MAKE THE WHISKEY GLAZE, on barbecue day, combine the honey and whiskey in a small saucepan. Bring to a boil over medium heat, stirring to blend. When the sauce thickens slightly, remove it from the heat. Set aside.

PREPARE A CHARCOAL FIRE until coals are covered with gray ash and smoldering.

GRILL THE RIBS over very low coals for about 1½ hours. Keep the barbecue covered and barely vented. This slow cooking (about 275° to 300°F) is what keeps the meat tender. Just before removing the ribs, brush with the glaze. Grill for 5 minutes, then brush again very lightly with glaze.

Serves 8 to 10 people for dinner, more as an appetizer

NOTES: Smoked Spanish paprika, known as pimontón, is sold by mail-order from Spanish markets. If you are an insecure barbecuer or do not have the time to stand by the barbecuing ribs for 1½ hours, rub the spice mixture on the ribs, let them marinate, and then wrap them tightly in foil. Bake in a preheated 250- to 275-degree oven for 1½ hours. Unwrap and finish the ribs on a slow grill for 30 minutes, turning to achieve some browning.

The Asador's Secrets

Here are the precautions followed by the asador, as handed down over four generations. It was difficult to wrench all of this information from asador Jeff Chavarria but he gave in finally: He couldn't stand the thought of too many people ruining their barbecue.

1. Put the meat on the grill when the fire passes the midpoint, with coals covered in gray ash. The meat will be blackened before it is cooked if the fire is too hot. Drip water over any flames.

2. Don't use too many soaked chips or green wood. Too much smoke causes a bitter aftertaste. Try soaking a few alder or applewood chips in wine or brandy for just 20 minutes before tossing on the coals.

3. Never use starter fluid. It can leave a horrible aftertaste.

4. Soaking meat too long in a liquid marinade can cause mushiness. Marinades flavor rather than tenderize. Marinades provide just surface tenderizing.

5. Never walk away from your fire.

6. A grill placed over stacked bricks or river rocks can provide as succulent a meal as an expensive grill.

7. Exact timing varies, depending on how hot the fire is and what type of cut you are grilling. Here are some estimated times:

- Flank steak (about 1¾ pounds): 20 to 25 minutes
- Chuck roast (3½ to 4 pounds): 1 hour
- Boneless top sirloin (2½ pounds): 35 minutes
- Tri-tip (1½ to 2 pounds): 35 minutes
- Chicken thighs: 40 minutes, turned frequently
- Chicken breasts with bone: 25 minutes, turned frequently
- Boneless chicken fillets: 10 to 12 minutes, turned once
- Baby back ribs (indirect heat): 1½ hours in a covered and vented grill

Colorful Side Dishes for a Barbecue

Half of the fun of a barbecue is the side dishes, which is why even a vegetarian can be satisfied. Certain classics were expected at rancho barbecues—like Red Enchiladas (page 9), thick frijoles, sarsa, and voluminous amounts of the delicate flour tortillas. The rest depended on the season and how celebratory the occasion was. You can add more salsas, corn on the cob, grilled vegetables, Chiles Flojos (page 65), and Chileña Pie (page 155). Any barbecue thrown in the summer had to have creek-chilled watermelon for dessert even if there were homemade pies and cakes.

charred corn

Since barbecues were held during the summer months, corn on the cob was an expected side dish. I have read recently that corn, cleaned of its silk but still in the husk, should be soaked in water to prevent charring. I don't believe soaking is necessary. Green husks don't burn too badly, and, besides, the smoky, charred flavor is desirable. In the old days people never rubbed anything on the corn itself, but we like a chile butter and the Mexican custom of drizzling on crema and cheese.

You may double and triple amounts as needed. Offer Mexican crema and crumbled cotija cheese for guests to drizzle and sprinkle over ears of freshly steamed or grilled corn on the cob.

    8 ears of corn with husks intact

    8 tablespoons (1 stick) butter, softened

    3 teaspoons red chile powder or 1 to 2 tablespoons puréed chipotle en adobo

    1 jar (15 ounces) crema mexicana, preferably Cacique brand

    1 cup grated or crumbled cotija cheese

CAREFULLY PEEL BACK the corn husks without tearing them. Remove all of the silk, rinsing off the corn under running water. Keep the husks intact.

MIX TOGETHER THE BUTTER and chile powder. Rub about 1 tablespoon of the chile butter over the kernels of each ear, then pull up the husks, smoothing them over the ears. If you want to cook the corn in a simpler fashion, as was done in the past, do not bother with the chile butter.

PREPARE A GRILL, preferably of wood or mesquite, until at medium heat.

GRILL THE EARS FOR 10 MINUTES, turning frequently. The husks will char and smoke a little, lending even more flavor to the corn.

DRIZZLE CREMA MEXICANA over your ear of corn, smear it around, and then sprinkle with cotija cheese.

Serves 8

chiles flojos

———————— ✕✕✕ ————————

Green chiles were placed at the side of the grill while the rest of the barbecue was cooking. Chiles Flojos, or lazy chiles, were charred, peeled, and sprinkled with olive oil and salt to be eaten with barbecued meat. They were also filled with soft queso fresco. Nowadays, we prefer a mixture of goat cheese and cream cheese. These are delicious with just a spoonful of sarsa on top, alone or with barbecued meats.

    8 to 10 long green Anaheim or New Mexican chiles, charred,
        peeled, andseedsed
    2 tablespoons olive oil
    1 teaspoon salt
    4 ounces goat cheese
    8 ounces cream cheese
    2 tablespoons minced Italian parsley
    2 tablespoons minced cilantro

CUT A SLIT DOWN THE SIDE of each chile. Carefully remove the seeds. Rub the chiles with olive oil and sprinkle with salt. Blend the goat cheese, cream cheese, parsley, and cilantro. Stuff about 2 tablespoons of this mixture into the length of each chile and press to seal the opening. Serve immediately.

Serves 8

THE olive
AND THE LANE

it was difficult for my grand-mother to give a recipe unless she started with, "First you take some olive oil. . . ." The use of olive oil was as necessary to authentic rancho cooking as the use of pure lard to classic Mexican cooking. Olive oil was the life force that animated all savory flavors, and if you took olive oil away from our cooking, there wouldn't be any cooking. The olive and the chile reigned supreme.

A young Aunt Dora pauses a moment on her pet horse,
Dolly, before heading back down to The Lane and the ranch house,
where she undoubtably removed that silly hat and helped
make enchiladas for dinner.

That given, it's understandable that one of the first things that José Loreto Higuera did upon receiving his Spanish land grant was to plant a copse of olive trees. In time, the trees formed into a mile-long silvery-green alley that became known as The Lane. Anyone coming by horse, *carreta*, or carriage entered into the world of Rancho Los Tularcitos through The Lane.

Sometime in the nineteenth century, The Lane was the setting for tragedy. One summer evening, the family waited for visitors, who were coming from a long way. They knew the carriage was close when they heard guitars and singing echoing down The Lane. The music was followed by an eerie silence. Assuming that the guests had arrived, the family went to greet them, but no one was there. Someone was sent down The Lane on horseback to check on the visitors only to find they had all been slaughtered by marauding Indians. Whenever this story was recounted on a dark night, you were asked to hush and listen for the Spanish songs that the visitors were singing that night. There was not one time when I did not hear the songs.

Only one quarter of The Lane remains, the rest having been consumed by the growth of Silicon Valley, but recently we went to visit it and stand under its green canopy. There is still a ghostly aura and I am sure that the carriage of singing guests returns on certain nights.

The Olive Press of the Rancho

The first trees planted by the astute padres who helped settle California were olive trees. They saw olive oil as an all-encompassing necessity. It could be eaten, used for cooking, for lamp oil, as a healing balm, and on occasion for the sacrament. A recent magazine article noted—incorrectly—that the early Californians only pressed olive oil to use for religious purposes. An anointing with olive oil was given on occasion with the sacrament or as a blessing in death. But nowhere in the United States was as large a crop of olive trees planted as in California in the 1770s. The missions and ranchos had more worldly uses for olive oil. Most of it was consumed as food.

On Rancho Los Tularcitos, they had their own granite crusher for grinding the olives into a purplish paste. This must have seemed like quite a step up from the method used in the earlier mission days when the olives were hand-crushed in mortars, boiled, and hung in sacks, which were then pressed between boards or in an olive press to extract the oil.

The missions and ranchos also cured olives for use in many dishes, they fried in olive oil, and dressed salad greens in olive oil. The asadors rubbed lamb, chicken, and beef with olive oil before grilling.

By the end of the nineteenth century, most ranchos no longer found it necessary to press their own oil. Good olive oil could be purchased in town. Still, they continued to cure whole olives in oak barrels because you couldn't buy good olives, let alone rancho-style olives. Many of the old-timers kept an olive barrel or crock on the back porch or in the cellar. I have found these addictive olives in only four places: my family's olive barrel, in Spain and Italy, and in the olive crocks of my friends, Barbara and Bill Spencer at Windrose Farm, where they harvest their own olives.

Curing Olives

The ancient practice of curing olives has seen a revitalization, especially among aficionados who cannot find the good olives they want to eat. Part of this interest is due to the increased appreciation of good olive oil not only for its flavor but also for its nutritional value. Also, many people in California have an olive tree in their yard or know someone with one.

The optimum time to pick olives is in the autumn, when the green olives are just beginning to show a slight purplish tinge. Olives at all stages of ripening are bitter because of glucosides. Curing purges the olives of this compound by drawing it out with water, salt, or lye.

All cures try to accomplish the same things: leach out the bitterness, develop flavor, and soften the fruit. A lye-cure can produce mild, sweet olives with no bitterness and a good olive flavor. Brine-cured and salt-cured olives will still have a residual bitterness which varies depending on the olives used, the stage of ripeness at which they were picked, and how long the cure. You may find that you like a bitter edge in an olive, as with Greek Kalamatas.

bill spencer's green olives

xxx

These are the true, almost nutty sweet olives, as they have been eaten for centuries in the Mediterranean, unsullied by too much vinegar and salt. The use of lye is necessary to leach away the olives' natural bitterness. Used with caution, this age-old cure is perfectly safe. In the past, water and wood ash were used as a natural form of lye cure. All of the olives that you buy, except the Kalamata or Greek-style olives, have been treated with a lye cure at some stage.

My Aunt Dede Santos, who cured olives up until a year before she died, still used the 1875 recipe from Rancho Los Tularcitos. Bill Spencer's technique closely matches that of the rancho, proving that curing olives is a timeless pursuit.

    5 gallons just-picked olives, still green and firm
    18 ounces of pure lye (caustic soda) with no additives
    15 gallon container, food-safe plastic bucket (do not use metal buckets)
    10 gallon container, plastic, to serve as a weight on olives
    2¾ cups sea salt

RINSE OLIVES 2 OR 3 TIMES in clean, cold water to rid them of dust and leaves. Remove any flawed or bruised olives.

WEARING GLOVES and guarding against splashes, measure 1 gallon room-temperature water into a 15-gallon food-safe plastic bucket and very slowly add 9 ounces of lye, stirring with a whisk or a long-handled wooden spoon to help the lye dissolve. Add 3 gallons of cold water, stirring well again.

USING A STRAINER, gently add the olives to the curing solution, again guarding against splashes. Make sure that the olives are completely covered in liquid; any olives that are not will turn dark.

CLEAN A BUCKET and add 2 gallons of water to it. Place on top of the olives to weight them down in the curing solution. Place in a cool, dark location. Let the olives stand for 8 hours. Drain the olives and add a fresh lye solution of the same proportions as above. Let stand for 8 to 10 hours. During the lye cure, the bitterness will be leached out and the olives will soften.

NOW YOU ARE READY FOR AN OLIVE TEST. Using tongs, remove an olive from the curing solution and rinse the olive under running water so you can handle it. Slice the olive to observe the depth to which the lye has penetrated which can be noted by the change of color in the olive flesh. You want a two-thirds to three-quarters pene-tation to the pit. This will take from 20 to 48 hours of curing. Generally, it is better to stop too soon. If the olives are left in the cure too long, they become soft and mushy.

WHEN YOU HAVE CHECKED THE OLIVE and the cure is complete (that is, three-quar-ters to the pit), drain off the curing solution. If the cure penetration is not yet there, let the olives stand for 8 hours more. Check again. Each time make sure that the olives remain submerged.

WHEN YOU ARE SATISFIED that the cure is complete, remove the olives and rinse 3 or 4 times in cold water. You can do this in a clean sink. Rinse out the cure bucket. Cover the olives with fresh cold water. Replace the weight bucket to hold the olives submerged so they do not come in contact with air. Place back in a cool, dark loca-tion.

RE-RINSE THE OLIVES EVERY DAY for 10 days and then rerinse every third day for a week. The water color will slowly change from coffee to thin tea. Drain off this "tea water."

AT THIS TIME, prepare a brine by combining 1¾ cups kosher or sea salt (do not use iodized salt) and 1 gallon of cold water. (I like to make sure the salt is well dissolved in a quart of warm water before I add it to the olives and cold water.) This brine cure will now purge the olives of any remaining lye.

AFTER 12 TO 14 HOURS, drain off the brine. Prepare a fresh salt brine and cover the olives a second time. Observe the color of the water after 1 week. If still dark, rinse the olives 2 or 3 times, prepare a fresh brine, and cover the olives. Soak for 1 week. If the water remains a light color, try an olive. The olive should taste sweet, creamy, nutty and there should be no aftertaste. Generally, it takes from 2 to 3 weeks to obtain the olives of your dreams.

TO STORE OLIVES, make a fresh salt brine of 1 cup sea salt to 1 gallon of water. Sub-merge the olives and store in the refrigerator for up to 6 months. Before serving, rinse the olives of the brine and garnish with fresh herbs, dried chiles, chipotle chiles, garlic cloves, and a dash of olive oil if desired.

Makes 5 gallons of olives

dry salt cure for olives

✕✕✕

This cure produces the more shriveled, Greek-style olives most of us are familiar with. I think this method is better than the wet cure for leaching out the natural bitterness, but the olives are saltier. After the cure, they can be soaked to remove some of the salt. Remember, the less you handle the olives with your hands, the better. Use utensils.

    2 gallons black, ripe olives
    10 pounds rock salt or sea salt
    Large plastic container poked with holes
    5-gallon crock or plastic, food-safe bucket (do not use metal)

PLACE A FEW CLEAN STONES in the bottom of a 5-gallon crock or food-safe plastic bucket to hold a large plastic container perforated with holes off the bottom. This will allow the bitter olive liquid to drip away. Fit the plastic container inside the crock.

PUT A LAYER OF SALT on the bottom of the plastic container. Add a layer of olives, a layer of salt, a layer of olives, and so on, until you have used all of the olives. Every olive should come in contact with salt. Place a plate with a weight on top to keep the olives submerged. (I use a brick as a weight.)

EVERY WEEK, remove the olives and discard any liquid at the bottom of the crock. If there is any excess liquid collected around particular olives, blot it off with clean paper towels. Repack using the same salt. Add more salt if necessary since salt prevents the forming of mold. If you see the slightest bit of mold, discard those olives. If you keep all of the olives submerged in salt, however, mold should not be a problem.

AFTER ABOUT 5 WEEKS, remove an olive, rinse it, and taste it. If most of the bitterness has been leached, take all of the olives out of the crock and rinse them in cold water. Allow the olives to soak in a bucket of clean water to rid them of some of the salt.

NEXT, PLACE THE OLIVES, 2 cups at a time, in a strainer and dip into boiling water for 10 seconds. Process all of the olives this way. Blot the olives with paper towels, sprinkle with sea salt, toss with olive oil, and store in jars in the refrigerator. You may season the olives further with vinegar, garlic, chipotle chiles, and herbs.

Makes 2 gallons of olives

platter of green salad

✕✕✕

One of the best ways to showcase fine extra virgin olive oil, unaffected by the heat of cooking, is in a salad. I like to garnish it with olives, home cured if possible.

I usually mix up the dressing just a few minutes before we sit down. The only thing I do different from my mother and grandmother is to add minced shallots or garlic and Dijon mustard, because I like the way the mustard makes the dressing emulsify. Sometimes I add a splash of balsamic vinegar, too.

I love to mix salad on a platter not only because you can toss it better but also because the salad stays crisper in one layer than when heaped in a deep bowl. You can use a bowl if you prefer.

1 tomato, halved
1 small cucumber, peeled and halved lengthwise
Sea salt and freshly ground black pepper
1 shallot, minced
2 teaspoons Dijon mustard
2 to 3 tablespoons sherry vinegar or red wine vinegar
5 to 6 tablespoons extra virgin olive oil
4 cups torn romaine (or your favorite lettuce), rinsed, dried, and crisped
1 handful of croutons (recipe follows)
Shavings of Parmigiano-Reggiano cheese
Green olives or salt-cured black olives, for garnish

USE A TINY SPOON to scoop out the seeds of the tomato and to scrape out the cucumber's seeds. Cut the tomato and cucumber into strips and dice. Put the tomato and cucumber on a paper towel to drain off excess liquid.

PLACE A GOOD PINCH OF SALT and a grind of pepper in a little bowl. Add the shallot, mustard, and vinegar. Whisk with a fork. Slowly drizzle in 5 tablespoons of the olive oil while beating with a fork. The dressing will thicken. Taste to see if you want to add more olive oil or salt. Remove the greens from the refrigerator and arrange them on a platter or wide bowl. Drizzle on 2 or 3 tablespoons of dressing and toss with your hands. Add more dressing and continue tossing with your hands until the leaves are just barely coated. Add the tomato, cucumber, and croutons. Drizzle a tiny bit of dressing over the top, grind some more pepper over all, sprinkle with the shavings of cheese, and garnish with olives.

Serves 4 to 6

Croutons

2 to 3 thick slices French or Italian bread, cut into ½-inch cubes

1 tablespoon olive oil

1 teaspoon dried herbs, such as oregano and basil (optional)

1 tablespoon grated Parmesan cheese (optional)

PREHEAT THE OVEN to 350°F (or use a toaster oven).

PUT THE BREAD CUBES in a pie pan and toss with the olive oil. Bake for about 10 minutes or until croutons are golden. Sprinkle with herbs or grated cheese, if desired.

Makes about 1 cup

The Olive Rule

The olive barrel kept in a cool spot on the verandah, near the back door, always beckoned. The rule was that you never reached in the barrel with your bare hands. For an olive taste, you used the wooden ladle.

THE tortilla

AND OTHER BREADS OF THE WEST

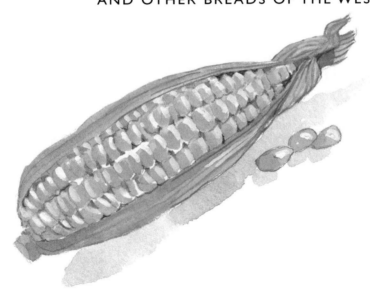

The tortilla, not sourdough, was the first bread of California. The flour tortillas, brought from Sonora by the Spanish colonists, were stretched large enough to hold dinner in an edible plate, the original burrito. At every stop along the trail, tortillas were cooked on a *comal*, or griddle, placed over coals. When California became more civilized with some

The whole family loved this car, but Aunt Emma (standing at the rear with her feet planted firmly on the ground) of tortilla fame refused to get in.

form of *cocina* (kitchen) and *horno* (outdoor oven), everyone still preferred tortillas, although eventually bread was made to satisfy Yankee and European tastes. The Californios grew quite fond of flour tortillas because often they were all they had to eat with their frijoles. Wheat was dry farmed in the valleys and practically took care of itself after it was broadcast in the spring. Like the cattle that roamed over the hills in endless pastures, the wheat required little effort on the part of the colonists and rancheros. The planting of corn was much more labor intensive, and corn also needed intermittent irrigation. In certain parts of California, they never ate the corn tortilla. Many of the missions and ranchos operated their own mills for grinding wheat to use for flour tortillas and horno breads.

Flour tortillas were so important in our family that they were treated like a rite of passage. All the girls learned to make them with varying degrees of success. If you married into the family, after the honeymoon it was tortilla school with Aunt Nicolassa, Aunt Emma, Grandmama, or Sister (my mother). When Uncle Jack married glamorous Faye from St. Louis, she was put under the tutelage of Sister, who was noted for patience and fun. Grandmama and the aunts were harder taskmasters. Success came after three or four sessions. Even Grandmama admitted that Aunt Faye's tortillas were quite good, even if she did come from Missouri.

From the age of eight, the job I coveted most in the kitchen was tortilla making.

Being in a position to eat as many warm tortillas as I wanted seemed like a sterling idea. After I endlessly badgered my grandmother, she finally gave me some dough to roll out. I used too much flour and overworked the tortilla into rubber. When she showed me how to gently lay it on the comal, it resembled an amoeba. As it baked, the little brown flecks formed and the holes I had poked in it almost closed up. I burned my fingers turning it over, but I ate the ugly thing as soon as I could get it off the griddle, thinking it the most delicious tortilla I had ever eaten. My grandmother and mother withheld judgment, which was probably the most profound way they had of teaching a skill. One was never criticized in this kitchen. Much later, when I finally accomplished a perfectly round tortilla, thin enough to read the newspaper through, everyone in the kitchen was overjoyed. Someone went to find Grandpa so he could see my perfect tortilla. He proposed that it be mounted under glass!

rancho flour tortillas

✕✕✕

Opinion was heatedly divided as to what constituted the perfect tortilla. One family swore by thick, leathery tortillas, which we thought might be better used as saddles, and we defended our thin, delicate ones, which the other camp thought were too insubstantial. We are shameless in thinking that the kind we make are the best. Personally, I love them all, thick and thin, for in the end the best is the warm tortilla you are eating at that moment.

The best rolling pin for tortillas is a 5- to 7-inch sawed-off broomstick or dowel.

> 4 cups unbleached all-purpose flour, plus more for kneading
> ⅛ teaspoon baking powder
> 2 rounded tablespoons vegetable shortening or lard (about ⅓ cup)
> 1½ teaspoons salt
> About 1½ cups warm water

STIR THE FLOUR and baking powder together in a large bowl with a whisk. Use a large fork or pastry blender to work the shortening into the flour mixture until it is mealy and there are no powdery remains of flour. Use your fingers to finish working the fat into the flour.

DISSOLVE THE SALT IN THE WARM WATER, then drizzle it slowly into flour mixture while stirring. Add most of water until you have a soft dough. Add the remaining water to any dry spots. Knead for 1 minute, adding flour as needed but not too much. Turn the bowl over to cover the dough. Let it rest for 25 to 45 minutes, to make the dough easier to handle.

PINCH OFF 12 PIECES OF DOUGH and form balls by turning the edges under as you rotate the ball in your hand. Oil a baking sheet to hold the balls of dough, covering them as they are formed. Flatten each ball with the heel of your hand. Cover with plastic wrap to prevent the dough from drying, and let rest for 20 to 30 minutes.

PREHEAT A COMAL OR GRIDDLE over medium heat. Take out 1 flattened ball and roll it into a thick circle, rolling from the center in short strokes. To make a round tortilla, not a violin-shaped one, turn the circle of dough after each stroke with the rolling pin. The tortilla should be about ⅛ inch thick and 9 to 10 inches across. You can hold it up and run your fingers underneath as you turn it to stretch it further; this step is not absolutely necessary but produces an even thinner tortilla.

GENTLY LAY THE FIRST TORTILLA on the comal or griddle. Turn over every 20 seconds. To turn, push your thumb and forefinger into the edge of the tortilla and turn it away from you. You will develop your own rhythm. Golden freckles will form over the surface of the tortilla, indicating its lightness. Sometimes the tortilla will inflate like a balloon. When the tortilla stops bubbling and forming freckles, it is done. Remove it immediately so it doesn't overcook.

WRAP COOKED TORTILLAS in a clean dishtowel. When cool, wrap in foil or put in a plastic bag. Heat tortillas on a griddle to warm them up before serving.

Makes 12 flour tortillas (minus one or two for the cook)

a granddaughter's
flour tortillas

———————————— ✂✂✂ ————————————

These tortillas are my updated version of the rancho tortilla. If you like to eat a lot of flour tortillas but worry about the type of fat the traditional ones require (shortening or lard), these are the tortillas for you. They are just as flaky, thanks to the trick of freezing part of the flour and the oil together so that the mixture simulates flour and shortening.

4 cups unbleached all-purpose flour
½ teaspoon baking powder
4 tablespoons canola oil
1½ teaspoons sea salt
1½ cups warm water

STIR THE FLOUR and baking powder together in a large bowl with a whisk. Transfer ½ cup of this mixture to another bowl and add all of the canola oil to it, blending with a fork. Place the oil-flour mixture in a plastic zipper bag and freeze for 1 hour.

USE A PASTRY BLENDER to blend the cold flour-oil mixture into the dry flour mixture until it resembles coarse crumbs.

MIX THE SALT INTO THE WARM WATER until dissolved. Stir into the flour mixture until a dough forms. Knead for 1 minute in the bowl. Cover the dough with plastic wrap and let it rest for at least 30 minutes.

FORM 12 BALLS OF DOUGH. Place on an oiled baking sheet and cover with plastic wrap. Flatten the balls with the heel of your hand (through the plastic is fine). Let rest for 30 minutes.

PREHEAT A COMAL OR GRIDDLE over medium heat. Take out 1 flattened ball and roll it into a thick circle, rolling from the center in short strokes. To make a round tortilla, keep turning the circle of dough after each stroke with the rolling pin. The tortilla should be about ⅛ inch thick and 9 to 10 inches across. You can hold it up and run your fingers underneath as you turn it to stretch it further; this step is not absolutely necessary but produces an even thinner tortilla.

GENTLY LAY THE FIRST TORTILLA on the comal or griddle. Turn over every 20 seconds. Push your thumb and forefinger into the edge of the tortilla and turn it away from you. You will develop your own rhythm. Golden freckles will form over the surface of the tortilla, indicating its lightness. Sometimes the tortilla will inflate like a balloon.

When the tortilla stops bubbling and forming freckles, it is done. Remove immediately so it doesn't overcook.

WRAP COOKED TORTILLAS in a clean dishtowel. When cool, wrap in foil or put in a plastic bag. Heat tortillas on a griddle to warm them up before serving.

Makes 12 flour tortillas

corn tortillas

xxx

Even though my family limited themselves to flour tortillas, corn tortillas were also a part of old California cooking. I had trouble mastering corn tortillas until I was advised by a Baja California cook to add a little white flour and oil to the masa to make the dough easier to handle. This version works, and it makes great quesadillas.

Instant masa harina is sold in supermarkets under the brand names of Quaker and Maseca.

   2 cups instant masa harina (tortilla flour)
   2 tablespoons all-purpose flour
   I cup and 2 to 4 tablespoons warm water, or more if needed
   3 teaspoons pure olive oil or canola oil

PLACE THE MASA HARINA and the flour in a large bowl or the workbowl of a food processor. Add the warm water and the oil. Mix with a large fork or whirl the ingredients in the processor just until combined. If the dough does not easily come together, add 2 more tablespoons of water. Blend again. The masa dough should stick together but not be gummy. Wrap the dough in plastic wrap and let it rest for 15 minutes.

PREHEAT A COMAL OR GRIDDLE over medium heat. Cut out 2 squares of plastic, slightly larger than your tortilla press. Place 1 square of plastic on the bottom half of the press. Place a walnut-size ball of dough in the middle. Cover with the second piece of plastic and lower the press to mold the tortilla. Open the press and peel off the top plastic starting from the sides. Flip the tortilla over and carefully peel off the remaining plastic from the sides. Lay the tortilla on the comal or griddle. Freckles will start to form. Turn over and cook for about 1 minute. Place in a dishtowel while you continue working. Store in plastic until needed.

Makes about 12 corn tortillas

sweet milk tortillas

When families traveled from rancho to rancho to visit, milk tortillas were wrapped in snowy-white tea towels and stored in baskets for the trip. Milk tortillas had better staying power than regular flour tortillas and were comforting to the children. I discovered the original version of this recipe in an 1850 book, and my family has become addicted to them. We have discovered how good milk tortillas are directly off the griddle, smeared with butter and sprinkled with cinnamon sugar. They taste more like a pastry and have become our tortilla version of cinnamon toast.

    2½ cups unbleached all-purpose flour

    ½ teaspoon salt

    ½ teaspoon baking powder

    3 tablespoons sugar

    4 tablespoons (½ stick) butter, cut into pieces

    2 tablespoons vegetable shortening

    ¾ cup regular or low-fat evaporated milk, warm, or more as needed

Tortilla Cinnamon Toast (optional)

    3 tablespoons sugar

    ½ teaspoon ground cinnamon

    About 3 tablespoons butter

COMBINE THE FLOUR, salt, baking powder, and sugar in a large bowl with a whisk. Work the butter and shortening into the flour mixture until mealy, as for pastry. Drizzle in the warm milk to form a soft dough. If the dough seems dry, add 1 to 2 tablespoons more milk. Knead for 1 minute in the bowl. Turn the bowl upside down over the dough and let it rest for 30 minutes.

FORM 8 BALLS OF DOUGH and place on an oiled baking sheet. Cover with plastic wrap. Flatten the balls. Let rest for 20 to 30 minutes.

TO FORM THE TORTILLAS, flatten each ball, rolling from the center to the edges. Keep turning the tortilla and rolling to keep the circle round. These tortillas will be a little thicker than plain flour tortillas, but they will bubble more on the comal, forming more layers. Wrap in a clean dishtowel as you cook each one. When cool, store in a plastic zipper bag.

PREHEAT A COMAL OR GRIDDLE to medium hot. Cook each tortilla for about 1 minute, turning over frequently. They are cooked when they have little golden brown flecks on both sides.

FOR TORTILLA CINNAMON TOAST, combine the sugar with the cinnamon. Spread about 1 teaspoon of butter on the surface of each tortilla, add a sprinkle of cinnamon sugar, fold, and eat.

Makes 10

cinnamon rolls

✕✕✕

It was my mother who made cinnamon rolls a rancho tradition. They are perfect to follow spicy Huevos Rancheros (page 128).

    1 recipe Grandmama's Potato Pan Rolls (page 95)
    ⅓ cup butter, softened
    ⅓ cup sugar
    1 tablespoon ground cinnamon
Icing
    1 tablespoon butter, melted
    3 cups powdered sugar
    2 tablespoons milk, hot
    ½ teaspoon vanilla extract
    Pinch of salt

PREPARE GRANDMAMA'S POTATO PAN ROLLS. Roll out the risen dough into an 18 x 12-inch rectangle. Brush with the softened butter. Mix the sugar and cinnamon and sprinkle evenly over the top. Roll up from the long side. Cut across into 2-inch pieces and place 3 inches apart on a greased jelly-roll pan. Cover and let rise for about 45 minutes.

PREHEAT THE OVEN to 375°F.

PLACE BAKING SHEETS in the middle of the oven and bake the rolls until golden, about 25 minutes, reversing once during baking time. Remove and let cool on a rack for 20 minutes.

TO MAKE THE ICING, blend the melted butter, powdered sugar, hot milk, vanilla, and salt. Pour over the top of the rolls, letting the icing run down the sides.

Makes about 14 large rolls

ma'dulce enchiladas
[strawberry enchiladas]

✕✕✕

The discovering of old recipes is one of my favorite pursuits. Santa Barbara *descendiente* Margarita Villa told me that in the old times, strawberries were called *ma'dulces*, meaning *más dulces*, or sweetness. I wanted to combine milk tortillas with strawberries for enchiladas, which make a wonderful treat if you can keep everyone away while you are making them.

Assemble no more than 1 hour in advance, so the tortillas don't become soggy.

Cream Cheese Filling

    8 ounces cream cheese
    ¼ cup sour cream
    1 teaspoon vanilla extract
    ½ cup powdered sugar

Strawberry Sauce

    1 tablespoon butter
    ¼ cup orange juice, preferably fresh
    ½ to ¾ cup sugar
    ¼ teaspoon salt
    ¾ cup fresh strawberries, puréed
    1 package (12 ounces) frozen unsweetened raspberries, thawed
    2 cups fresh strawberries, sliced

Assembly

    6 Sweet Milk Tortillas (page 84), or other thin flour tortillas
    Powdered sugar, for dusting

PLACE THE CREAM CHEESE, sour cream, vanilla, and powdered sugar in the bowl of a stand mixer and beat until fluffy. Set aside the filling.

TO PREPARE THE SAUCE, combine the butter, orange juice, sugar, salt, and puréed strawberries in a 3-quart saucepan. Place the raspberries in a wire strainer and push them through with a wooden spoon. Scrape off any purée clinging to bottom of strainer. Add the raspberry purée to the mixture in the saucepan. Simmer over medium heat until the mixture thickens into a sauce, about 8 minutes. Remove from the heat and stir in the sliced strawberries.

TO ASSEMBLE THE ENCHILADAS, place about 2 rounded tablespoons of filling down the center of each tortilla. Fold over the sides. Place, seam side down, in a buttered 13 x 10-inch baking dish.

PREHEAT THE OVEN to 350°F. Bake the enchiladas for 8 to 10 minutes, or just until the filling is puffed. Place each enchilada on a dessert plate, pour a generous ¼ cup of Strawberry Sauce on each enchilada, dust with powdered sugar, and serve.

Serves 6

NOTE: Thin uncooked flour tortillas are sold in some supermarkets. They are the closest to homemade and could also be used for the enchiladas if you are pressed for time. This type of tortilla requires about a minute each to cook for enchiladas.

semítas

These sweet, flat biscuits were traditionally pierced across the tops with a fork before they were put in the oven. They were enjoyed more like scones at tea time than for breakfast. They are delicious with jam or lemon curd.

    3 cups all-purpose flour
    4 tablespoons sugar
    5 teaspoons baking powder
    1 teaspoon baking soda
    1½ teaspoons salt
    ¼ cup vegetable shortening or lard
    4 tablespoons (½ stick) butter
    1 egg
    1 to 1¼ cups sour milk or buttermilk

SIFT THE FLOUR, sugar, baking powder, baking soda, and salt into a mixing bowl. Drop teaspoons of shortening and butter into the flour mix. Using your hands, work the mixture together until it is crumbly and there are no dry spots remaining. Beat the egg and whisk it into 1 cup sour milk or buttermilk. Drizzle into the flour mixture, adding the last ¼ cup of milk if dough seems dry.

PREHEAT THE OVEN to 400°F. Pat out onto a floured board until ¾ inch thick. If you like higher biscuits, pat to 1 inch thick. Cut with a floured 4-inch biscuit cutter. (I use an empty, clean tuna can.) Do not twist the cutter when forming the semítas, as this will affect the rise. Place on ungreased baking sheets, and puncture 2 rows of holes across the tops, using a fork. Bake for 12 to 15 minutes, until golden brown across the tops. Serve immediately with butter and jam.

Makes 8 semítas

biscochuelos

⋊⋉⋊

These rich buns, made for special occasions, were the closest that rancho cooking came to brioche. The extravagance and variety of rich *pan dulce* as enjoyed in the Mexican capital never reached California until the twentieth century. For special breakfasts, I dip each Biscochuelo in Chocolate Topping (recipe follows) before baking.

    1 package active dry yeast
    1 teaspoon sugar
    ¾ cup lukewarm water (110°F)
    ¾ cup sugar
    1 teaspoon salt
    4 eggs
    8 tablespoons (1 stick) butter, very soft, or more as needed
    4 cups unbleached all-purpose flour, plus about ½ cup flour for kneading
    1 egg yolk, beaten with 1 tablespoon water, for glaze
    1 teaspoon ground cinnamon

DISSOLVE THE YEAST and 1 teaspoon sugar in warm water in a large bowl and allow to proof for 10 minutes until foamy. Meanwhile, warm the eggs in a bowl of hot water for 2 minutes.

ADD ½ CUP OF THE SUGAR, salt, and eggs to the yeast mixture. Whisk in 1 cup of the flour. Add the butter in small pieces. Use the whisk to continue blending, making sure that the butter is well incorporated. Add the remaining 3 cups of flour, ½ cup at a time. The dough will be soft.

KNEAD THE DOUGH on a well-floured board for 3 to 5 minutes. The dough will be sticky so you may find it easier to use a dough scraper to lift it up and fold it over for kneading. Rub the dough with some soft butter. Place in a warm bowl and cover well with plastic wrap. Let rise until doubled, about 1½ hours.

AFTER THE DOUGH HAS RISEN, pinch it into 12 pieces and form into balls. Place on oiled sheet or on parchment paper–lined baking sheets. Brush with the egg yolk and water glaze. Combine the remaining ¼ cup of sugar and the cinnamon and sprinkle over the dough. Let rise until puffy, about 45 minutes.

PREHEAT THE OVEN TO 375°F. Bake until the biscochuelos are golden, about 15 minutes. Place on a rack to cool. Serve for tea time or breakfast.

WRAP IN FOIL or store in plastic zipper bags for up to 2 days. These freeze well also.

Makes 12 biscochuelos

chocolate topping

This topping, which I sometimes use instead of cinnamon sugar on Biscochuelos, is not a traditional rancho recipe but something that we have come to love. I believe in revitalizing the old by adding something new.

3 ounces semisweet chocolate, melted

2 tablespoons butter

1 ½ tablespoons flour

3 tablespoons powdered sugar

Biscochuelos (page 88)

COMBINE THE MELTED CHOCOLATE, butter, flour, and powdered sugar in a small bowl. Freeze for 30 minutes. Process into a crumblike texture in a food processor. Spread the chocolate crumbs on a flat plate.

BRUSH EACH BISCOCHUELO with the egg glaze, then turn it upside down into the plate of chocolate and press so the top is covered with chocolate crumbs. Place the Biscochuelos, chocolate side up, on a greased jelly-roll pan. Cover and let rise for 40 minutes.

PREHEAT THE OVEN to 375°F. Bake for 15 minutes. Cool Biscochuelos on a rack.

Makes enough for 12 biscochuelos

adobe oven bread

⋊⋉⋊⋉

Adobe Oven Bread, or horno bread, always contained a low amount of fat, as did all the mission and rancho breads except Biscochuelos. Good fat, such as the pure lard used for pastries, flour tortillas, breads, and tamales, was not always available unless a pig had recently been slaughtered. I remember Grandmama treating her bucket of homemade lard like a pot of gold.

This recipe was given to me by Rancho La Purísima where they frequently still bake in their outdoor horno oven for large groups.

Adobe bread was always eaten shortly after it came out of the oven. If, by some rare chance, there was leftover bread the next day, it was traditional to make Capirotada (page 92) or bread pudding.

The recipe can be tripled.

> 2 teaspoons active dry yeast
> Pinch of sugar
> ¼ cup lukewarm water (110°F)
> 2 cups warm water, preferably potato water
> 2 tablespoons honey or brown sugar
> 2 teaspoons salt
> 2 tablespoons melted lard or butter
> 4½ cups unbleached all-purpose flour, plus about ½ cup flour for kneading

DISSOLVE THE YEAST AND SUGAR in the lukewarm water and pour into a large bowl to proof for 5 minutes, until foamy. Add the warm potato water, honey, salt, melted lard, and 1 cup of the flour. Use a whisk to blend well. Continue adding flour, 1 cup at a time, to make a soft dough. Knead for about 5 minutes, adding flour gradually as you knead. Pat the dough into an oiled mixing bowl and put it in a cool place. Let it rise slowly until doubled, 3 to 4 hours or overnight.

GENTLY PUSH DOWN THE DOUGH, being careful not to deflate all of the air bubbles, and divide it in half. Form 2 round loaves and place in greased 8-inch cake pans. Let rise until doubled, 45 minutes to 1 hour.

PREHEAT THE OVEN to 450°F. For the kind of heat provided by the adobe oven, line the oven rack with unglazed clay tiles or a baking stone.

PLACE THE PANS right on top of the tiles or baking stone. Bake until golden brown and crusty, about 45 minutes. Cool on racks.

WRAP IN FOIL TO STORE.

Makes 2 loaves

pan casero

xxx

This homemade white bread was developed late in the nineteenth century when breads began to share an equal footing with tortillas. Such ingredients as yeast, butter, lard, and evaporated milk were available at the grocery store in town. My friend and supreme bread baker and cookbook author, Beth Hensperger, shared this recipe, which is like a richer version of horno bread.

 1 package active dry yeast
 Pinch of sugar
 ⅓ cup lukewarm water (110°F)
 1 can (13 ounces) evaporated regular or goat's milk, warm
 3 tablespoons honey
 2 tablespoons lard or butter, melted
 2 teaspoons salt
 4 to 4½ cups unbleached all-purpose flour, plus flour for kneading
 2 tablespoons melted butter or lard, for brushing

DISSOLVE THE YEAST AND SUGAR in the water in a small bowl and let it proof and become foamy, about 5 minutes.

COMBINE THE MILK, honey, lard, salt, and 1½ cups of the flour. Add the yeast mixture and beat on low speed for 1 minute. Add the remaining flour, ½ cup at a time, mixing on low speed until a soft shaggy dough just clears the sides of the bowl.

SPRINKLE A COUPLE OF TABLESPOONS OF FLOUR on a board and knead the dough for a few minutes, or until smooth and springy. Place in a greased container, turn over once to coat the top, and cover with plastic wrap. Let it rise until double, about 1½ hours.

GREASE TWO 8½ X 4½-INCH LOAF PANS. Gently punch down dough, being careful not to entirely deflate it. Divide in half and form 2 rectangular loaves. Place in prepared pans. Cover loaves loosely with plastic wrap. Let dough rise until almost doubled, about 1 hour.

ABOUT 30 MINUTES BEFORE BAKING, preheat the oven to 400°F.

BRUSH LOAVES WITH MELTED BUTTER. Bake for 15 minutes, then turn oven down to 375°F and bake for 20 minutes more. The loaves should be golden brown on top and a lighter tan on the sides. Use a knife to loosen bread around the edges of the pan and release the loaves. Tap on the bottoms of the loaves to see if they sound hollow. If not, bake a minute or two more.

PLACE ON RACKS TO COOL. Wrap in foil to store. Pan Casero keeps well for a few days and freezes well for 1 to 2 months.

Makes 2 loaves

capirotada

✕✕✕

Capirotada, though considered a pudding, is made without eggs or milk. It remains a popular Lenten food among Hispanics. The sweetness imparted by the syrup can be counterbalanced by serving the Capirotada with unsweetened lightly whipped cream or crema mexicana. Slices of day-old Pan Casero, Adobe Oven Bread, or even French bread can be used quite effectively for Capirotada.

2 cups (packed) dark brown sugar or 2 large cones *piloncillo*

4 cups water

2 teaspoons ground cinnamon

Pinch of ground cloves

I tablespoon pure vanilla extract

I loaf Adobe Oven Bread (page 90), Pan Casero (page 91), Bolillos (page 94),
   or French bread

4 tablespoons (½ stick) butter, softened, plus I tablespoon for baking dish

2 cups grated Monterey Jack cheese

8 ounces cream cheese

½ cup golden raisins

¼ cup sliced almonds, toasted

½ cup roasted peanuts (not dry-roasted)

I cup lightly whipped cream or crema mexicana

Minced peanuts, for garnish

COMBINE THE BROWN SUGAR, water, cinnamon, and cloves in a large saucepan. Simmer, uncovered, over medium-low heat until thick and syrupy, about 15 minutes. Remove from the heat and add the vanilla. Reserve ½ cup syrup and set it all aside.

PREHEAT THE OVEN to 350°F.

SLICE THE BREAD and toast it on a baking sheet until golden but not overly browned, about 10 minutes. Remove from the oven and spread with the butter. Place one-third of the bread in a buttered 4-quart baking dish. Sprinkle on a layer of grated cheese, dot with cream cheese, raisins, almonds, and peanuts. Continue layering and then pour the syrup (except for the reserved ½ cup) over all.

COVER THE BAKING DISH WITH FOIL and bake for 20 minutes. Pour the reserved syrup over all, cover, and continue baking for 15 minutes. The pudding should appear firm, and most of the liquid will be absorbed.

SERVE WARM, topping each serving with whipped cream and sprinkling with peanuts.

Serves 10

NOTE: Sometimes a peeled and diced apple was added to the filling along with the raisins and nuts.

molletes

Molletes are one of the best-kept secrets for using up stale Bolillos (besides Capirotada) and leftover beans. If you do not have Bolillos, substitute French or Italian long crusty rolls.

Molletes are eaten for breakfast, lunch, or snacks.

> 1 tablespoon olive oil or lard
> 1½ cups cooked pink beans or Frijoles de la Olla (page 108)
> 3 Bolillos (page 94) or French rolls, split
> About 1½ cups grated white cheese, such as Monterey Jack or Italian Fontina

IF YOU ARE USING THE FRIJOLES DE LA OLLA, which are already thickened, you can delete the next step.

HEAT THE OIL IN A SKILLET over medium heat and add 1 cup of beans, including some of the liquid. As soon as the beans are hot, begin mashing them with a large spoon or wooden bean masher. When they are thick, add the rest of the beans and mash again. Simmer until thickened enough to spread on the bread.

SPREAD ABOUT ¼ CUP MASHED BEANS on top of each bolillo half in a thin layer. Sprinkle on ¼ cup grated cheese. Place on a baking sheet and broil until the cheese is bubbly and the edges of the rolls are toasted. Serve at once.

Serves 4 to 6

NOTE: Canned refried beans can be used in a pinch.

bolillos

✕✕✕

These crusty, elongated rolls, shaped like spindles, are still baked in *panaderías* (bakeries) from Mexico City to San Francisco to Santa Fe and beyond. European-inspired Bolillos date from the nineteenth century; they have crossed many borders. At their best, they have a crusty exterior and a creamy, soft interior.

Sponge

  1 package active dry yeast

  ¼ cup lukewarm water (110°F)

  1 tablespoon sugar

  1½ cups lukewarm water (110°F)

  2 cups bread flour

Bread Dough

  1 cup lukewarm water (110°F)

  3 teaspoons salt

  1 teaspoon baking soda

  2½ cups bread flour

  2 tablespoons butter, softened, plus 1 tablespoon for rubbing

  ½ cup all-purpose flour for kneading and forming rolls

  1 egg white, beaten with 2 tablespoons water, for glaze

TO MAKE THE SPONGE, proof the yeast with the ¼ cup water and the sugar. When the yeast mixture is foamy, in about 5 minutes, combine with the 1½ cups water in a large mixing bowl. Add the flour and stir until the dough forms strands when the spoon is lifted. Cover the sponge and let it ferment for 1 hour.

TO MAKE THE DOUGH, combine the sponge, 1 cup water, salt, baking soda, bread flour, and butter. Add the flour ½ cup at a time. As you add the flour, stir vigorously with a wooden spoon or use a dough hook on a stand mixer. Knead the dough for about 4 minutes. Place the dough on a floured board and finish kneading by hand until the dough is smooth. Rub soft butter over the dough and put it back in the bowl. Cover with a damp cloth or plastic wrap. Let rise until doubled, about 1½ hours.

DEFLATE THE DOUGH GENTLY, leaving some of the air bubbles. Using a dough scraper, cut off 12 pieces of dough. Form rolls by taking each piece of dough and turning in the ends. Use the edge of your palm to create a crease in the center of the dough, bringing up the sides and pinching together. Roll back and forth to make the Bolillo shape. Pinch both ends into tips. Holding the tips, swing the Bolillo back and forth to round out the shape. Place the Bolillos on 2 parchment paper–lined baking sheets.

PREHEAT THE OVEN to 425°F.

AFTER LETTING DOUGH RISE 30 MINUTES, use a sharp paring knife or single-edge razor to slash each Bolillo lengthwise down the middle. Cut deeply enough so that the slash opens, as this assures the distinctive look of a Bolillo. Brush with the egg glaze. Let rise for 10 minutes more. Sprinkle 1 tablespoon of water under the parchment in the corner of each baking sheet, to help create steam. Place both sheets on the middle rack of the oven and bake for 20 minutes, reversing sheets once. Turn the heat down to 400°F and bake for 15 to 20 minutes more, or until dark golden and crusty.

Makes 12 bolillos

grandmama's potato pan rolls

xxx

These velvety rolls were so good, Grandmama didn't need to bake any other bread except flour tortillas. No one remembers where the recipe originated, but Rancho Los Tularcitos' big black oven could turn out potato pan rolls as fast as anyone could eat them. For picnics, the rolls were split, buttered, and filled with ham or chicken and Calera Creek's watercress.

    I large russet potato, peeled and quartered
    3 cups water
    6 tablespoons (¾ stick) soft butter
    I package active dry yeast
    I teaspoon sugar
    2 large eggs
    2 teaspoons salt
    ¼ cup sugar
    6 cups unbleached, all-purpose flour
    I egg, blended with I tablespoon water for glaze

SIMMER THE POTATO IN THE WATER over medium heat until very tender when pierced with a knife, about 25 minutes. Drain off the potato water and reserve. Mash the potato with a potato or bean masher or push it through a ricer. Add a little potato water to help make it creamier. Measure 1¼ cups of mashed potatoes, add the butter, and blend. Set aside.

STIR THE YEAST AND SUGAR into ½ cup of warm (110°F) potato water. Let it proof and become spongy, 5 to 10 minutes. Beat the eggs, salt, sugar, and another cup of warm potato water in a large mixing bowl until blended. Add the mashed potato mixture and blend. Stir in the yeast mixture. Add 1 cup of flour and use a whisk to combine. Add a second cup of flour. Use a wooden spoon to stir in the remaining 4 cups of flour, ½ cup at a time. Sprinkle ½ cup of flour on a breadboard and knead the dough until smooth, 8 to 10 minutes. Add flour by the tablespoon if necessary to keep the dough from sticking. This is a soft dough at its best.

PLACE THE DOUGH IN A GREASED BOWL. Cover with plastic wrap and let rise until doubled, about 1½ hours. Punch down, cover with plastic wrap, and refrigerate for 3 hours or overnight. The long chilling of the dough helps its flavor to develop.

LIGHTLY PUSH THE DOUGH DOWN, being careful not to completely deflate it. Form into 20 portions for large rolls. Make balls by turning the rolls and tucking in the sides. Place the rolls, as you form them, about 2 inches apart on greased baking sheets or parchment paper–lined sheets. Let rise for 30 to 40 minutes.

PREHEAT THE OVEN to 375°F. Brush the rolls with the egg glaze and bake until golden, about 25 to 30 minutes.

Makes 20 dinner rolls

RANCHO **comfort** FOOD

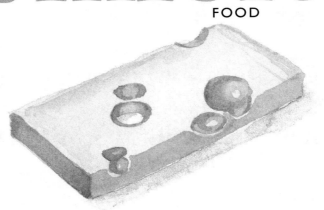

my great-uncles who over-saw the land remained bachelors, growing old and bent as the hundred-year-old pear trees along Calera Creek. The well-pruned trees still held the promise of fruit every year, and the uncles tended to the fruit. Part of their after-dinner ritual was to sit on the verandah of the adobe, smoking cigars, and wryly discussing the agricultural expert who had told

The rancho crew needed a lot of comfort food like Pastel de Tamal after loading, hauling, and delivering a wagonful of beets.

them that the trees were too far past their prime to bear good fruit. With sweet revenge, Uncle John and Uncle Charlie sipped their port accompanied by wedges of succulent, sweet pears from trees that were too old.

Ranch life, in spite of resident ghosts in the adobe and down The Lane, was thought to be healthful for children, so brothers Frank and Louis, who lived in town with their families, sent out one or two from the flock to keep company with the bachelor uncles and Aunt Nicolassa, who let them run free as squirrels. This was during the 1920s and '30s, a quiet period when the rancho made its living from small crops of walnuts, peaches, apricots, and cherries.

While their mothers in town hoped for some of the old Spanish ways to rub off, the children sent to the quiet countryside obliged by seeming to stay out of trouble most of the time. They were always instructed by their parents to help their uncles and not be a bother to Aunt Nicolassa. All of these children, who are now in their late eighties or long gone, used to fondly recall the rancho method of discipline, which was no discipline. Yet Uncle John and Uncle Charlie could make a guilty child remorseful by their silent treatment—never scolding or issuing punishment—which was what happened when one of the cousins rode Dolly, the pet horse, into the swampy tules near the Bay. Dolly sunk up to her knees in mud. Leaving the horse in the quagmire, the cousin (no one ever told who it was) ran back to the ranch for Uncle John. Two horses were silently hooked up to the wagon, which went forth to pull the horse out of the tules. Never was a word of chastisement spoken to the boy, who felt humiliated.

Later all the other cousins tried to guess who the bad boy was. The guilty boy, backed up by his uncle, was never identified. It was probably my mother's younger brother, Jack. He was the youngest and the most fearless. Jack spent most of his time stalking darkened rooms in the upper story of the house, which were kept locked for years because of some untimely death. He thought he could face off any ghost. The barn, which was inhabited seasonally by migrant workers who came to work in the fruit trees, was Jack's domain; he refused to be daunted by creaking noises and footsteps on the stairs at night.

At the end of the day or night, everyone wanted to know where Jack had been. Not just because of the mischief he caused but because he always had a story to tell. He was the one who later became a great asador.

The days slipped by quietly with no rush. The uncles and Aunt Nick had the rancho back to themselves during the weekdays. They welcomed the rhythm of the ordinary that they were used to, which gave them enough time to dally in the kitchen, to make an apricot pie just for themselves, to enjoy the songs of the red-breasted linnets they had tamed and kept in an aviary on the verandah, and to listen to Jack's stories.

Sister (my mother) and Jack were usually the ones sent to look for eggs. Since the chickens roamed freely and no one was ever sure where the eggs were, it was a daily Easter egg hunt. But Sister and Jack knew the chickens loved the cool banks of Calera Creek, so they looked there first, sometimes finding a dozen eggs at a time secreted in the tall grass.

Simple meals with no fanfare were provided by the incomparable Aunt Nicolassa. These were the kinds of soul-satisfying meals that went from pot to bowl; the kitchen fed several people the rancho's brand of comfort food, like Sopa de Albóndigas or Tamale Pie, for days on end. I still hunger for these foods when I feel a wintry chill or just need to "chase the coyote from the door." It's called taking your comfort in a bowl.

chicken soup with fideos

✕✕✕

The most luxurious chicken broth is made by simmering a whole, cut-up chicken. Everything else is extraneous, especially if the broth is meant to pamper someone with a bad cold. You don't want to assail the invalid with too many exotic ingredients. You can do that later when wellness is imminent. If you were really sick, you just got broth. By the second or third day, when you were better, you were rewarded with broth and soft fideos. More garlic, up to 6 cloves, was added for bad colds.

    3 to 4 pounds chicken parts or a whole chicken
    2½ quarts of water
    1 clove garlic
    1 onion, chopped
    2 carrots, peeled and sliced
    1 stalk celery, sliced
    Handful of parsley
    2 teaspoons salt
    ½ cup fideos or vermicelli noodles, broken up
    1 cup finely diced carrot or potato (optional)
    2 tablespoons minced parsley

USING POULTRY SHEARS and a well-sharpened knife, cut the chicken parts into smaller pieces. They will give even more richness to the broth. Snip off any excess fat. Cover with water and bring to a simmer, skimming off surface foam for the first 20 minutes.

ADD THE GARLIC, onion, carrots, celery, parsley, and salt. Simmer for 1½ hours, removing the breast after 25 to 30 minutes so it does not become overcooked. Cool the chicken breast and reserve. You can chop or shred it later to add back to the soup or use for sandwiches or enchiladas.

WHEN THE BROTH HAS SIMMERED long enough, pour it through a wire strainer lined with damp cheesecloth. Discard the scraps in the strainer.

RETURN THE STRAINED BROTH TO THE POT, bring to a gentle simmer, and add the fideos. Simmer for 8 minutes. Add tiny diced vegetables like carrots and potatoes, if you like. Do not add strong vegetables like broccoli. Sprinkle each serving of soup with 1 teaspoon minced parsley.

Serves 6

sopa de albóndigas
[meatball soup]

✕✕✕

This classic soup continues to be a favorite of children, who love to scoop up the little meatballs. You can add more of your favorite vegetables to make the soup even heartier. The soup broth is enriched by a seasoning paste since we like everything spicier.

Seasoning Paste

    1 tablespoon olive oil

    2 medium tomatoes, peeled, seeded, and chopped

    2 cloves garlic, minced

    2 to 3 tablespoons New Mexican chile powder

    ½ teaspoon cumin seeds, crushed

Sopa (Soup)

    2½ quarts Caldo (page 103), chicken broth, or home-style canned broth

    ½ onion, diced

    2 stalks celery, sliced

    4 carrots, peeled and sliced

    1 russet potato, peeled and diced

    1 turnip, peeled and diced

    1 chayote (mirliton), peeled and diced

    Salt

Albóndigas (Meatballs)

    1 pound ground sirloin

    1 egg

    ¼ onion, minced

    1 clove garlic, minced

    ¼ cup minced parsley

    ¼ cup minced mint

    1 teaspoon dried oregano

    ½ cup bread crumbs

    ½ teaspoon salt

    Freshly ground black pepper

TO MAKE THE SEASONING PASTE, heat the olive oil in large pot over medium heat and add the tomatoes. Sauté for several minutes. Add the garlic, chile powder, cumin seeds, caldo, onion, celery, carrots, potato, turnip, and chayote. Simmer for 15 minutes, taste, and add salt.

TO MAKE THE ALBÓNDIGAS, combine the meat, egg, onion, garlic, parsley, mint, oregano, bread crumbs, salt, and pepper in a large bowl. Use you hands to gently mix. Wet your hands and form meatballs, a little larger than a walnut. Drop them into the simmering soup and cook, partially covered, for 20 minutes. Ladle into bowls, giving at least 3 meatballs per person.

Serves 6

caldo

The foundation of many everyday soups was a rich Caldo, or broth, which was started with meaty, gelatinous bones, marrow bones, chicken wings, vegetables, and herbs, and whatever else might intrigue the cook. My grandmother adored chicken feet for the flavor they gave to Caldo, but I have gone on to other flavorings. Caldo was never thought of as too much trouble; just wait until there are enough good bones and put them on to simmer.

About 2½ pounds marrow bones, ham bone, chicken parts, or whole chicken
I quart water per pound of bones and meat
I head of garlic, top sliced off
I ancho chile, rinsed and halved
I tomato, halved
I onion, halved
2 bay leaves
I sprig of Italian parsley
I sprig of cilantro, with stem
2 to 3 teaspoons salt

COVER THE BONES WITH THE WATER in a stockpot or pressure cooker, taking care that all is submerged. Add the garlic, chile, tomato, onion, bay leaves, parsley, cilantro, and salt. Simmer over low heat for 1½ hours or pressure cook for 45 minutes. During the first 30 minutes of simmering, skim off and discard any foam. After cooking, strain the Caldo, discarding the solids. Pour the broth into a container to chill. Once the fat is congealed, remove and discard it. Use the Caldo as a base for soup, stews, and sauces.

Makes about 2½ quarts

beef vegetable soup

———— ✕✕✕ ————

Meat was always braised before it was added to soups. The caramelized essences, acting like a secret ingredient, are left in the pot to add more flavor to the soup.

Braised Beef

    2 pounds beef brisket, cut into 2-inch chunks
    I tablespoon oil
    I onion, roughly chopped
    3 cups water

Soup

    2 quarts Caldo (page 103), broth, or water
    2 teaspoons salt
    2 whole dried red chiles, such as California or New Mexican
    ½ cup chopped onion
    I tablespoon minced garlic
    I stalk celery, with leaves, diced
    I cup chopped tomatoes, fresh or canned ready-cut
    2 carrots, peeled and cut into chunks
    4 ounces (½ cup) bow-tie pasta or macaroni
    Minced Italian parsley, for garnish

PREHEAT THE OVEN to 350°F.

DRY THE MEAT WITH PAPER TOWELS. Heat the oil in a Dutch oven over medium heat and brown the meat in batches, removing it as it browns. Add more oil if necessary.

RETURN ALL THE MEAT TO THE POT and add the onion and water. Cover tightly and bake for 2 hours, checking a couple of times to make sure the liquid has not evaporated. If necessary, add water, about ½ cup at a time. You want the pot to collect a lot of concentrated juices, so don't allow precious brown essences to burn away. When the meat is tender, remove the pot from the oven. You should have about ¼ cup rich collected juices. If there is excess oil, blot the surface with paper towels to remove.

TO FINISH THE SOUP, add the Caldo to the pot, stirring to dislodge brown bits. Add the salt, dried chiles, onion, garlic, celery, tomatoes, and carrots and simmer for 15 minutes. Add the pasta and cook for 12 minutes more.

LADLE SERVINGS INTO WIDE BOWLS and sprinkle with parsley.

Serves 6

thick lentil soup

✕✕✕

This a lift-your-spirits soup. My brother would have nothing to do with the idea that a clear, crystalline broth was needed for healing, when what he craved was something thick and hearty. During Lent, this soup made its appearance minus the bacon.

1 pound lentils

3 quarts Caldo (page 103) or water (or a combination)

1 tablespoon olive oil

1 cup chopped onion

2 cloves garlic, minced

2 green or red bell peppers, veins removed, chopped

4 carrots, peeled and chopped

2 stalks celery, sliced

2 cups canned tomato purée

Salt and pepper

6 slices meaty bacon, chopped

2 ounces diced jarred pimiento

WASH THE LENTILS IN A SIEVE, checking for twigs and stones. Place in a soup pot, add the Caldo, and simmer over medium heat.

HEAT THE OLIVE OIL IN A SKILLET over medium heat and sauté the onion until softened. Add the garlic, bell peppers, carrots, and celery. Sauté for 5 minutes, stirring occasionally.

AFTER THE LENTILS HAVE SIMMERED for 30 minutes, add the vegetable mixture and the tomato purée. Continue to cook the soup over low heat. Season with salt and pepper to taste.

MEANWHILE, FRY THE BACON in a separate skillet over medium heat to render some of the fat. When the bacon is almost crisp, drain it and add it to the soup. Simmer the soup for 30 minutes longer. Add the pimientos and additional salt and pepper if needed toward the end of the cooking time. If the soup thickens too much, thin with water or broth.

Serves 6

NOTE: Spicy sausages (about 8 ounces) can be substituted for bacon. Just slice and sauté them separately before adding to lentils.

enchilada soup

xxx

Many times when I am cooking, I fall back on my family's favorite way of adding flavor to savory dishes. Caramelized onions were almost as important as sea salt and olive oil as an ingredient. This soup, like enchiladas in a soup bowl, uses the ever-present onions along with frijoles and red chile.

1 tablespoon olive oil
2 onions, chopped
4 cloves garlic, minced
2 cups Frijoles de la Olla (page 108)
8 cups water
1 teaspoon salt
6 dried California or New Mexican chiles
1 cup water, for puréeing
4 tomatoes, peeled and seeded
1 teaspoon ground cumin
2 teaspoons dried oregano
1 tablespoon New Mexican chile powder, or more as needed (optional)
½ cup sliced black olives

Garnish

2 cups crushed tortilla chips
2 cups grated medium-sharp Cheddar cheese
½ cup minced green onions

HEAT THE OLIVE OIL in a large pot over medium-low heat and add the onions. Cook until caramelized, at least 15 minutes. Add the garlic toward the end of the cooking so it doesn't burn. Stir in the frijoles, 8 cups water, and salt.

MEANWHILE, STEAM THE CHILES for 20 minutes. Using tongs, remove the chiles to a blender. Add 1 cup water and the tomatoes and purée. Add more water if needed.

STIR THE RED CHILE–TOMATO PURÉE into the beans. Add the cumin, oregano, and chile powder. Simmer for 30 to 45 minutes to meld flavors. Taste for seasonings and add more salt or chile powder if necessary. During the last few minutes of simmering, stir in the black olives.

LADLE INTO SERVING BOWLS, sprinkling each with crushed tortilla chips, cheese, and green onions.

Serves 6 to 8

Frijoles Fit for a King

There is nothing sweeter cooking on the back burner than a pot of frijoles. The air is charged with fragrance, making whoever enters the kitchen hungry. You will get used to hearing, "Are the beans done yet?" When done right, they can be fed to a king.

Rancho families were so enamored with beans they could have shared the title of Bean Eaters with the Tuscans. Even though beans were served for every meal except tea and *merienda,* no one seemed to tire of them. The ranchero had only pink beans and garbanzos, not the great variety we have available today. Even so, most of the rancheros were staunchly loyal to the pink bean.

My mother and grandmother made the best frijoles, thick and creamy, and they were expected to provide them for every barbecue, even if they went to someone else's barbecue. I didn't pay much attention to how they were done until I was on my own. I added a long list of ingredients to the pot, while, I was sure, my Grandmother's muse was shaking her head in dismay. Eventually I came to my senses and went back to beans, water, onion, an occasional ham bone, and salt. The lesson can be applied to all cooking. More is not necessarily better. I also learned from an aunt about an important step I had left out. A good portion of the cooked beans have to be mashed with some of their juices to produce a kind of bean velvet.

frijoles de la olla
[creamy rancho beans]

✕✕✕

Only small pink beans were used on the rancho because it was believed that they had more flavor than the starchier pintos. I still cook them rancho style using that unique way of thickening, the secret to their flavor.

At home the beans were served from the cooking vessel, either a clay *olla* or a pot. This recipe can be tripled or quadrupled for a large fiesta.

1 pound dried pink beans
1 cup chopped onion
2 cloves garlic, minced
10 cups water
2 teaspoons salt
1 ham hock or ham bone (optional)
2 tablespoons lard, preferably homemade, or pure olive oil
½ teaspoon freshly ground black pepper

PLACE THE BEANS IN A STRAINER and run water through them to clean. Check for stones or foreign matter. Place the beans, onion, garlic, ham hock, and water in a 4-quart pot. (In the old days, a clay olla was used and some bean cooks think the olla added to the flavor.) Bring to a simmer over medium-high heat and cook, partially covered, over low heat until the beans begin to soften, about 1 hour. Add the salt. Add hot water to the simmering beans if the liquid reduces below the surface of the beans. Continue cooking until the beans are completely tender, 1 to 1½ hours more. Turn off the heat and let them sit for 1 hour.

HEAT THE LARD in a large cast-iron skillet over medium heat and sprinkle in the pepper, averting your head from the pepper fumes, and pour in 2 cups of the warm beans. As the beans absorb the fat, mash them with a potato masher or wooden bean masher. Add ½ cup bean liquor from the pot. Simmer and add another cup of beans and another ½ cup of bean liquor. Simmer the thickening beans in the open skillet, uncovered, over medium-high heat. Keep mashing to create creaminess. Continue adding beans and bean liquor to the skillet until you have a thick unctuous mess of beans that take up at least half the pot.

STIR THE THICKENED BEANS back into the pot with the unthickened beans and cook together over medium heat to blend. (I like to keep stirring the beans with a wooden bean masher.) To serve, bring the beans to the table in the pot.

Serves 8 to 10 as an accompaniment

NOTE: Beans were never soaked. It was believed that soaking sapped flavor. Besides, if you were cooking 20 pounds of beans for a fiesta, you would need a reservoir of water to soak the beans!

refritos
[refried beans]

Crispy refried beans, almost bean pancakes, were always in demand for breakfast with eggs and chorizo or Huevos Rancheros (page 128). It is wise to cook more beans than you need so as to have leftovers for Refritos. *"Frijoles, frijolitos, y frijoles refritos!"* ("Beans, little beans, and refried beans") was a saying that reaffirmed that life without beans was not life at all.

> 2 tablespoons lard, preferably homemade, pure olive oil, or bacon grease
> 2 to 3 cups cold Frijoles de la Olla (page 108), cooked the day before
> 2 tablespoons grated Romano or cotija cheese

HEAT THE LARD in a cast-iron skillet over medium heat and add the beans all at once. Press them into a large pancake and let them sizzle 3 to 4 minutes, to create a crust, considered the best part of refried beans. When the beans are crispy around the edges but still creamy in the center, they are ready. Sprinkle with grated cheese and serve.

Serves 4 to 6 as a side dish

VARIATION: Frijoles Chinitos. To make this rich version of refried beans, fry 8 ounces of chorizo or *longaniza* sausage and drain on paper towels. Leave 1 to 2 tablespoons of the fat in the pan (or use pure olive oil) and add 3 cups of cooked beans. Add the sausage to the beans. Cook until crisp around the edges. Season with grated Romano or cotija cheese and serve.

colache

✕✕✕

Another popular side dish was Colache, a "broken down" mélange of zucchini, tomatoes, corn, and string beans. Grandmama was the best Colache cook, probably because she used more olive oil—about six tablespoons in this recipe—and lots of Parmesan cheese that she bought in hunks from the Italian grocery store in San José. Colache was served from mid-summer to October when all the called-for vegetables were in season.

I have found it easy to cut down on the large amount of olive oil that Grandmama used for sautéing, but just before serving the warm Colache I drizzle a few teaspoons of first-press olive oil over the top so that the flavor of the olive oil can be saved for last.

2 tablespoons olive oil

1 medium onion, chopped

2 pounds zucchini, trimmed and thickly sliced

4 cloves garlic, minced

½ cup cut-up string beans (optional)

2 medium tomatoes, peeled, seeded, and chopped

1 teaspoon dried oregano

1 tablespoon minced fresh basil

1 teaspoon sea salt

Freshly ground black pepper

3 ears of corn, husked and cut into 4-inch pieces

2 to 4 teaspoons extra-virgin olive oil

¼ cup freshly grated Parmesan or Romano cheese

IN A HEAVY-BOTTOMED POT, heat the olive oil over medium heat and sauté the onion until softened, about 10 minutes. Push to 1 side and add the zucchini slices. Sauté the zucchini until golden on both sides. Sprinkle the garlic over the zucchini. Add the string beans, tomatoes, oregano, basil, salt, and pepper to taste. Simmer, covered, on low heat for 20 minutes. Bury the corn in the vegetables. Simmer, covered, on low heat for 10 minutes more.

BEFORE SERVING, drizzle on olive oil and sprinkle the cheese over the top.

Serves 6 as a side dish

grandmama's rice

⋙⋘

One afternoon, I caught a whiff of the toasty, almost popcorn smell of my grand-mother's rice coming from my Mexican kitchen where María, our maid, was fixing lunch. I rushed to the kitchen to find her frying the rice kernels until golden, a step that I had previously omitted and one that is necessary for traditional Mexican and rancho rice. The toasted rice flavor makes it seem as though some mysterious spice has been added.

> 2 to 4 tablespoons olive oil
> I cup long-grain rice
> ½ onion, minced
> I clove garlic, mashed with 1½ teaspoons salt
> 3 teaspoons chile powder
> 2½ cups water

HEAT THE OIL IN A HEAVY POT over medium heat, add the rice, and fry it until golden. If you worry about fat, use the lesser amount of oil; if you worry about flavor, use the greater amount. There is a fine line between golden and too brown, so watch carefully. The rice will give off a toasty, popcorn smell when done. Drain off and discard any excess oil. Add the onion, garlic, and salt and sauté for 1 minute more. Add the chile powder and "two fingers of water," as Grandmama would say. I figure that to be about 2½ cups. Cook over medium heat until you see little holes forming in the surface of the rice, like craters, about 10 minutes. This indicates that most of the liquid has been absorbed. Turn the heat to low, put on a lid, and steam for 4 to 8 minutes longer, just until the rice has absorbed all the liquid and is tender.

Serves 6

NOTE: It's okay to peek at the cooking rice to check on it. It's an old wive's tale that the rice will be ruined if you lift the lid. It's far better to check than to overcook the rice. When rice is overcooked, the kernels look flowered and the rice is too soft.

grandmama's infamous eight chicken wing spaghetti sauce to feed ten people

✕✕✕

When my grandmother entered the corner grocery store on Twelfth Street in San José, the butcher visibly steeled himself. She was one of his best customers and his worst nightmare. The oft-repeated negotiations between the two adversaries often ended with Grandmama striking a deal. She believed that she knew better than the butcher what to do with scraps. She never left without a few free chicken wings or a marrow bone for the dog, and she didn't have a dog. Scraps were glorified by Grandmama. If available, the chicken neck and gizzards were also cooked in this sauce along with the chicken wings.

I once tried making the sauce without the wings and neck, and it had no soul. The title of the recipe comes from Grandmama's reputation of being able to feed an endless number of people by adding one more chicken wing and another handful of spaghetti to the pot.

4 tablespoons olive oil

1 large onion, chopped

4 cloves garlic, minced

1 celery stalk, with leaves, minced

1 carrot, peeled and chopped

Several needles of fresh rosemary, minced

2 tablespoons minced fresh Italian parsley

1 teaspoon dried oregano

1 teaspoon dried basil

1 can (6 ounces) tomato paste

2 cups water or half wine and half water

1 can (28 ounces) tomato purée

1 can (28 ounces) crushed tomatoes

2 teaspoons salt, or more as needed

Freshly ground black pepper

8 chicken wings, tips cut off and saved for stock

1 chicken neck and gizzard (optional)

1¼ cups grated Romano cheese

2 pounds spaghetti

HEAT 1 TO 2 TABLESPOONS OF THE OLIVE OIL in a deep, heavy pot (4 quart) over medium heat. Add the onion and sauté for about 5 minutes. Add the garlic, celery, and carrot and sauté for 3 minutes. Stir in the rosemary, parsley, oregano, basil, tomato paste, water, tomato purée, crushed tomatoes, salt, and pepper to taste. Simmer on low heat, partially covered, for 20 minutes while you prepare the chicken wings.

HEAT 2 TABLESPOONS OF THE REMAINING OLIVE OIL in a skillet over medium heat and sauté the chicken wings until golden on both sides. Season the wings with salt and pepper to taste. Add the sautéed wings and the chicken neck and gizzard, if using, to the sauce. Reduce the heat and simmer, covered, for 1½ hours on very low heat. Stir frequently. Toward the end of the cooking time, stir in ¼ cup of the Romano cheese.

JUST BEFORE SERVING, cook the spaghetti in a large pot of boiling salted water until al dente, about 10 minutes. Drain. Transfer to a platter, toss with half of the remaining Romano cheese, top with three quarters of the sauce, the wings, and more Romano. Serve right away.

Serves 8 to 10

aunt polanco's pastel de tamal

XXX

This elegant pastel is rich and meant for someone special. I was able to recreate the recipe from researching old Mexican recipes, again showing the strong connection between the cooking of Old California and Mexico.

Ancho Chile–Pork Filling

    1½ pounds boneless pork tenderloin
    2 tablespoons olive oil
    1 onion, sliced
    Salt and freshly ground black pepper
    2 cups water
    1 bay leaf
    4 ancho chiles
    1½ cups chopped onion
    1 tablespoon white wine vinegar
    ⅓ cup raisins, soaked in sherry
    2 teaspoons sugar
    1 teaspoon salt

Masa-Chile Crust

> 2 cups masa harina
>
> 1/4 cup sugar
>
> 1 1/2 teaspoons salt
>
> 1/2 teaspoon baking powder
>
> 2 1/2 cups chicken broth, hot
>
> 1/3 cup pure olive oil, not extra virgin
>
> 2 eggs
>
> 10 dried corn husks *(hojas)*, soaked in hot water for 30 minutes (see page 162)

PREHEAT THE OVEN to 350°F.

TO PREPARE THE FILLING, dry off the meat with paper towels and cut into large chunks, about 6 pieces. Heat 1 tablespoon of the oil in a Dutch oven over medium heat and add the pork and onion. Sauté for about 10 minutes or long enough to brown the meat on all sides. Season with salt and pepper to taste. Add the water and bay leaf. Cover and bake until the meat is very tender when pierced with a fork, 45 minutes. Use a fork to break up and shred the meat while warm. Reserve the braising liquid.

WHILE THE MEAT IS COOKING, soak the chiles for 25 minutes, then purée in a blender with 1/2 cup water or braising liquid. Reserve 2 tablespoons of the ancho purée for the crust.

HEAT THE REMAINING TABLESPOON OF OLIVE OIL in a 4-quart skillet over medium heat and sauté the onion. Add the ancho purée, shredded meat, vinegar, raisins, and 1/2 cup of the braising liquid. Simmer for 15 minutes. Season with sugar and salt.

TO PREPARE THE CRUST, stir the masa harina, sugar, salt, and baking powder together with a whisk in a large bowl. Combine the broth and olive oil. Add this liquid to the masa mixture, stirring it into a very soft dough. Add the eggs and reserved 2 table-spoons chile purée, blending well.

PREHEAT THE OVEN to 350°F.

SPREAD HALF OF THE MASA DOUGH on the bottom of a deep, oiled 10-inch baking dish. Spread the filling on top and finish with the remaining masa. Cover with oiled aluminum foil or soaked corn husks, pressing the husks into the masa layer and tucking the edges down into the pastel so it is well sealed.

BAKE FOR ABOUT 40 MINUTES. When done, the masa should be firm yet still moist when the foil or husks are lifted. Remove the foil or husks and let rest for 15 minutes before serving.

Serves 6

pastel de tamal
[tamale pie]

xxxx

Tamale pie used some of the same ingredients as tamales, but it was also a good way of using up leftover cooked chicken or pot roast. Tamale Pie was served not only during the week but also at small barbecues.

Chicken or Beef Filling
- 1 tablespoon olive oil
- 1 medium onion, chopped
- 1 clove garlic, minced
- 1 red or green bell pepper, seeds removed and chopped
- 4 Anaheim chiles, charred, peeled, seeded, and chopped
- 3 medium tomatoes, peeled, seeded, and chopped
- 1 to 2 tablespoons chile powder
- 1 tablespoon dried oregano
- 1½ teaspoons cumin seeds, crushed
- 1 teaspoon salt
- Freshly ground black pepper
- 4 ears of corn, kernels cut off
- 1 chicken (3 pounds), roasted or poached, meat removed and diced, or 1 pound diced pot roast (see page 31)
- 1 cup pitted black olives

Masa-Cheese Crust
- 1⅓ cups masa harina
- ¾ teaspoon salt
- 2 teaspoons red chile powder
- ½ teaspoon baking powder
- 2 cups chicken broth, hot, or more as needed
- ¼ cup pure olive oil or canola oil
- ⅔ cup grated sharp Cheddar cheese
- 8 dried corn husks (hojas), soaked in hot water for 30 minutes (see page 162)

TO PREPARE THE FILLING, heat the oil in a large skillet over medium heat and sauté the onion until softened, about 5 minutes. Add the garlic and cook briefly. Add the bell pepper, chiles, tomatoes, chile powder, oregano, cumin, salt, and pepper to taste. Simmer until the sauce thickens, about 15 minutes. Add the corn, chicken or roast, and olives. Simmer for 10 minutes more. Set aside.

TO PREPARE THE CRUST, stir the masa harina, salt, chile powder, and baking powder together with a whisk in a large bowl. Combine the broth and the oil. Add the liquid to the masa mixture, stirring to form a very soft dough. Add a little more broth or warm water if it seems too thick. Add the grated cheese.

PREHEAT THE OVEN to 350°F. Oil a long, deep, 3-quart ovenproof dish.

SPREAD HALF OF THE MASA DOUGH on the bottom of the dish. Spread the filling on top and finish with a layer of masa dough. Cover with oiled aluminum foil or soaked corn husks, pressing the husks into the masa layer and tucking the edges down into the pastel so it is well sealed. Bake until the masa crust is firm to the touch, 45 to 50 minutes. Remove the foil and let rest for 15 minutes before serving. The corn husks remain to add an earthy touch to the Pastel de Tamal. They are peeled off at the table, just before serving.

Serves 6

roasted peppers

xxxx

Every cook should have some *sorpresas* (surprises) that seem to be pulled out of a hat but are, in reality, prepped behind the scenes. Having a fridge or pantry filled with surprises is like having insurance. These peppers qualify as such a surprise. Keep them on hand for adding to salads or sandwiches, or to top Tortilla Española (page 126).

> 3 tablespoons olive oil
> 4 red bell peppers, scrubbed
> 2 tablespoons sherry vinegar or red wine vinegar
> 1 teaspoon salt
> 1 teaspoon dried oregano

RUB 2 TEASPOONS OF THE OLIVE OIL over the surface of the peppers. Place in a preheated broiler and broil, turning frequently, until slightly blackened with the skins separating from the pepper flesh, about 20 minutes. Place under wet paper towels to steam for 10 minutes. Use the paper towels to slide off the blackened skins. Remove the cores and slice peppers into thin strips. Place in a shallow dish and dress with sherry vinegar, salt, oregano, and the remaining olive oil. Warm peppers will absorb more of the marinade. Serve immediately or refrigerate for up to 5 days.

Makes 1 quart

NOTE: For a great sandwich, spread marinated roasted pepper on a slice of country bread, cover with strips of Italian Fontina cheese and broil.

mostaza
[wild mustard greens]

✕✕✕

Depending on the late winter rains, the first mustard with its tender leaves might herald spring as early as February. The potency of wild mustard was so valued that after pots of the greens were cooked, the liquid was drained off and bottled. All the children were lined up and given their dose of mustard water as a spring tonic. My mother's brother Jack once feigned a mustard water seizure, thinking that he wouldn't have to drink any more of the green stuff. He was sternly given his draught after the performance was over.

Mustard greens have a definite taste of their own. They are quite delicious when combined with fresh spinach. I often add half a pound of spinach during the last five minutes of cooking the mustard.

1 ½ pounds wild mustard greens, spinach, or Swiss chard
¼ cup water
2 tablespoons olive oil
¼ cup minced onion
3 cloves garlic, minced
1 teaspoon sea salt
Freshly ground black pepper
Crushed red pepper

PULL OFF THE TOUGH STEMS of the greens. Wash the greens thoroughly in a sink of cold water until clean. You may need to change the water a couple of times. Place the greens in a large pot with the water and cook for 5 minutes. Drain the greens. When cool enough to handle, squeeze out excess liquid and roughly chop. Heat the olive oil in a skillet over medium heat and sauté the onion and garlic until softened. Add the greens and continue to sauté for 5 minutes more to blend flavors. Season with salt, black pepper, and red pepper to taste.

VARIATION: Mostaza was often combined with leftover pink beans. After sautéing the greens, add 2 cups of cooked beans and simmer for 15 minutes longer. Do not cook too long, or the greens will become bitter.

Serves 6 as a side dish

fried squash blossoms

✕✕✕

Squash blossoms have a flavor all their own, slightly mushroomy and flowery with the tiniest hint of squash. During mid to late summer, the male zucchini and pumpkin blossoms were harvested in the early morning before the petals closed up in the heat. My mother often dipped the blossoms in a beer batter and deep-fried them, but I have switched to an easier technique that is less time-consuming.

12 male zucchini or pumpkin blossoms, grown on the long stems, freshly picked

3 eggs

¼ cup ice water

½ teaspoon salt

2 cups coarse bread crumbs (see Note)

2 ounces queso fresco or mild goat cheese

1 tablespoon minced parsley and basil

½ cup pure olive oil or canola oil, or more as needed

IF THE BLOSSOMS ARE PARTICULARLY DUSTY, dip them in a bowl of ice water and drain. Wrap in paper towels, place in a plastic bag, and store in the refrigerator. Just before cooking time, trim off the stems and pull out the pistil at the center of each blossom. Use your hand to gently flatten the blossom near the stem end.

BEAT THE EGGS AND ICE WATER until well blended. Stir the salt into the bread crumbs and spread the crumbs on a flat plate or piece of wax paper. Set aside.

MIX THE CHEESE WITH THE HERBS. Hold each blossom open and stuff with 2 teaspoons of the cheese filling. Press the blossom so the cheese spreads a little. Extend the petals so the flower shape is evident. Fill all the blossoms in this manner.

DIP EACH BLOSSOM IN THE EGG BATTER to coat both side, but don't allow egg to run inside the blossom. Place the blossom on top of the crumbs, using your fingers to sprinkle more crumbs on top. Lightly press in more crumbs. Set them on a tray. Continue coating all the blossoms.

HEAT THE OIL IN A 10-INCH SKILLET over medium heat. Fry 4 blossoms at a time, turning once, until very golden brown. Drain on paper towels. Continue frying all the blossoms. If at any time the oil becomes congested with crumbs, remove the crumbs with a slotted spoon. Or pour the oil into a heatproof cup. Wipe out the skillet with a wad of paper towels and add fresh oil. Heat and continue frying.

Serves 4 as an appetizer

NOTE: Grandmama saved slices of Italian bread to make crumbs. When dry, they were crushed with a heavy rolling pin. I turn 3-day-old French or Italian bread into crumbs in my food processor. Even easier is to buy the unauthentic but superb Japanese panko crumbs. They are sold in cellophane packets in the Asian section of many supermarkets.

squash blossom quesadillas

xxx

It was an old Indian belief that eating squash blossoms brought fertility. It seemed as though the Californios loved squash blossoms more than the squash itself, and it was not uncommon to find fifteen children at many family tables. Perhaps some credence can be given to the Indian wise men.

2 tablespoons pure olive oil

1 cup diced mild red onion

2 fresh Anaheim or poblano chiles, charred, peeled, and seeded

6 epazote leaves (optional), minced

1 clove garlic, minced

10 cleaned squash blossoms, cut into strips

½ teaspoon sea salt

½ cup cubed melting cheese, such as Monterey Jack

6 flour tortillas or 8 corn tortillas

HEAT THE OIL IN A SKILLET over medium heat and sauté the onion until softened, about 10 minutes. Cut the prepared chiles into strips and cook for 5 minutes with the onion. Stir in the epazote, garlic, and blossoms. Continue to cook for another 5 minutes. Season with salt and add the cheese. Turn off the heat and stir until the cheese is melted.

TO MAKE THE QUESADILLAS, place ¼ cup filling on half of each of 6 flour tortillas. Use less for a smaller corn tortilla. Press into a half-moon shape and heat on a comal or a nonstick pan over medium heat for about 2 minutes on each side or until quesadilla is golden.

Makes 6 or 8 quesadillas

squash blossom budín

———— ✕✕✕ ————

A *budín,* in the Spanish vernacular, refers to a pudding, which can be either savory or sweet. It's also a brilliant way to use up a few vegetables and stale tortillas but still extravagant enough to serve to guests. The Californios were magicians at concocting budíns like this.

Tortilla Croutons

    10 stale corn tortillas, diced into ½-inch pieces

    2 tablespoons pure olive oil or canola oil

    ½ teaspoon sea salt, mixed with 1 teaspoon chile powder

Vegetable Filling

    1 tablespoon pure olive oil, for sautéing

    1½ cups diced mild onion

    3 poblano chiles, charred, peeled, and seeded

    2 cups squash blossoms, pistils and stems discarded

    2 small zucchini, trimmed and diced

    2 ears of corn, kernels sliced off

    Salt

    1 cup thick cream, such as crema mexicana or sour cream

        thinned with 3 tablespoons milk

    1½ cups grated Monterey Jack cheese

PREHEAT THE OVEN to 350°F.

TO PREPARE TORTILLA CROUTONS, stir the tortilla pieces in a bowl with 2 tablespoons oil. Spread them out on a baking sheet. Bake, stirring once, until golden, about 10 minutes. Remove and sprinkle with the salt and chile powder.

HEAT 1 TABLESPOON OLIVE OIL in a large skillet over medium heat and sauté the onion for 5 minutes, until translucent. Cut the chiles and squash blossoms into strips and add. Add the zucchini and corn kernels. Cook for 10 minutes more. Season with salt to taste.

PREHEAT THE OVEN to 350°F. Oil a 3-quart shallow baking dish.

SPRINKLE ONE THIRD OF THE TORTILLA CROUTONS over the bottom of the dish. Cover with a third of the vegetable mixture, half of the cream, and ½ cup of the cheese. Continue layering the tortilla croutons, the vegetables, the cream, and the cheese. Sprinkle the top with the remaining croutons and cheese. Bake for 20 minutes.

Serves 6 as a side dish

NOTE: The croutons are also delicious in Mexican salads or on top of soups.

braised string beans and tomatoes

✕✕✕

Olive oil, the preferred fat for cooking, was frequently used to braise vegetables. In summer, when string beans were in season, this dish was served for lunch with just bread and cheese.

I pound string beans, preferably very young and thin

2 tablespoons olive oil

I cup minced onion

I clove garlic, minced

2 medium tomatoes, peeled, seeded, and chopped

I to 2 tablespoons red wine vinegar

½ teaspoon sea salt

Freshly ground black pepper

IF NECESSARY, pull the strings off the string beans. If you are using larger beans, French-cut them lengthwise so they will cook up more tenderly.

HEAT THE OLIVE OIL in a skillet over medium heat and sauté the onion until softened. Add the garlic and cook briefly. Add the tomatoes and string beans. Cover and simmer until the beans are tender, 10 to 12 minutes. Sprinkle in the wine vinegar. Cook off the vinegar for 1 or 2 minutes in the uncovered skillet over medium heat, and season with salt and pepper to taste.

Serves 6 as a side dish

don miguel acosta's tortilla omelet

✕✕✕

If I could manage it, I would call up Mike Acosta (full name: Don Miguel Dominguez y Yuarez Acosta), a Santa Barbara *descendiente*, every morning to find out what he was fixing for breakfast. Even his smallest meal is prepared with the utmost of care. After eighty-four years, he still wakes up with new ideas. The following recipe is one of those inspirations, and every person who has eaten the tortilla omelet loves it.

2 eggs
2 tablespoons water
1 tablespoon cornmeal
¼ teaspoon garlic salt
¼ teaspoon salt
1 tablespoon minced cilantro
1 tablespoon finely minced onion
2 corn tortillas
1 tablespoon pure olive oil
4 tablespoons grated Monterey Jack cheese

Additions (optional)
Green salsa (Mike recommends the Herdez brand)
Minced onion
Minced cilantro
Olive oil

BEAT THE EGGS, water, cornmeal, garlic salt, salt, cilantro, and onion. Set aside while you heat up the tortillas in a skillet or over the gas flame of your stove, as Mike does. Heat the oil in a nonstick 10-inch skillet over medium heat. Pour in a fourth of the egg batter and place a warm tortilla on top, pushing the tortilla down into the batter. Pour another fourth of the batter on top. Once the tortilla omelet begins to set up but is still a little moist on top, flip it over and sprinkle 2 tablespoons of the grated cheese on top. Drizzle on a little green salsa, some minced onion, more minced cilantro, and a drizzle of olive oil. Repeat with the second tortilla.

Serves 2 or 1 generously for breakfast, lunch, or light dinner

green chiles en escabeche

✕✕✕

Rancho kitchens valued their red chile sauces but this didn't mean that they ignored green chiles, which were often brined in crocks. Escabeches were the dominant Spanish technique for preserving foods and adding flavor. The pickled chiles, slightly tamed from the soaking, were then ready for a myriad of dishes from rajas to Chiles Rellenos con Queso (page 125).

    8 Anaheim or New Mexican green chiles
    2 cups white wine vinegar or apple cider vinegar
    I cup water
    2 tablespoons fruity olive oil
    2 tablespoons sea salt or kosher salt
    2 tablespoons sugar
    2 cloves garlic, crushed
    I tablespoon cumin seeds, crushed
    I bay leaf
    I teaspoon dried oregano
    2 carrots, peeled and cut into 2-inch pieces

CHAR THE CHILES OVER A FLAME or grill until the surface is blackened. Place wet paper towels over the chiles to help them steam to loosen the skins. Gently slip off the blackened skins, using paper towels to rub them off. Cut a lengthwise slit down the side of each chile. Remove the seeds, being careful not to tear the flesh. Set aside.

COMBINE THE VINEGAR, water, olive oil, salt, sugar, garlic, cumin, bay leaf, oregano, and carrots in a large saucepan. Bring to a simmer over medium heat just to dissolve the salt and sugar. Place the chiles in a large glass bowl or a 2-quart crock and pour in the hot marinade. Marinate from 1 hour to 1 week. If marinated for the short time, they are perfect for chiles rellenos. After a full day of marinating, they taste more pickled and are best used as flavoring or for layering into sandwiches. Use the pickled carrots for appetizers or chopped in salads.

Makes 1 quart

chiles con ensalada ruso

—— xxx ——

The Chiles en Escabeche can be removed early from their brining and anointed with olive oil. Filled with *ensalada ruso* (Russian salad), or chicken or seafood salad, the stuffed chiles are delicious for a first course or to bring to a picnic.

> 6 to 8 Green Chiles en Escabeche (page 123)
>
> 1 tablespoon olive oil

Russian Salad

> 4 red-skin new potatoes, scrubbed and diced
>
> 1 carrot, peeled and diced
>
> ¼ cup small green or frozen petite peas
>
> 2 tablespoons minced sweet onion
>
> 1 tablespoon minced parsley
>
> 1 tablespoon minced cilantro
>
> ½ teaspoon salt
>
> ½ teaspoon dry mustard
>
> ¼ cup crema mexicana plus 2 tablespoons for garnish
>
> 2 tablespoons mayonnaise
>
> Lettuce leaves, for garnish

REMOVE THE CHILES FROM THE MARINADE after 1 hour, reserving the marinade. Place the chiles on a plate and drizzle with olive oil.

TO PREPARE THE RUSSIAN SALAD, simmer the potatoes and carrots in 1 inch of water over medium heat for about 10 minutes. Do not let them overcook. Add the peas during last minute. Drain the vegetables in a colander while you mix the dressing.

COMBINE THE ONION, parsley, cilantro, salt, mustard, crema, mayonnaise, and about 3 teaspoons of the escabeche marinade. Blend and taste. You might want a little more of the marinade. Stir the cooked vegetables and dressing together. Fill each chile with about ¼ cup of Russian Salad and place on a salad plate garnished with lettuce. Drizzle 1 teaspoon of crema over each chile.

Serves 6

VARIATION: Stir ½ to 1 cup of cooked chicken or shrimp (diced prawns or baby shrimp) into the salad. Add 1 or 2 more tablespoons of mayonnaise to the dressing and adjust the seasonings.

chiles rellenos con queso

———————✕✕✕———————

Rancho cooks roasted green chiles filled with cheese on the top of the kitchen's big iron stove. The chile was then wrapped in a warm flour tortilla, the perfect way to enjoy pure chile essence. Use this technique if you want just one chile for yourself or if you need eight chiles for many eaters. I have made bread-crumbed chiles by the dozen for parties.

> 1 to 8 fresh Anaheim, New Mexican, or poblano chiles
> ½ cup grated cheese per chile, such as Monterey Jack, Italian Fontina,
>   or Mexican Chihuahua
> 1 to 8 flour tortillas, warm (optional)

CHAR EACH CHILE OVER A FLAME or on a grill (I use the little asador grill that fits on one burner) and place under wet paper towels to steam for at least 10 minutes. Use a paper towel to help wipe off the charred skin. Leave bits of charred skin on for flavor. Slit the chile down the side and shake out the seeds, or pull out the heavier seed pod of the poblano if using that. Fill the chile with grated cheese. Place the chile on a dry griddle and cook until the cheese melts. Eat as is or wrapped in a tortilla, if desired.

Serves 1 to 8

VARIATION: Crusty Chiles. Dip each cheese-filled chile in 2 eggs beaten with 2 tablespoons water. Spread ¼ cup bread crumbs per chile on a piece of waxed paper and place the chiles on top. Press the crumbs into the chiles. Place the chiles on an oiled baking sheet. Drizzle each chile with about 2 teaspoons of olive oil or melted butter. Bake in a preheated 375-degree oven until golden, about 15 minutes.

NOTE: Place 4 to 5 slices of day-old French or Italian bread into a food processor. Add 2 sprigs parsley, 1 clove of garlic, and 2 tablespoons grated Parmesan cheese. Grind bread into fluffy crumbs.

tortilla española

⨯⨯⨯

This tortilla, really a thick potato omelet, is related only in name to the flat breads that we know as tortillas. The version cooked on the rancho, with partially cooked potatoes, required less olive oil in the frying step than the traditional Spanish tortilla. A Spaniard would be aghast at the scrimping of olive oil, but we prefer the less oily tortilla. It resembles a thick, golden potato cake, barely held together with egg.

    7 Yukon Gold potatoes, scrubbed (about 1½ pounds),
        or 2 russet potatoes, scrubbed
    3 tablespoons flavorful olive oil, or more as needed
    1 onion, thinly sliced
    1 teaspoon sea salt
    Freshly ground black pepper
    4 eggs
    2 tablespoons minced Italian parsley

IF USING YUKON GOLDS, parboil for 6 minutes; if using russets, parboil for 10 minutes. Drain in a colander and let cool for at least 30 minutes. Peel the potatoes and slice ⅛ inch thick.

HEAT 1 TABLESPOON OF THE OLIVE OIL in large skillet over low heat and sauté the onion slices for 10 minutes. Drizzle in 1 tablespoon more oil and add the potato slices. Sprinkle with a little salt. Cover the skillet and cook over low heat. Every 3 or 4 minutes, uncover and turn the potatoes and onions to prevent browning. Add a little salt and pepper every time you turn the potatoes. Drizzle in more olive oil if needed. Cook the mixture for 15 minutes, then place in a colander to cool.

BEAT THE EGGS in a large mixing bowl and add the slightly cooled potatoes and onions and the parsley. Let soak for 15 minutes.

HEAT OLIVE OIL in a deep 10-inch nonstick skillet (this is untraditional but it works) over low heat. Once the pan is hot, pour in the egg-potato mixture. Using your fingers, press it into a flat, even potato tortilla. Cook for 5 minutes on low heat. The bottom will turn golden brown but the center might still be a little soft. Turn off the heat. With your hands in oven mitts, place a flat 12-inch dish on top of the omelet pan and turn over. A little liquid egg may run onto the plate. Slide the tortilla back into the omelet pan along with any liquid egg. Cook until the bottom is golden, about 3 minutes.

IMMEDIATELY SLIDE THE TORTILLA onto a flat serving dish. Let sit for at least 20 minutes before serving; it has maximum flavor when cooled down. The potato tortilla actually is at its best a couple of hours later, making it great to bring to picnics. Cut into wedges to serve.

Serves 4 as a light lunch or 6 as an appetizer or for a picnic

scrambled eggs and nopalitos

xxx

Nopalitos, or cactus paddles, have long been considered a delicacy in Mexico, California, and the Southwest. When prepared correctly and cut into string-bean shapes, they are usually mistaken for tender beans because they are similar in flavor. People cannot believe that they are eating cactus. Except for Huevos Rancheros (page 128), you cannot find a more traditional breakfast than eggs and nopalitos. Serve them with Frijoles de la Olla (page 108) for a truly authentic rancho breakfast.

I small *nopal* or cactus paddle
3 quarts water
I tablespoon olive oil
¼ cup diced red onion
I jalapeño or güero chile, seeded and minced
6 eggs
I tablespoon water
2 tablespoons minced cilantro
½ cup crumbled fried corn tortillas or good-quality corn chips
½ cup queso fresco

PURCHASE ALREADY TRIMMED AND DESPINED CACTUS in a Latino market or prepare your own according to the directions given on page 33.

BRING THE 3 QUARTS WATER TO A BOIL and blanch the cactus pad for 1 minute. Drain in a colander under cold running water, rinsing well. Cut the cactus into narrow strips about the width of a green bean and then into 2-inch pieces. Rinse again in cold water.

HEAT THE OLIVE OIL IN A SKILLET over medium heat and sauté the cactus, onion, and chile until the onion is softened, 5 to 8 minutes. Beat the eggs with the water and pour into the skillet. Let the eggs cook gently for 2 minutes, swirling the pan. While the eggs are still partially liquid, stir in the cilantro and crumbled chips. Stir very gently for 2 minutes more, removing from the heat while the eggs are still moist. Sprinkle the queso fresco on top of the eggs and serve immediately.

Serves 4 to 6

huevos rancheros

✕✕✕

A batch of ranchero sauce was always on hand to pour over a steak, stuffed chiles, or eggs. Huevos Rancheros, or rancho-style eggs, remains a favorite breakfast and Sunday night supper. In this version, the eggs and sauce are served on top of a flat quesadilla. If you can, prepare the ranchero sauce the night before your breakfast.

Serve Huevos Rancheros with Frijoles de la Olla (page 108) or fruit.

    ¼ cup oil
    12 corn tortillas
    1½ cups grated Monterey Jack cheese
    12 eggs

Ranchero Sauce

    ½ cup chopped onion
    2 cloves garlic, minced
    1 to 2 jalapeño chiles, seeded and minced
    1 can (28 ounces) ready-cut tomatoes or plum tomatoes, roughly puréed
    2 fresh tomatoes, diced
    1 teaspoon dried oregano
    ½ teaspoon ground cumin
    1 to 2 tablespoons New Mexican chile powder
    1 cup water
    1 teaspoon sugar
    1 teaspoon salt
    1 tablespoon apple cider vinegar
    Freshly ground black pepper
    ½ cup crumbled cotija cheese (optional)

LAY OUT THE OIL, tortillas, grated cheese, and eggs.

TO PREPARE THE SAUCE, combine the onion, garlic, jalapeños, puréed tomatoes, fresh tomatoes, oregano, and cumin in a deep saucepan and simmer over low heat. Dissolve the chile powder in ½ cup of the water, add the remaining water, and add to the sauce. Add the sugar, salt, and vinegar. Cook for 15 to 20 minutes longer. Season with freshly ground pepper to taste. Keep warm while you fix the quesadillas and eggs.

PREHEAT THE OVEN to 200°F and put 6 large dinner plates in the oven to keep warm. Heat 2 teaspoons of the oil in a 12-inch nonstick skillet and add 1 tortilla. Spread on ¼ cup of the grated cheese and top with a second tortilla, pressing together. Fry for 1 minute, turn over, and cook for 1 minute more. Place the quesadilla on a baking sheet. Continue frying the remaining 5 quesadillas, adding oil to the pan as needed. Put the quesadillas in the oven to keep warm.

HEAT MORE OIL IN THE SAME SKILLET as for the quesadillas, add 4 eggs, and cook over low heat, turning once. Cook for 4 minutes for soft or up to 8 minutes for well-done eggs. You can use a second skillet, if desired, to fry the other 4 eggs, to speed up the process. Cook the last 4 eggs.

TO SERVE HUEVOS RANCHEROS, place a quesadilla on a warm plate, top with 2 fried eggs, and smother with a generous ½ cup sauce. Sprinkle crumbled queso cotija over the top, if desired.

Serves 6

seafood

BY THE BAY

for most Californios, life as experienced from the saddle was the sweetest and the only sporting life a man needed. Around the 1840s, it was noted by an American that the rancheros would fish only if they could ride their horses out into San Francisco Bay and fish from their saddles. San Francisco Bay and Monterey Bay were bursting with fish but none came to the table on a regular basis.

*Family and friends share seafood and
salads in the al fresco dining room.*

For years the only seafood enjoyed by the rancheros was the type that could be foraged along the shores with no need of a fishing pole. From Rancho Los Tularcitos in Milpitas, they sent out the boys to scavenge down at the Bay at low tide for mussels and abalone. Many a breakfast included fried abalone with eggs, frijoles, and tortillas.

When California was inundated with seaworthy Portuguese, Italians, and Chileans, it wasn't long before fishing became a flourishing livelihood in San Francisco Bay. Dungeness crab, prawns, salmon, petrale sole, sand dabs, and oysters became classics on San Francisco menus. Crab suppers over spread-out newspapers were a favorite during Dungeness crab season from November to May. Foraging for mussels was as much a family ritual for us as tamale-making. The entire extended family of uncles, aunts, children, Grandpa, and Grandmama went to Half Moon Bay every October. Part of the attraction was the raucous camaraderie that accompanied plucking mussels from dangerous rocks, as much a rite of machismo as the bull's head barbecue.

The men waded with their pants rolled up to their knees at low tide. Uncle Ed was always good at spotting the blue-black shells of mussels clinging to the rock walls by their whiskers. Only mussels with closed shells, indicating they were alive, were removed. If the musselers stayed out too long, the water started to rise and we children watched our fathers from the beach. Finally, when the fog began to come in, the men walked like heroes to the warm campfire where coffee and eager antici-pation awaited them. The mussels were rinsed off in a bucket of fresh seawater, cleaned, and stacked in the blue enamel mussel pot, which had been placed over beach rocks circling the fire. There is a special quality to eating hot garlicky mussels in your wet, sandy beach clothes with the fog rolling in.

chileña seafood pie with corn topping

xxx

My favorite part of the traditional Chileña Pie (page 155) has always been the corn topping, which is my inspiration for this seafood version. It has two layers instead of the usual three, so it is a little easier to make.

> 2 cups mixed cooked seafood, such as cooked Dungeness crabmeat,
>   prawns, lobster, or halibut
> ¾ cup Velvet Tomato-Chipotle Sauce (page 142)
> 4 to 5 ears of corn
> 5 tablespoons crema mexicana or heavy cream
> Pinch of salt
> 1 teaspoon sugar
> 2 tablespoons slivered basil

PREHEAT THE OVEN to 350°F.

COMBINE THE SEAFOOD with the sauce and pour into an oiled shallow 1-quart baking dish. Grate the corn using a corn grater or the big hole of a box grater. This method extracts the sweet heart of each kernel. Mix the grated corn with 4 tablespoons of the crema, salt, sugar, and basil. Pour over the top of the seafood. Bake for 15 min-utes. Drizzle the remaining tablespoon of crema over the top of the corn layer. Place the baking dish 8 inches below a preheated broiler for 1 to 2 minutes and broil until the pie turns golden. Remove immediately. Let the pie set up for 5 to 10 minutes before serving.

Serves 6 as a side dish

garlicky steamed mussels

⋈⋈⋈

This recipe works equally well for cultivated or farmed mussels or for the mussels you might still be lucky enough to harvest along rocky coastal areas of the Pacific Coast. Rinse the mussels under cold, running water and debeard them if necessary by pulling off the beards or running a sharp paring knife around the mouth of the shells. If a mussel is open, squeeze it. If alive, the shell will close; if the shell remains open, discard it.

When we cooked mussels on the beach, the bread for dunking was impaled on a stick and balanced over the coals until the crust was crackly. It was then perfect for dunking. We were always reminded, as if we hadn't heard it a hundred times, that drinking mussel liquor added ten years to your life.

    5 pounds mussels
    2 to 6 tablespoons butter, olive oil, or a combination
    1 tablespoon minced garlic
    ¼ cup minced parsley
    2 tablespoons minced cilantro
    2 cups water
    1 cup dry white wine

PREPARE THE MUSSELS by cleaning and debearding.

MELT THE BUTTER and/or olive oil in a 6-quart pot and sauté the garlic over medium heat just until fragrant. Add the parsley, cilantro, water, and white wine. Bring to a simmer on medium-high heat and add the mussels. Cover and steam just until they open, 3 to 6 minutes. Remove the mussels as soon as they open, discarding any unopened ones. Lift the mussels out onto a platter, reserving the broth. Serve each person a bowl of mussels with broth.

Serves 6

NOTE: It has always been our practice to steam extra mussels for Paella Salad (page 140) or, if it was near Thanksgiving, for turkey stuffing.

grilled mussels
with salsa de nopalitos

xxx

This salsa is purely a modern invention. My grandmother never would have made salsa de nopalitos, but she would have understood that we live in a salsa-mad world. This is another example of how I take liberties with the old ways.

I cactus paddle, despined (see page 33)
2 teaspoons olive oil
I ear of corn
¼ cup diced red onion
2 cloves garlic, minced
I red bell pepper, cored and diced
2 serrano chiles, finely minced
½ teaspoon salt
I teaspoon sugar
2 tablespoons lime juice
I tablespoon olive oil
¼ cup minced cilantro
¼ cup crumbled cotija cheese
24 to 30 mussels, cleaned and debearded

BRUSH THE CACTUS PADDLE with olive oil and grill over medium heat for 8 minutes, turning frequently. Brush some olive oil on the corn and grill at the same time until slightly blackened.

DICE THE CACTUS. If it seems sticky, place in a colander and rinse with cold water. Blot with paper towels. Shave off the corn kernels. Place in a bowl with the diced cactus and the onion, garlic, bell pepper, and serrano chiles. Make a dressing by combining the salt, sugar, lime juice, and olive oil. Blend well and pour over the vegetables. Sprinkle with cilantro and cotija cheese.

TO GRILL THE MUSSELS, place over coals that are covered in white ash, or a medium-hot gas grill. Turn once with tongs. They will pop open in 3 to 4 minutes. Lift off the grill immediately and serve with salsa spooned over the top of the mussel inside.

Serves 6 as an appetizer

norma's mussel stuffing

⋙⋘

Norma Thomas, one of the best cooks I have ever known, lived on a ranch in San Luis Obispo and made frequent forays to the pier in Avila Beach for the freshest fish and mussels in season. Once, a war nearly broke out in her house when someone sacrilegiously threw out the mussel broth she'd saved for moistening the stuffing.

I loaf 2 to 3 day-old French bread, lightly toasted if too fresh

4 tablespoons (½ stick) butter

I tablespoon flavorful olive oil

I onion, minced

2 pints mussels, steamed and chopped, broth reserved and strained
  (see page 135)

I teaspoon dried basil or I tablespoon fresh basil

¼ cup minced Italian parsley

I egg, beaten

Freshly ground black pepper

I chicken (3½ pounds) or I turkey (10 to 12 pounds)

Sea salt

Olive oil

Handful of Italian parsley

TO BAKE THE STUFFING in a baking dish, preheat the oven to 350°F.

TRIM THE CRUST FROM THE BREAD. Cut bread into 1-inch cubes. Heat the butter and olive oil in a large, deep skillet over medium heat and sauté the onion until translucent, about 5 minutes. Add the chopped mussels, the bread cubes, basil, and parsley. Stir to combine. Remove from heat. Add the egg and about 1 cup of the reserved mussel broth. Season with pepper to taste. Add just enough more broth to make the bread cling together without being soggy. Place the stuffing in a buttered 2-quart baking dish or stuff into a chicken or turkey. If using a baking dish, cover with foil and bake for 25 minutes.

TO STUFF A CHICKEN OR TURKEY, preheat the oven to 425°F. Rub salt and olive oil inside the cavity and outside of the chicken or turkey, gently lifting the skin and sliding your fingers underneath to loosen. Slip 5 or 6 whole parsley leaves underneath the skin along with some salt and olive oil. The leaves will show underneath the translucent skin. Place the stuffing inside the cavity.

ROAST THE CHICKEN OR TURKEY at 425°F for 20 minutes. Turn the heat down to 350°F and roast or until juices run clear when a thigh is pierced, about 45 minutes for a 3½-pound chicken and about 2½ to 3 hours for a 12-pound turkey. Let stand before carving.

Serves 6 to 8

paella

✕✕✕

We treated paella like a rich man's Arroz con Pollo (page 168), with the added seafood making it more appropriate for celebrations. California paella was likely to have mussels, abalone, and prawns, but you can add and subtract seafood according to what you can find. All you need with this is a salad dressed lightly with olive oil and wine vinegar, maybe some cold artichokes, some crusty bread, and red wine.

    1 pound boneless chicken, cut into small pieces
    1 teaspoon dried oregano
    2 cloves garlic
    ½ teaspoon freshly ground black pepper
    1½ teaspoons sea salt
    1 tablespoon vinegar
    1 tablespoon olive oil
    8 ounces chorizo sausage
    6 cups water or a combination of clam broth, seafood, and chicken
        broth, and white wine
    1 pound bay scallops
    1 pound medium or large shrimp
    1 dozen mussels or clams, scrubbed
    4 lobster tails, sliced through the shells following the natural rings (optional)
    1 teaspoon salt
    ¼ teaspoon Spanish saffron threads
    3 tablespoons olive oil
    1 onion, minced
    1 red bell pepper, diced
    2 cups Arborio rice or short-grain Spanish rice
    2 medium tomatoes, peeled, seeded, and chopped
    1 teaspoon Spanish paprika
    2 tablespoons capers, drained
    1 cup frozen petite peas, thawed
    1 jar (4 ounces) Spanish pimiento, blotted and cut into strips

DRY THE CHICKEN PIECES WELL with paper towels. Mash the oregano, garlic, pepper, and salt into a paste using a mortar and pestle or a chef's knife. Add the vinegar and olive oil. Rub the paste over the chicken pieces. Set aside to marinate.

SAUTÉ THE CHORIZO SAUSAGE for 5 minutes and drain on paper towels. Set aside.

BRING THE WATER OR STOCK TO A SIMMER in a 3-quart saucepan over medium heat. Add the scallops and poach for 2 minutes. Lift out immediately. Add the shrimp and the mussels to the poaching liquid and cook for about 3 minutes. Remove immediately. Add the lobster, if using, and cook for 2 to 3 minutes. Lift out of the stock and set aside. Pour the liquid through a strainer and reserve for cooking the rice. Measure out 4½ cups and add salt and saffron.

HEAT 2 TABLESPOONS OF THE OLIVE OIL in a 14-inch paella pan over medium heat and sauté the onion until translucent, about 5 minutes. Add the bell pepper and cook briefly. Push to the side of the pan, add 1 tablespoon more olive oil, and sauté the marinated chicken pieces until brown on all sides, 10 minutes. Remove chicken as it browns. Add the rice to the pan, sautéing for 1 or 2 minutes. Add more olive oil if needed. Add the tomatoes, sautéing to reduce some of their liquid.

ADD THE RESERVED CHICKEN PIECES, chorizo, and 4½ cups strained stock. Sprinkle in the paprika and capers. Simmer the paella on low heat for 10 minutes. Bury the shrimp, scallops, and lobster pieces, if using, in the rice. Cover the pan with a lid or a wide piece of foil to help the rice steam. Continue simmering on low heat for 5 minutes more. Uncover and sprinkle peas over the top and arrange the strips of pimiento around the pan in a pinwheel. Bury the mussels in the rice a little. Cover the pan, turn off the heat, and allow the paella to set up in its own fragrant steam for 5 minutes. Remove the lid and serve immediately.

Serves 6 to 8

NOTE: Whenever I steam mussels or poach shrimp or lobster, I save the leftover broth and freeze it for later use in paella or soups. Shrimp shells or lobster shells can be simmered for 30 minutes in chicken or clam broth and white wine to make a good seafood stock. Use 1 quart of liquid for every 2 cups of shells.

paella salad

✕✕✕

This beautiful salad, one of our favorites, is great for a summer lunch or dinner. The rice is cooked in a seafood broth that is flavored with a chipotle chile, which is not traditional but is very good, and it is then dressed, while still warm, with a sherry vinaigrette. Serve the salad with bread, wine, and fruit.

Rice

    2 cups chicken broth

    2 cups seafood stock or clam broth

    2 teaspoons flavorful olive oil

    I teaspoons sea salt

    I chipotle chile

    1/8 teaspoon ground saffron

    I bay leaf

    2 tablespoons tomato paste

    1/2 cup diced onion

    2 cups long-grain rice, such as basmati

    I cup frozen petite peas, thawed

Sherry Vinaigrette

    I shallot, finely diced

    I teaspoon Dijon mustard

    Pinch of salt

    1/4 cup sherry vinegar

    2 tablespoons rice vinegar

    1/2 cup flavorful olive oil

    1/4 cup minced cilantro

Chicken and Seafood

    I pound boneless and skinless chicken breast, cut into strips

    3 cups water

    1/2 cup white wine

    I pound shrimp

    I pound mussels

Vegetables for Garnish

    2 tomatoes, diced

    1/2 cup diced mild onion

    1/2 cup diced red bell pepper

¾ cup diced artichoke hearts, fresh or canned

10 stuffed olives

1 tablespoon capers, drained

¼ cup minced cilantro or Italian parsley

COMBINE THE CHICKEN BROTH, seafood stock, olive oil, salt, chipotle chile, saffron, bay leaf, tomato paste, onion, and rice in a 3-quart saucepan. Bring to a simmer over medium heat and cover. Cook over low heat for 12 minutes. Add the peas and cook for 2 minutes more. Remove from the heat and, with the lid still on, let steam for 3 minutes. Fluff with a fork and transfer to a wide bowl to cool.

TO PREPARE THE VINAIGRETTE, combine the shallot, mustard, salt, sherry vinegar, rice vinegar, and olive oil in a small bowl. Whisk to emulsify. Add the cilantro.

POUR ¼ CUP OF THE SHERRY VINAIGRETTE over the chicken strips and let marinate for 20 minutes. Grill the chicken in a ridged grill pan on the stove or on a gas grill. Cook for a total of 8 minutes, turning once.

TO PREPARE THE SEAFOOD, bring the water and wine to a simmer in a 3-quart saucepan. Add the shrimp and mussels, cover, and cook until the shrimp turns pink and the mussels open, 3 to 4 minutes. Lift out the seafood immediately, discarding any mussels that haven't opened. Reserve the broth for another use.

WHEN COOL ENOUGH TO HANDLE, pull the mussels from the shells and cut in half. Shell the shrimp.

STIR ¼ CUP OF THE VINAIGRETTE into the rice. Dice the grilled chicken and stir it into the rice with the mussels, shrimp, tomatoes, onion, bell pepper, artichoke hearts, olives, and capers. Drizzle another ¼ cup over all and sprinkle with cilantro. The extra vinaigrette can be passed at the table.

Serves 8

seafood enchiladas with velvet tomato-chipotle sauce

XXX

This recipe embodies many old rancho and Mexican techniques, such as roasting and charring vegetables, and combines them with chiles to make a sauce as complex as any French sauce. No, they most likely did not use chipotles in the rancho days, but for the last twenty years I have had a love affair with chipotles and they are my own addition to rancho cooking. I cure my own red jalapeños over apricot wood in a little water smoker every autumn when the jalapeños are ripening.

Be sure to add the velvet touch—crema mexicana—to the sauce. If crema mexicana is not available, substitute sour cream thinned with milk.

Velvet Tomato-Chipotle Sauce

½ onion

1 head of garlic, top sliced off

2 teaspoons olive oil

2 teaspoons dried oregano

1 pound Roma or plum tomatoes, halved

1 tablespoon olive oil

½ teaspoon salt

2 cups water

3 chipotle chiles, rinsed

3 dried red chiles, preferably New Mexican

1 bay leaf

1 teaspoon sugar

Salt

¼ cup crema mexicana

Seafood Filling

1 cup chopped onion

2 teaspoons olive oil

2 cups cooked mixed seafood, such as shrimp, crab, lobster, and scallops

2½ cups grated Italian fontina cheese

Assembly

8 corn tortillas

2 teaspoons oil

Extra shrimp or slices of lobster, for garnish (optional)

Sprigs of cilantro, for garnish (optional)

PREHEAT THE OVEN to 375°F.

TO PREPARE THE SAUCE, place the onion and garlic on a piece of aluminum foil. Drizzle with 2 teaspoons olive oil and sprinkle 1 teaspoon oregano on top. Wrap up and bake for 35 minutes.

PLACE THE TOMATOES ON A BAKING SHEET, cut side up, and sprinkle 1 tablespoon olive oil and salt over the tops. Place under a broiler until they begin to caramelize and brown on top, about 20 minutes. Remove immediately.

POUR THE WATER INTO A 2-QUART SAUCEPAN and add the chipotle chiles, red chiles, 1 teaspoon of the oregano, the bay leaf, the broiled tomatoes, and the roasted garlic and onion. Bring to a simmer over medium heat and cook for 20 minutes, stirring from time to time. Make sure that the chiles are immersed in liquid. Turn off the heat and let cool for 30 minutes.

TRANSFER THE TOMATOES, onion, 4 cloves of the garlic, the chipotles, red chiles, and ¼ cup liquid from the pot into a food processor or blender. Discard the bay leaf. Purée and then push through a wire strainer to remove the seeds and skins. Be sure to scrape off the bottom of the strainer. Pour all the liquid from the pot through the strainer. Put the purée back into the saucepan. Simmer over medium heat for 5 minutes. Add the sugar and salt to taste. Add the crema mexicana. Simmer for 5 minutes more to concentrate the flavors. Set aside to cool slightly.

TO PREPARE THE SEAFOOD FILLING, sauté the onion in the olive oil in a sauté pan over medium-low heat until translucent, about 5 minutes. Turn off the heat and add the seafood and ⅓ cup of the sauce. Stir to combine. Add 1 cup of the cheese.

SOFTEN THE CORN TORTILLAS in a skillet with a little oil and stack them on a plate.

PREHEAT THE OVEN to 375°F. Oil a large shallow baking dish.

DIP A TORTILLA IN THE VELVET SAUCE and lay it on a dinner plate for easier handling. Place a scant ¼ cup seafood filling down the middle. Fold over the sides and place, seam-side down, in the baking dish. Continue dipping and filling. When finished, drizzle ½ cup of sauce over the tops of the enchiladas. Sprinkle on the rest of the cheese. Bake until the cheese is melted, about 8 minutes. Remove immediately. Garnish with pieces of seafood and sprigs of cilantro, if desired. Serve.

Makes 8 enchiladas

NOTE: This recipe makes 1 quart Velvet Tomato-Chipotle Sauce. You will have from 1 to 1½ cups sauce left over, which you can use with pasta, enchiladas, over eggs (for an elegant Huevos Rancheros, see page 128), or Chileña Seafood Pie with Corn Topping (page 134).

grilled trout
wrapped in fig leaves

xxx

The rancheros, who were happiest on their horses, were not fishermen, but eventually our family turned one out in the person of Uncle Jack, who also reigned as asador. Jack often brought along a little barbecue grill right to a trout stream to grill his freshly caught fish. My friend Mary Stec carried the fish grilling even further by stuffing the trout with fresh rosemary and thyme, massaging the outside with olive oil, and wrapping it in fresh fig leaves. The leaves add flavor and also serve to protect the fish from sticking to the grill. Edible leaves work as nature's nonstick covering.

Sea salt or kosher salt

1 golden trout (1½ to 2 pounds)

2 sprigs of rosemary

1 sprig of oregano

2 sprigs of marjoram

3 tablespoons olive oil

Freshly ground black pepper

2 large fig leaves, stems trimmed even with leaves, or grape leaves,
    Swiss chard leaves, or romaine lettuce leaves

4 bamboo skewers, soaked in cold water for 20 minutes

1 tablespoon white wine, mixed with 1 tablespoon olive oil

Fresh herbs or watercress, for garnish

START A WOOD FIRE 30 minutes before grilling time. Brush the grill rack to make sure that it is clean.

SPRINKLE SALT INSIDE THE CAVITY OF THE TROUT and stuff with the rosemary, oregano, and marjoram. Rub 2 teaspoons of the olive oil on the skin of the fish and sprinkle with ½ teaspoon salt and pepper to taste. Place the leaves in opposite directions, stem ends together. Lay the fish on the leaves and wrap them over the fish, securing with the bamboo skewers. Brush olive oil on the leaves. They are going to char, but this will add considerable flavor.

JUST BEFORE PLACING THE TROUT ON THE GRILL, lightly brush the hot grill rack with the remaining oil. Lay on the trout enrobed in the fig leaves. Grill for about 6 minutes. Brush with the wine–olive oil mix and turn the trout over. Grill for 6 minutes more. Let the leaves char. Remove to a platter garnished with herbs or watercress and serve.

Serves 4 to 6

Overleaf: A bowl of green olives, barrel-cured on the rancho, awaits snackers.

Far left: Chiles Rellenos—stuffed with cheese, rolled in breadcrumbs, and baked until golden—are a popular dish at fiestas.

Left: Rancho meals often ended with fruit, such as these plums.

Below: A cool pitcher of Agua Fresca de Sandìa, freshly made watermelon juice.

Above: Palillis reach back in time to gentler days on the rancho but are still appreciated when served today.

Far right: Stacked Enchilada Pie, a tower of corn tortillas dipped in red chile sauce, layered with cheese and onions, and lavishly garnished.

Right: Two freshly picked peaches.

Left: Paella Salad, perfect for a picnic or outdoor entertaining.

Above: Great-Grandma Silva's Chilean Empanadas, traditional fried turnovers, are filled with spicy picadillo.

Right: Vino tinto, red wine, was often made from the rancho's own grapes.

Above: Chileña Pie, topped with grated corn in place of pastry.

Far right: Apricot Pie appeared during the summer months, Walnut Pie in the autumn.

Right: Figs, one of the most revered fruits brought from the old country.

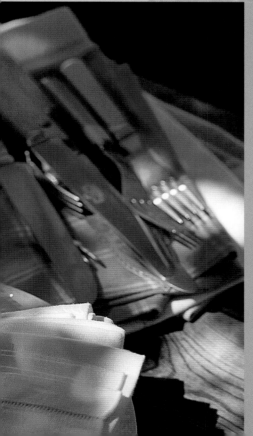

Far left: Thin and delicate Rancho Flour Tortillas pair well with California's original salsa, called sarsa by the rancheros.

Above: Butterflied Lamb in Pomegranate Juice is marinated before being grilled and served with Salsa Verde.

Left: Napkins and silver brought outdoors for a meal.

Above: Californio Rancho Tamales are extra fat because there are two additional corn husks spread with masa dough and wrapped around the center tamale.

Far right: Rancho cooks often rubbed meat and poultry with seasoning paste. Mama's Spicy Chicken, served here with Layered Potato Salad, is a delicious example.

Right: Flowers grace an everyday table.

Far left: Fig Empanadas, made of rich cookie dough folded over a fig and walnut filling.

Above: Classic Red Enchiladas, one of the oldest and best loved rancho dishes.

Left: Grilled Mussels have long been an appreciated delicacy along the West Coast. Our version is topped with Salsa de Nopalitos, cactus salsa.

Following page: An outdoor table, laden with delicious offerings, was preferred to the dining room when weather permitted.

escabeche de pescado

—— xxx ——

Even though many of the foods cooked in California were those the Spaniards had adopted from Mexico, the techniques often were the only Spanish part of a recipe. They possessed a love of grilling and the use of escabeches to preserve vegetables and seafood. Escabeche is one of Spain's contributions to the kitchen, and it was a practice that went beyond simple pickling. With the passage of time, sherry vinegar, olive oil, aromatic spices, and herbs all played a part in this version of preserving. In this recipe, the escabeche marinade not only adds flavor but gives keeping power to the fish. It tastes wonderful the next day.

3 cups combined seafood stock, white wine, and clam broth

2 pounds fillets of salmon, halibut, or rock cod

Escabeche

2 cloves garlic, minced

I teaspoon sea salt

¼ cup olive oil

½ cup white wine

3 tablespoons sherry vinegar

2 bay leaves

Pinch of sugar

¼ teaspoon cayenne pepper

I teaspoon dried oregano

Freshly ground pepper

I teaspoon capers, drained

2 tablespoons minced parsley

Cilantro Pesto Sauce

2 cloves garlic

I teaspoon sea salt

2 tablespoons lemon or lime juice

2 cups cilantro leaves, with some stems

3 tablespoons fragrant olive oil, or more if needed

PUT THE STOCK, wine, and clam broth in a 3-quart saucepan wide enough to not crowd the fish, and bring it to a simmer over medium heat. Lower in the fish. Poach just until the fish is barely firm, about 8 minutes. Lift out immediately and place in a shallow dish.

TO PREPARE THE ESCABECHE, combine the garlic, salt, olive oil, wine, sherry, bay leaves, sugar, cayenne pepper, and oregano in a saucepan. Simmer over medium heat for 5 minutes. Remove from the heat and season with pepper to taste. Add the capers and parsley. Let cool for 20 minutes, then pour over the fish. Marinate, refrigerated, for at least 2 hours, turning the fish a couple of times.

TO PREPARE THE PESTO SAUCE, place the garlic, salt, lemon juice, cilantro, and olive oil in a food processor and purée. Add a little more olive oil if needed. Makes about ¾ cup. Serve with the fish or with any seafood as a salsa.

Serves 6

bouillabaisse chili

———— ✕✕✕ ————

As with classic San Francisco cioppino, this bouillabaisse-cum-chili has evolved through the years within the family. Originally, it didn't even have chiles. It's gotten spicier with each generation. I, of course, had to add one of my favorite ingredients: chipotle chiles. The seafood is varied depending on what is the freshest.

Serve the bouillabaisse with crusty bread or, here in keeping with the spirit of the dish, warm tortillas.

Vegetables
  1 pound plum tomatoes, halved
  2 teaspoons olive oil
  1 teaspoon salt
  2 red bell peppers, seeded, and halved
  3 Anaheim chiles
  2 chipotle chiles, rinsed
  4 cups water
  1 bottle (8 ounces) natural clam juice

Aromatics
  1 tablespoon flavorful olive oil
  1 cup diced onion
  1 cup diced celery, including leaves
  6 cloves garlic, finely minced
  2 bay leaves
  1 tablespoon cumin seeds, toasted and finely crushed in a mortar or spice mill
  1 tablespoon New Mexican chile powder, preferably Dixon
  2 teaspoons freshly ground black pepper
  Salt

Seafood

   1 pound halibut, cut into 2-inch pieces

   1 pound scallops

   1 pound shrimp, shelled

   ¼ pound cleaned and prepared Monterey squid, cut into rings

   ½ cup minced cilantro

TO PREPARE THE VEGETABLES, spread the tomatoes, cut side up, on a baking sheet. Drizzle with olive oil and sprinkle with salt. Place the peppers and Anaheim chiles on the same baking sheet. Broil until slightly charred, turning the chiles over once, about 20 minutes. Remove from broiler. Place the peppers and chiles in a paper bag to steam further.

COMBINE THE TOMATOES, chipotle chiles, water, and clam juice in a 4-quart pot. Simmer over medium heat for 25 minutes. Using a slotted spoon, transfer the tomatoes and chipotles to a food processor and purée. Pour into a wire strainer placed over a large bowl and push through the strainer. Place the peppers and chiles into the processor bowl and purée. Pour into the strainer and push through to remove skins and seeds. Scrape the bottom of the strainer. Pour the liquid from the pot used to simmer the tomatoes through the strainer into the mixture. Set the purée aside.

TO PREPARE THE AROMATICS, heat the olive oil in a large saucepan over medium heat and sauté the onions until translucent, about 5 minutes. Add the celery, garlic, bay leaves, and cumin. Sauté for 2 minutes. Add the chile powder, pepper, vegetable purée, and salt to taste. Simmer for 20 minutes, adding water if the mixture seems too thick.

ADD THE HALIBUT, scallops, and shrimp. Add water if necessary to cover the seafood. Simmer for 8 minutes and then stir in the squid rings. Simmer for 5 minutes more, adding the cilantro at the last minute.

Serves 8

fast crab soup

✕✕✕

Many times when I needed to fix a quick meal, I've prepared this soup. It is cioppino inspired but does not claim to be close to the extravagance of a real San Francisco creation. In a pinch, I have even used canned minced clams and their liquor in place of the crab. I'm very close to adding a chipotle chile to this soup also.

1 tablespoon olive oil

½ cup diced onion

½ cup diced red bell pepper

3 cloves garlic, minced

1 carrot, peeled and diced

1 stalk celery with leaves, diced

4 ripe tomatoes, peeled, seeded, and diced

1 bottle (8 ounces) clam juice

2 cups water

¼ cup white wine or rosé wine

1 teaspoon dried oregano

1 teaspoon dried basil

2 tablespoons minced Italian parsley

1 cup Dungeness crabmeat or shrimp, mussels, or halibut

Sea salt

Freshly ground black pepper

Dash of cayenne pepper

HEAT THE OLIVE OIL in a 2-quart saucepan over medium heat and sauté the onion until translucent, about 5 minutes. Add the bell pepper, garlic, carrot, and celery and sauté for 1 minute. Add the tomatoes, clam juice, water, wine, oregano, basil, and parsley and simmer for 10 minutes. Stir in the crabmeat or your choice of seafood. Taste and adjust the seasoning with salt, pepper, and cayenne.

Serves 2 or 3

grandmama's codfish croquetas

These little delicacies were Grandmama's triumph over Friday fish night and the lean days of Lent. These croquetas have been known to fool people into thinking that they were eating crab cakes. The key is to seek out the best *bacalao*, preferably boneless. Bacalao, or dried cod, resembles a fishy board but when reconstituted it will be unctuous. Allow time for an overnight soak to draw the salt out of the bacalao.

1 pound boneless salt cod (bacalao)
4 cups milk
1 ½ cups diced potatoes
2 tablespoons butter
¼ cup minced onion
¼ teaspoon cayenne pepper
4 tablespoons finely minced parsley
2 egg yolks
Freshly ground pepper
1 ½ cups coarse bread crumbs
¾ cup oil, such as pure olive oil or grapeseed oil, for frying

COVER THE SALT COD WITH COLD WATER and soak overnight, changing the water several times. The next day, remove the cod from the water. Place it in a colander and rinse under running water. Separate into pieces, put in a pot, and cover with the milk. Simmer gently until the fish flakes easily, 15 to 20 minutes. Drain in a colander, discarding the milk.

SIMMER THE POTATOES IN WATER to cover over medium heat until tender when pierced with a knife, about 12 minutes. Remove from the heat and drain. Put back in the pan and mash with a large spoon or potato masher, adding the butter and onion.

FLAKE THE COD INTO A LARGE BOWL. Add the mashed potato mixture, using your hands to blend. Add the cayenne, parsley, and egg yolks and mix well. Season with pepper to taste.

FORM THE COD MIXTURE INTO PATTIES like fat crab cakes or, as Grandmama preferred, into finger-shaped croquetas. Roll in the bread crumbs, coating evenly.

HEAT THE OIL UNTIL HOT and fry the croquetas until golden brown on both sides. Drain on paper towels, blotting the tops. Serve hot.

Serves 6

celebración

at the heart of every-thing in the life of the Californios was *celebración*. They would die if they could not make an occasion over all of life's moments. If by chance they found out it was your birthday, time would stop while they put you on a pedestal for that day. This eagerness was often viewed as an affliction by someone who was not a Californio. In reality, it was a need to reaffirm each little

A romantic couple waits to enjoy the festivities and dancing of a typical celebración on the rancho.

detail of life. Woven into celebración was the ritual of food, so savored that while Californios were eating, time stood still. Food and celebración were inseparable.

The world where celebración had a better fit than today was that of my rancho family, whose life revolved around the first peach, the first corn, the last corn, the first dried red chiles, the last tomatoes of October, the first wild mushrooms harvested in the fields around the rancho. The taste of each season waited for my family as they anticipated the ripening fig and imagined its flavor. If you were told the walnuts had just been harvested and Sister was making her famous walnut pies, please come my child, my friend. You were there. Wild horses couldn't keep you away—or more likely wild horses actually brought you there. No one was ever too busy, too far away, too distracted, or too weight conscious.

Of all the things from the past that I long for it is celebración and the ceremony of eating. It is not just the huge occasion that serves celebración well but the smallest. When I take the time to peel an apple like Grandpa in one long artful strip, cut two wedges of Gorgonzola, and pour two glasses of port for me and Robert, we're so close to celebración, we can taste it.

María Higuera's Wedding

Many things brought change to the ranchos, but in our family it was a wedding, the ultimate celebración. The wedding defined our history, gave us the acceptable reason for losing the rancho. "The wedding of María Higuera, it was the wedding of María Higuera," was repeated until it became the truth.

The morning of her wedding, the silk ribbon stirrup broke as María Higuera mounted her godfather's horse for the procession to Mission Santa Clara, where she was to marry Nicolas Chavarria. This omen haunted the bride the rest of her life.

The wedding mass proceeded without incident and after their vows, María and Nicolas rode under the arches of flowers held by well-wishers waiting for them along the road home. When they finally arrived at Rancho Los Tularcitos, the real celebración began. There was an invisible web connecting all of the Californio families. News spread by messengers, and the families came together for important occasions. Guests came from as far away as San Diego and as close as San Francisco for what some called one of the last great weddings of a Californio girl. Wedding celebraciones typically lasted three days. María's lasted for a week. Special foods were served daily, including Chileña Pie made especially for Nicolas who was from Chile. Asadors and tortilla makers worked nonstop.

Dancing went on until daybreak or until the men dropped. There is no mention of the women dropping, only that they wore out several pairs of dancing slippers. María's father, Don Valentín, playing the role of generous patriarch, sent for more of everything—dancing slippers, brandy, cigars, wine, and cakes. Endless tabs were signed.

The omen of the broken stirrup was fulfilled ten years later, when most of Rancho Los Tularcitos was consumed by debt. The wedding extravagances were blamed. The lavish wedding for María Higuera may have been the rancho's undoing, but it was Don Valentín's wedding gift of ten acres to her and Nicolas that became the family's refuge. Five years later Nicolas bought more land to add to the wedding parcel, and it was on his land that the family continued to live out their legend, surrounded by the crumbling adobes of Rancho Los Tularcitos.

chileña pie

xxx

Deep pans of the layered Chileña Pie were made for María Higuera's wedding, as well as barbecues, festivities, and September 18, the National Day of Chile, which Nicolas always celebrated. It was only made in the summer when corn was in season. On the rancho, someone made a special corn grater that extracted the hearts of the kernels. Toothpicks were placed by Grandmama on the corn pudding layer over spots where the best chicken could be found. Only her favorite people knew the meaning of the toothpicks.

Picadillo Layer

    2½ pounds round or flank steak

    Water to cover

    1 onion, sliced

    1 clove garlic, whole

    1 carrot, scraped and chopped

    2 tablespoons olive oil

    1 onion, chopped

    1 clove garlic, minced

    3 teaspoons dried oregano

    2 teaspoons cumin seed, crushed

    2 tablespoons ground red chile powder, California or New Mexican

    1 teaspoon salt

    ¼ cup raisins, plumped in hot water

Chicken Layer

    2½ to 3 pounds chicken, from the breast, drumsticks, and thighs

    1 quart cold water

    1 teaspoon salt

    2 tablespoons olive oil

    1 jalapeño chile, seeded and minced

    Salt and pepper

Corn Layer

    10 ears of corn, husks removed

    2 tablespoons butter, melted

    1 teaspoon salt

    1 tablespoon sugar

    ⅓ cup heavy cream

    1 to 2 tablespoons fresh basil leaves, slivered

    2 tablespoons brown sugar

Garnish

    Basil leaves

TO PREPARE THE PICADILLO LAYER, place the meat in a large pot with the onion, garlic, carrot, and cold water to cover. Simmer over low heat for 1½ hours. Cool the meat in the broth for 20 minutes. Finely chop the meat using a chef's knife or a food processor. Do not overprocess. Reserve the broth.

HEAT THE OLIVE OIL IN A SKILLET over medium heat and sauté the onion until softened and lightly browned, about 10 minutes. Push to the side and add the chopped meat and garlic. Season it with oregano, cumin, chile powder, and salt. Add the plumped raisins and ½ cup of the reserved broth. If the mixture seems dry, add a little more broth. Set aside and prepare the chicken.

TO PREPARE THE CHICKEN LAYER, place the chicken in a large pot, cover with cold water, and add the salt. Bring to a boil, poach over low heat for 10 minutes, and cool in the cooking broth until just warm to the touch. Remove the bones and skin from the chicken and cut the meat into a large dice. Heat the olive oil and sauté the chicken until lightly browned. Season with the jalapeño chile, and salt and pepper to taste. Set aside.

TO PREPARE THE CORN LAYER, push the ear of corn across the spikes of a corn grater, if you have one, to remove the hearts of the kernels. Lacking a corn grater, grate the corn on the big hole of a box grater or cut off the kernels and purée them in a food processor. With a processor, the corn will not be as delicate as with a grater, but the layer will still be good. Combine the corn, melted butter, salt, sugar, cream, and basil.

PREHEAT THE OVEN to 375°F.

TO ASSEMBLE THE PIE, grease a deep 14 x 10-inch baking dish. Spread the picadillo over the bottom, layer the chicken on top, and finish with the corn layer. Sprinkle brown sugar over the top. Bake until golden, 30 to 40 minutes. Garnish with basil leaves.

Serves 8

NOTE: When making Chilena Pie, it is helpful if you prepare the picadillo and the chicken the day before you assemble the pie.

pastel de maíz

✕✕✕

This pastel is a cousin to the Chileña Pie and a sister to the green corn tamales that many rancho families made from July to October, when corn was in season. Instead of green corn tamales thickened with cornmeal, we like this pastel, simplified to the pure essence of corn. The pan is lined with green corn husks for extra flavor and rustic charm.

To grate the corn, I use a corn grater that is a small version of the one used on our rancho. It is made of maple wood and has an inset of raised spikes that release the corn's essence.

    12 ears of corn, husked and washed of corn silk
    Boiling water
    ¼ cup plus 2 to 3 tablespoons heavy cream
    1 teaspoon salt
    8 large fresh basil leaves, cut into slivers
    2 tablespoons sugar

TRIM OFF BOTH ENDS of each ear of corn. Carefully peel or unfurl the husks. Do not pull off the tender husks or they will tear. You will need 15 to 20 husks. Place the widest husks in a large heatproof bowl and cover with boiling water. Let steep for 10 minutes. Line a rectangular or oval 2-quart baking dish with the softened husks.

PREHEAT THE OVEN to 350°F.

TO PREPARE THE CORN, stand a box grater in a wide bowl and run the kernels against the large holes of the grater to release the corn essence. Add the ¼ cup cream, salt, and basil slivers and pour into the husk-lined dish. Drizzle the 2 to 3 tablespoons of cream over the top. Sprinkle sugar on top. I use my fingers to spread the cream and sugar around. Bake until golden on top, about 35 minutes.

THE PASTEL WILL CONTINUE TO SET UP as it cools.

Serves 6 to 8 as a side dish

great-grandma silva's chilean empanadas

✕✕✕

Grandmama's mother, Cecilia Silva, came from Valparaiso, Chile, when she was about eight. Cecilia, like Nicolas Chavarria, my Chilean great-grandfather, remained a mystery. All Cecilia brought with her to California was a small trunk of clothes and a handmade doll, which I still possess.

Empanadas were always made for Christmas and to carry on picnics. The juxtaposition of salty and sweet reflects the Moorish Spanish influence on many Chilean foods. Great-grandma Silva's memory of empanadas was further enriched by letters from Chilean relatives.

Picadillo Filling

2½ pounds round steak or flank steak, cut into chunks

1 clove garlic

1 onion, stuck with 3 cloves

1 carrot, peeled and chopped

1 bay leaf

1 tablespoon olive oil

1 onion, minced

3 teaspoons dried oregano

3 teaspoons cumin seeds, crushed in a mortar

1 to 2 tablespoons ground red chile powder

1 teaspoon salt

1 cup black raisins

½ cup sherry

1 tablespoon sugar

¼ cup slivered almonds

1 cup sliced black olives or ½ cup sliced stuffed green olives

Empanada Dough

3 cups unbleached all-purpose flour

¼ cup vegetable shortening

2 tablespoons butter

1 teaspoon salt

½ cup plus 1 tablespoon water

Assembly

2 cups canola or grapeseed oil

2 tablespoons sugar, for sprinkling

TO PREPARED THE PICADILLO FILLING, place the steak in a large pot with the garlic, onion, carrot, and bay leaf and cover with cold water. Simmer gently over low heat for 2 hours. Cool in the broth for 30 minutes. Drain the broth and reserve. Finely chop the meat with a knife or food processor. Do not overprocess.

HEAT THE OLIVE OIL IN A SKILLET over medium heat and sauté the onion until softened, about 5 minutes. Push the onion to the side and add the chopped meat, oregano, cumin, chile powder, and salt. Add enough broth, about ½ cup, to make the meat glisten. Cook for about 15 minutes.

MEANWHILE, steep the raisins in the sherry to plump. Add the sugar, almonds, and olives to the picadillo. If the mixture seems dry, moisten with leftover raisin sherry or the meat broth. Set aside and cool.

TO PREPARE THE EMPANADA DOUGH, put the flour in a large bowl. Rub the shortening and butter into the flour until crumbly. Stir the salt into the water and drizzle it on to make a soft, pliable dough. Knead on a floured board for no more than 1 minute, just until dough is smooth, as for a biscuit dough. Break off a piece of dough the size of a walnut and roll it into a 6-inch circle. Place ½ cup of the picadillo filling on the bottom half of the circle and fold over the top half, pressing together. Crimp the edges as for a turnover.

HEAT THE OIL IN A DEEP SKILLET until hot. Fry each empanada for 2 minutes, spooning hot oil over the surface. Turn and fry until golden. Remove immediately to a baking sheet lined with paper towels. Blot with paper towels. Sprinkle lightly with sugar. Continue frying, one empanada at a time. Serve immediately or cool down and store, wrapped, in the refrigerator. Reheat in a preheated 350°F oven for about 10 minutes.

Makes about 12 very large empanadas

californio rancho tamales

✕✕✕

There was never a Christmas or New Year's without the staging of a *tamalada*, or tamale fest, with a roomful of laughing people assembled at the kitchen table, which was spread with newspapers, damp *hojas*, or corn husks, piled in a roasting pan, and rolls of cotton string. Emotions ran high during tamale making. There was arguing, yelling, joking, and port wine drinking. The amount of port consumed could lower or raise the barometer.

Everyone had a role to play. The hoja man (or woman) soaked the corn husks, checking that they were free of dried insects and corn silk. The all-important tamale boss, usually Grandmama, cooked the meat and red chile for the filling. The masa spreaders had to make sure that it wasn't spread too thin or too thick. Californio tamales were wrapped with an extra hoja spread with masa, making them extra fat. This precautionary measure also helped safeguard against chile juices leaking into the pot. The extra masa is my favorite part, for I love peeling off the first hoja and eating pure corn essence.

When preparing tamales, cook the meat filling and chile sauce the day before so the flavors will steep together.

The day before the tamalada, purchase the pure masa from a Mexican grocery store or tortilla factory. Do not buy already prepared dough, often called masa preparada, which has added seasonings and cheap lard.

Incidentally, my grandmother never added baking powder to the tamale dough, but I have found that it considerably lightens the dough.

Tamale Filling

 3½ pounds chuck roast or boneless pork butt, trimmed of most fat

 2 tablespoons oil

 Cold water, Caldo (page 103), or beef stock

 I onion

 2 cloves garlic

 I tablespoon dried oregano

 Freshly ground black pepper

Red Chile Sauce (Salsa Colorado)

 15 dried California or New Mexican chiles, or a combination

 1½ cups water, for puréeing chiles

 2 tablespoons oil or lard

 2 tablespoons flour

 I clove garlic, minced

 I teaspoon salt

    1 tablespoon vinegar

    2 teaspoons dried oregano

    1 teaspoon cumin seeds

Tamale Dough

    3 cups lard, preferably freshly rendered (1½ pounds), or 1½ cups vegetable
        shortening and 1½ cups butter

    ¼ cup flavorful olive oil

    4 pounds pure, freshly ground masa

    2 tablespoons sea salt

    ¾ cup broth

    2 teaspoons baking powder

Assembly

    1 package dried corn husks (hojas), soaked in hot water for 30 minutes
        (see page 162)

    1½ cups pitted black olives

PREHEAT THE OVEN to 350°F.

TO PREPARE THE TAMALE FILLING, dry the meat with paper towels. Heat the oil in a large Dutch oven over medium heat and brown both sides of the roast. Cover with cold water. Add the onion, garlic, oregano, and pepper to taste. Put on the lid and bake for 2 hours. Cool for 1 hour in the broth. Reserve the broth and cut the meat into 1½-inch cubes.

TO PREPARE THE CHILE SAUCE, use scissors to cut off chile stems and cut the chiles in half. Shake out the seeds. Steam the chiles in a steamer basket over simmering water for 25 minutes. Place the chiles in a blender jar and purée in batches, adding about ½ cup fresh water to each batch. Add more water if necessary. Reserve ¼ cup of the chile purée to add to the tamale dough later. Heat the oil in a skillet over medium heat and brown the flour to a light golden roux. Cook for 2 minutes. Whisk in the chile purée, garlic, salt, vinegar, oregano, and cumin. If the sauce is too thick, thin out with reserved beef broth or water. Simmer for 10 minutes. Add the cubed meat and simmer for 30 minutes more. Set aside to cool, then refrigerate until tamale-making time.

TO PREPARE THE TAMALE DOUGH, whip the lard, using a stand-up mixer, for 5 to 10 minutes, or until it mounds up like whipped butter, adding olive oil as an additional flavoring toward the last. With the mixer going, add dollops of masa so that it is slowly incorporated. Stir the salt into the broth and drizzle it into the dough. Whip for 3 minutes longer. Drop ½ teaspoon of batter into a glass of cold water for a test. The dough is sufficiently light if it floats on top of the water. If it doesn't float, keep whipping until it does. Add the reserved ¼ cup chile purée to give the tamales a rosy hue. Fold in the baking powder.

ARRANGE A TAMALE ASSEMBLY LINE: the soaked husks, the tamale dough, the red chile sauce, the meat filling, black olives, and string cut into 8-inch lengths.

CHOOSE THE WIDEST HUSKS. Spread about ½ cup tamale dough inside the curve of a husk, allowing a ½-inch border along 1 side. Place a spoonful of meat filling and 2 olives in the center. Fold over the sides to the center. To follow Californio tradition, spread 2 tablespoons more dough on another husk and wrap it around the filled tamale. Tie off each end of the tamale with a piece of kitchen string. Alternatively, tear off strips of corn husk and tie off tamales with these. Continue filling and wrapping tamales.

POUR 3 INCHES OF WATER into the bottom of a tamale steamer and place 3 pennies in the bottom. When you do not hear dancing pennies, you've run out of water. Lay tamales across the steamer rather than stand them up. Cover the tamales with a layer of husks and steam for 50 to 60 minutes. Remove a tamale to check. If the dough pulls away from the husk easily, it is done. Transfer the tamales to a platter. At this point, the tamale is at its most tender and delicate, and you should definitely try one now. They will keep for a couple of days, stored in zipper-type plastic bags, in the refrigerator. Reheat in the steamer for 10 minutes or, wrapped in foil, in a preheated 350-degree oven for 15 minutes. You can also microwave a tamale for 1 minute on high.

Makes about 30 large tamales

NOTE: In another break from tradition, I use a multilayered Chinese steamer. You can freeze raw tamales in plastic zipper bags and steam them later.

Hojas

The corn husks, or hojas, dried for use in tamale-making are from field corn and hence are wider than hojas from the hybrid sweet corn varieties. The hoja should be at least 7½ inches across the bottom. You can overlap two smaller hojas if necessary. The day you are going to use them, soak the corn husks for 30 minutes in a sink filled with hot water. Choose the widest and longest husks, and rinse off any corn silk. Drain the husks on several layers of paper towels.

tamales dulces
with vanilla raisins

xxx

These richer, sweet tamales were served only at Christmas as a separate holiday treat with Champurrado (page 174) for children or with a glass of port for the adults. The raisins macerated in vanilla are my later edition. Minced apples and walnuts or strawberry jam also make good fillings.

Vanilla Raisin Filling
- 1 cup moist black raisins
- 2 tablespoons pure vanilla extract
- 1 tablespoon hot water
- ½ cup brown sugar

Sweet Tamale Dough
- 1 cup vegetable shortening or home-rendered lard (see page 164)
- 4 tablespoons (½ stick) butter
- 1 cup sugar
- 1½ tablespoons salt
- 4 cups mild chicken broth
- 4 cups masa harina
- ¼ teaspoon baking powder

Assembly
- ½ package dried corn husks (hojas), soaked in hot water for 30 minutes (see page 162)

TO PREPARE THE FILLING, rinse the raisins in a sieve held under running water and then steep them with vanilla and hot water for several hours. Add the brown sugar.

TO PREPARE THE TAMALE DOUGH, use an electric mixer to whip the shortening and butter until very fluffy, about 5 minutes. Add the sugar and continue whipping.

PUT THE MASA HARINA in a large bowl. Dissolve the salt in the broth and drizzle it into the masa harina. If the dough seems dry, add a little water. Knead for 2 or 3 minutes to make a smooth dough. With the mixer going, drop pieces of the masa dough into the creamed fat mixture. Continue adding dough in small amounts. Whip until very light. Mix in the baking powder. To test, place ½ teaspoon of dough in a glass of water. If the dough floats, it is light enough. If it doesn't float, keep whipping.

BLOT THE CORN HUSKS DRY with paper towels. Lay out a double thickness of paper towels to work on. Sweet tamales are made smaller than savory ones, so spread a scant ¼ cup dough thinly on a husk. Spoon on 1 tablespoon of raisin filling in the middle and roll up the tamale. Tie off each end of the tamale with cotton string or a strip of husk. Continue until all are done. You will have about 24 small tamales depending on how large you make them.

LAY THE TAMALES IN THE BASKET of a steamer set over 2 inches of water. Steam the tamales for 30 minutes. Test by removing a tamale. Let it cool for a minute and then peel back the husk. If the masa dough separates easily from the husk, the tamales are ready. Serve immediately or cool down and place in plastic bags for later. Tamales also freeze well in plastic bags or wrapped in foil.

Makes about 2 dozen sweet tamales

NOTE: I prefer to lay the tamales in the steamer insert instead of standing them upright. When they stand on end, a lot of the fat drips out, leaving the tamales drier.

How to Render Lard

Which fat to use in tamale-making is endlessly debated. I have found that a little fruity olive oil adds wonderful flavor to savory tamales. Hydrogenated shortening can be used in place of home-rendered lard, but I never use the hydrogenated *manteca*, or lard, sold in red boxes in the supermarket. Lard, by the way, has less cholesterol than butter.

To render lard, get 4 pounds of pork fat from your market (you may have to request this in advance) and cut it into small pieces. Pour 1 cup of water into a Dutch oven and add the fat. (The water will slowly evaporate, but it keeps the fat from browning.) Cover with a lid and place the pot in a 325-degree oven for 1½ hours. Check from time to time to make sure the lard doesn't brown. You should have about 3 cups pure lard.

NOTE: Discard cracklings or use in cooking beans.

pavo adobada y asada
[chile rubbed and roasted turkey]

——————— xxx ———————

It was typical for any festive occasion to have at least one if not many roasted turkeys, burnished a deep amber from a good rubbing with chile paste. A favorite stuffing or relleno consisted of tamales, another glorification of leftovers.

Chile Adobo Rub

    8 dried New Mexican or California chiles
    ½ cup water
    2 cloves garlic
    1 teaspoon dried oregano
    1 teaspoon salt
    1 tablespoon apple cider vinegar
    2 tablespoons olive oil

Turkey

    1 turkey (12 pounds)
    2 teaspoons sea salt
    1 teaspoon freshly ground black pepper
    1 recipe Tamale Relleno (page 166) or 2 apples, halved, and 1 onion, halved
    1 cup white wine
    ¼ cup olive oil

TO PREPARE THE RUB, break the chiles in half and remove the seeds and stems. Steam the chiles in an insert over simmering water for 20 minutes. Place half of the chiles in a blender with ½ cup fresh water, the garlic, oregano, salt, vinegar, and olive oil, and purée. Repeat with the remaining batch of chiles, then combine the two for the rub.

PREHEAT THE OVEN to 350°F.

TO PREPARE THE TURKEY, rinse it in cold water and pat dry with paper towels. Rub salt and pepper in the cavity and on the outside of the turkey. Rub the turkey all over, inside and out, with ¼ cup of the rub. If you put on too much rub at this point, it will burn. Fill with the relleno or the apples and onion. Arrange the turkey in a roasting pan and place in the oven. Combine the wine and olive oil, and baste with this mixture every 20 minutes. After 2 hours, begin basting with the remaining rub every 15 minutes until you have given the turkey at least half a dozen coats. Watch carefully as chile tends to burn. Cover with heavy foil if necessary to prevent excessive browning. When the turkey reaches an internal temperature of 172°F, remove it from the oven. Let stand for 20 minutes before carving. If you have used the Tamale Relleno, remove it immediately.

Serves 8 to 12

tamale relleno
for holiday turkey

xxx

This relleno is so delicious, it's worth it to make tamales (or buy good tamales if you have a source) so you can stuff a turkey with it. I have also placed Tamale Relleno in an oiled dish and baked prebrowned turkey fillets or pork chops on top of it.

    2 tablespoons butter or olive oil
    1 medium onion, chopped
    1 teaspoon cumin seeds, crushed in a mortar
    1 teaspoon dried oregano
    1 tablespoon chile powder
    ¼ cup water
    ¼ cup sherry
    ¼ cup black raisins
    ½ cup dried pears or 1 fresh apple, minced
    4 leftover beef or chicken tamales or 8 leftover sweet tamales, husks removed
    3 cups day-old corn bread (see page 167)
    ¼ cup lightly toasted pine nuts or pecans
    1 egg, beaten
    ½ to 1 cup chicken broth
    1 turkey, prepared for roasting (see page 165)

HEAT THE BUTTER OR OIL in a skillet over medium heat and sauté the onion until translucent, about 5 minutes. Add the cumin, oregano, and chile powder. Combine the water and sherry in a small saucepan. Add the raisins, and dried pears or fresh apple. Simmer for 2 minutes, or until the raisins are plump and the pears have absorbed some moisture.

BREAK THE TAMALES INTO SMALL PIECES and crumble the corn bread into a large bowl. Add the sautéed onion and the fruit mixture, with any juices in the pan. Stir in the pine nuts, egg, and ½ cup of broth. If the relleno seems dry, add more broth. The relleno should cling together but not be soggy.

PREHEAT THE OVEN to 350°F.

STUFF THE RELLENO into the main cavity of the turkey for roasting or lightly press into a buttered 2-quart baking dish and cover with foil. Bake the dish for 30 minutes.

Makes about 6 cups, enough for a 12-pound turkey

la beth's famous corn bread

✕✕✕

The recipe below, given to me by my friend, Beth Hensperger, has supplanted all other corn bread, traditional and nontraditional. Maybe it's the vanilla. It is good warm, cold, toasted in slabs, as a base for eggs with a spicy sauce, or as part of a relleno.

    1 cup fine stone-ground cornmeal, preferably from a mill or
        health food store
    1 cup all-purpose flour
    ½ cup powdered sugar
    ½ teaspoon salt
    ½ teaspoon baking powder
    1 teaspoon baking soda
    2 eggs
    1½ cups cultured buttermilk
    1 tablespoon vanilla extract, preferably Madagascar Bourbon
    5 tablespoons unsalted butter, melted

PREHEAT THE OVEN to 375°F. Mist or lightly coat an 8-inch square pan with oil.

COMBINE THE CORNMEAL, flour, sugar, salt, baking powder, and baking soda in a bowl and whisk to blend. In a separate bowl, whisk the eggs, buttermilk, and vanilla. Pour over the dry ingredients. Stir once and add the melted butter, stirring just until barely blended. Take care not to overmix. Pour the batter into the prepared pan and bake until golden around the edges with golden speckles on top, 30 to 40 minutes. Cut into wide squares and serve warm or let cool in pan.

8 servings

arroz con pollo

xxx

This was one of Grandmama's favorite dishes to fix when she had a lot of people in the house. Something fancy wasn't in order, just something to fill them up, but delicious. I actually save up bits of chorizo, ham, and andouille sausage in the freezer until we have enough for a good Arroz con Pollo. I like to fix this the day after Christmas or New Year's.

3 cloves garlic, minced

1 teaspoon sea salt

2 teaspoons chile powder

1 teaspoon cumin seeds

1 tablespoon olive oil

1 chicken (3½ pounds), disjointed and with breast quartered

4 tablespoons olive oil

8 ounces chorizo or Italian sausage

1½ cups chopped onion

1½ cups long-grain rice (preferably basmati)

1 slice ham, cut into strips

4 cups water, chicken broth, or a combination

2 tablespoons dry sherry

1 teaspoon smoky Spanish paprika

1 cup frozen petite peas

2 tablespoons jarred Spanish pimiento

MASH THE GARLIC, salt, chile powder, and cumin into a paste using a mortar and pestle or a large knife. Place in a little bowl and add olive oil to make a seasoning paste.

DRY THE CHICKEN WELL with paper towels and cut off any excess fat. Rub all the surfaces with seasoning paste. Let stand for about 20 minutes.

SAUTÉ CHICKEN IN THE OLIVE OIL in a skillet over medium heat, using 1 tablespoon oil at a time, until golden brown. Remove the pieces as they brown on both sides. Allow at least 15 minutes for this step. Cook the chorizo in the same skillet for 8 to 10 minutes. Remove and drain on paper towels when done.

HEAT THE REMAINING 2 TABLESPOONS OLIVE OIL in a 12-inch skillet shaped like a paella pan and sauté the onion until softened, about 5 minutes. Push to the side and fry the rice until lightly toasted. Add the browned chicken, the ham strips, sausage, water, and sherry. Bring to a gentle simmer and keep on low to medium heat, uncovered, until craters or holes appear on the surface of the rice, about 12 minutes.

Sprinkle on the paprika and peas. Lay the pimiento in decorative strips on top. Cover and steam the rice on low heat for 8 minutes more. Check the rice. All the liquid should be absorbed and the rice should be just tender but not overcooked.

Serves 6

spanish cocido

───────────✕✕✕───────────

Puchero and *olla podrida* were simpler stews made to feed large families and the numerous guests who magically appeared for dinner almost on a daily basis. The Spanish Cocido, with an extravagance of ingredients, was the grand stew reserved for special occasions. A simpler cocido was made without the chicken and sausages and with fewer vegetables.

1 brisket of beef (4 pounds)
1 chicken, halved lengthwise (4 pounds)
Salt and pepper
1 tablespoon paprika
2 to 3 tablespoons olive oil
4 bay leaves
1 sprig of oregano or thyme
10 peppercorns, crushed
1 head of garlic, top sliced off
1 onion, peeled and halved
4 dried red chiles, California or New Mexican
1 chipotle chile
3 quarts water
4 cups cooked chickpeas (garbanzo beans)
10 carrots, peeled
5 potatoes, peeled and halved
2 chayote, peeled and sliced
4 leeks, trimmed, rinsed, and sliced
1 medium cabbage, quartered
3 pounds sausage, such as garlic sausage, *longaniza,* or chorizo
1 tablespoon olive oil
2 cloves garlic, minced

Salsa Verde

    1 cup minced Italian parsley

    1 tablespoon dried oregano

    4 cloves garlic, minced

    1 to 2 güero chiles, seeded and minced

    ¼ cup fruity olive oil

    2 tablespoons wine vinegar

    Salt

DRY THE BRISKET AND CHICKEN WELL with paper towels. Season with salt and pepper to taste and the paprika. Heat some of the olive oil in a heavy pot over medium heat and brown the brisket well on both sides. Brown the chicken in a separate skillet using the rest of the oil.

PLACE THE BRISKET AND CHICKEN in a 10-quart Dutch oven or stew pot. Add the bay leaves, oregano, peppercorns, the head of garlic, onion, chiles, and chipotle. Cover with 3 quarts water and bring to a simmer. Turn the heat down to low, cover the pot, and simmer for 1 hour. Skim off the foam during the first 15 minutes. After 45 minutes, remove the chicken and set aside.

CONTINUE TO SIMMER THE BRISKET for 1½ hours more. It should be tender when pierced with a fork. Add the chickpeas, carrots, potatoes, and chayote and cook until tender. Bring 1 quart of water to a boil in a separate pot, add the leek slices and cabbage quarters, and simmer just until tender, about 12 minutes. Return the chicken to the pot with the brisket to reheat for 5 minutes.

MEANWHILE, SAUTÉ THE SAUSAGES in a skillet with the olive oil. Sprinkle with minced garlic at the last minute. When browned, drain the sausages and set aside.

TO PREPARE THE SALSA VERDE, combine the parsley, oregano, garlic, chiles, olive oil, vinegar, and salt to taste. The salsa can be minced in a food processor.

ON 1 OR 2 LARGE PLATTERS, arrange the brisket in slices, pieces of chicken in the center, and with the sausages arranged in a circle. Ladle some of the pot broth over the meats. Artistically arrange the vegetables, alternating colors. Ladle over more broth and drop bits of the salsa verde over the meats. Strain the remaining broth.

GIVE GUESTS LARGE SHALLOW BOWLS for their meats and vegetables. Pass more broth at the table to moisten everything. Serve the Spanish Cocido with Salsa Verde and bread.

Serves 10

NOTE: We prefer to save most of the broth so that it can be degreased and served the next day as a soup.

pumpkin empanadas

xxx

The rancheros used pumpkin as much for dessert as for a vegetable. Sweet pumpkin empanadas often took the place of pumpkin pie at Thanksgiving and Christmas. The only ingredient not readily available is the feathery leaves of anise that Californios were fond of using to add a natural sweetness to desserts. It grew wild and was abundant in the coastal canyons surrounding the ranchos. You can still find it in natural canyons when you are out hiking. Commercially raised anise can be found seasonally in grocery stores and farmers' markets.

Pumpkin Filling

2 cups puréed pumpkin, canned, or freshly steamed and puréed

¾ cup (packed) brown sugar

1 teaspoon ground cinnamon or 2 teaspoons minced feathery wild anise

½ teaspoon salt

½ cup raisins

1 egg, beaten

1½ teaspoons pure vanilla extract

Empanada Pastry

2 cups all-purpose flour

1 teaspoon baking powder

½ teaspoon salt

1 tablespoon sugar

½ cup vegetable shortening

4 tablespoons (½ stick) butter

5 tablespoons cold milk

1 tablespoon brandy

2 tablespoons sugar, mixed with 1 teaspoon ground cinnamon

TO PREPARE THE FILLING, combine the pumpkin purée, brown sugar, cinnamon, salt, and raisins in a 2-quart saucepan. Simmer over low heat for 3 minutes, stirring so the purée doesn't stick. Remove from the heat and slowly whisk in the beaten egg and vanilla. Put back on the heat and stir for just 1 minute. Set aside to cool while you prepare the pastry.

PREHEAT THE OVEN to 400°F.

TO PREPARE THE PASTRY, combine the flour, baking powder, salt, and sugar. Cut in the shortening and butter until the size of peas. Stir the milk and brandy together and sprinkle over the dough. Stir with a fork until the dry ingredients are moistened.

Place the dough on a floured board and knead with the heel of your hand 3 or 4 times. Wrap and chill in the refrigerator for 10 minutes.

DIVIDE THE DOUGH, chilling one half while rolling out the other into a thin circle. Cut into 4-inch circles. Place about 2 tablespoons pumpkin filling on the bottom half of a circle. Fold over and press with a fork to seal the edges. Roll out the other half of the dough and repeat. Place the empanadas on a baking sheet.

BAKE UNTIL GOLDEN BROWN, 15 to 18 minutes. Sprinkle with cinnamon sugar when you remove the empanadas from the oven.

Makes 12 to 14 empanadas

VARIATION: Sweet Bean Empanadas. One of the most beloved empanadas among the rancheros was filled with sweetened frijoles that had just been cooked with water and salt (no garlic or onion here). Substitute 2 cups puréed cooked pink beans for the pumpkin purée and add a pinch of nutmeg and cloves with the cinnamon. Omit the raisins and vanilla. All other ingredients are the same. Whisk together in a saucepan, heating gently for 2 to 3 minutes. Cool before filling the empanadas.

fig empanaditas

✕✕✕

As the Californios re-created a little Mediterranean outpost in California, the fig reminded them of Spain, no matter how far removed they were. It was the most revered of all the fruits that they had introduced here. During their short season in the fall, figs were served with walnuts for dessert. They were also preserved, so they could be enjoyed the rest of the year. These empanaditas are like delicate pastries and were always made by my mother for Christmas, other special occasions, and to bring to picnics.

Fig Filling

1½ cups dried mission figs

¼ cup sugar

¼ cup water

¼ cup milk

1 teaspoon grated lemon zest

1 tablespoon lemon juice

1 tablespoon butter

½ cup minced walnuts

Empanadita Dough

8 tablespoons (1 stick) unsalted butter
½ cup shortening
½ cup sugar
1 egg
2 teaspoons pure vanilla extract
2½ cups all-purpose flour
¼ teaspoon baking soda
1 teaspoon baking powder
½ teaspoon salt
¼ cup milk, mixed with 1 teaspoon vinegar to sour
2 tablespoons flour, mixed with 2 tablespoons sugar

TO PREPARE THE FIG FILLING, place the figs and sugar in a food processor and grind until finely minced. The sugar will keep the figs from becoming too sticky. Place in a saucepan with the water, milk, lemon zest, lemon juice, and butter. Simmer for 10 minutes or until filling is juicy and a bit thickened. Cool and stir in the walnuts.

TO PREPARE THE DOUGH, use the paddle of an electric mixer to beat the butter and shortening together until creamy. Add the sugar, egg, and vanilla. Beat until combined well. Whisk the flour, baking soda, baking powder, and salt together. Add half of the flour mixture to the butter mixture and blend. Drizzle in the soured milk, then stir in the rest of the flour mixture. Blend well. This will be a very soft dough. Flatten into a large circle on a square of plastic wrap and wrap the dough up. Chill for 2 hours before rolling out.

PREHEAT THE OVEN to 375°F.

ROLL OUT HALF OF THE DOUGH AT A TIME, keeping the other half chilled. Sprinkle a board or pastry cloth with the flour and sugar mixture. Roll the dough into a circle ⅛ inch thick. While rolling, keep lifting up the dough with a spatula and turning, to keep the circle even. Cut out 3-inch circles. Place a couple of heaping teaspoons of fig filling on half of each circle and fold to make a turnover or empanadita. Press the edges with a fork to seal. Use a fork to poke a row of holes across the tops. Place on an ungreased baking sheet, preferably lined with parchment paper. Bake until golden around the edges, about 15 minutes.

Makes 14 to 16 small empanaditas

champurrado
[chocolate atole]

✕✕✕

This thick chocolate drink is a perfect example of how colonial Spaniards blended their ingredients of sugar and milk with the native Indian ingredient of corn. Californios adopted the Mexican technique, and it is still one of the most requested recipes of the *descendientes*. It was served for breakfast or merienda, or with buñuelos for Christmas celebrations. Champurrado is a supreme comfort food. The fortuitous combination of earthy masa and the chocolate was a discovery made centuries ago. Huge pots of champurrado go quickly at fiestas. The recipe can be easily doubled or tripled.

⅓ cup finely ground masa harina
1 tablespoon *maizena* or cornstarch
½ cup cold water
4 cups milk
¾ cup (packed) dark brown sugar
1 ounce bittersweet or semisweet chocolate, chopped
Dash of ground cinnamon
1 piece (2 inches) vanilla bean, split to expose seeds, or 1 teaspoon
    vanilla extract
Cinnamon sticks, for garnish

ADD THE MASA HARINA and maizena to the cold water and whisk to dissolve lumps. Add the mixture to the milk and brown sugar in a saucepan deep enough to allow room for whisking. Stir over very low heat. Once the Champurrado has begun to slightly thicken, after about 10 minutes, add the chocolate, cinnamon, and vanilla bean. The tiny granules of corn will take about 20 minutes to swell and thicken, and suddenly the Champurrado will become smooth and velvety thick. Serve garnished with cinnamon sticks.

Serves 4

buñuelos

✕✕✕

Many Californio families traditionally served Buñuelos on Noche Buena (Christmas Eve) just as is still done in Mexico and the Southwest. Our cousin Louie García Robinson remembers his childhood in East L.A., when the Christmas Eve bonfires were accompanied with Buñuelos and Champurrado (page 174).

Syrup

    1 cup honey

    ½ cup water

    2 tablespoons butter

    ½ teaspoon ground cinnamon

    1 teaspoon vanilla extract

Buñuelos

    3 cups unbleached all-purpose flour

    1 teaspoon baking powder

    1 teaspoon salt

    3 tablespoons shortening or butter

    ½ cup milk, or more as needed

    2 eggs

    1 quart canola or grapeseed oil, for frying

    ½ cup sugar, mixed with 1 teaspoon ground cinnamon

TO PREPARE THE SYRUP, combine the honey, water, butter, and cinnamon in a small saucepan. Simmer over low heat for 5 minutes. Remove from the heat and add the vanilla. Set aside.

TO PREPARE THE BUÑUELOS, whisk the flour, baking powder, and salt together in a large bowl. Using a fork or pastry blender, mix the shortening into the dry ingredients until coarse crumbs are formed. Whisk the milk and eggs together in a separate bowl and drizzle over the dry ingredients Push together to form a dough. If the dough seems too dry, add a little more milk. Knead just until smooth but do not overwork. Wrap the dough in plastic wrap and let it rest for 10 minutes.

PINCH OFF 12 TO 15 PIECES OF DOUGH and form into balls. Place on a greased baking sheet and cover with plastic wrap or damp towel. Let the balls rest for 15 to 20 minutes.

POUR 2 INCHES OF OIL into a heavy, deep-sided pan and heat over low heat while you begin rolling out the dough. Flatten a ball with your hand and begin rolling from the center to the edge. Keep lifting and turning the dough while you roll the ball out to a paper-thin circle less than ¼ inch thick. Stack the rolled-out circles between pieces of wax paper.

WHEN THE OIL IS AT 375°F, gently lower a circle of dough into it. After the buñuelo is golden on 1 side, turn over and fry the other side. Do not spoon hot fat over the buñuelo, as you don't want it to puff. Place the golden buñuelo on paper towels and blot with another paper towel. Sprinkle with 1 teaspoon of the cinnamon sugar. Continue frying the rest of the buñuelos.

FOR SERVING, stack the buñuelos into a tower, pouring the syrup down the sides, or simply place a buñuelo on a plate and allow the guest to add a drizzle of syrup. When served, many people immediately shatter their buñuelo so more surfaces are exposed to the syrup.

Serves 12 to 15

palillis

✕✕✕

Palillis are not in any culinary lexicon or Spanish dictionary, but they were one of the most beloved of celebración foods of the Californios. Our family continues to make them several times a year, especially around Christmas. When my son, Ian, brought home Tracy, the girl who was eventually to become his wife, he asked me to make palillis. Now she helps me roll them out.

Palillis remain one of my most dreamlike memories of the rancho kitchen. My hands barely reached the table where at eye level I saw platters of Palillis, so enormous they looked like sugary clouds. I was given one but wanted them all.

3 cups unbleached all-purpose flour
3 teaspoons baking powder
I teaspoon salt
3 tablespoons vegetable shortening
I to I¼ cups warm evaporated milk, preferably Pet brand
I quart canola or grapeseed oil
Powdered sugar, in a shaker or sieve
Pourable honey (optional)

SIFT THE FLOUR, baking powder, and salt together into a large bowl. Using a pastry blender or your fingers, work the shortening into the dry mixture until it resembles coarse meal. Gradually add enough warm milk to bring the dough to a soft consistency. Push the dough together and when it adheres and is no longer dry, stop adding milk. Knead the dough for 2 to 3 minutes, or until it is smooth. Wrap the dough in plastic wrap and let it rest for 45 minutes to 1 hour.

UNWRAP THE DOUGH and cut it into quarters. Remove one quarter and rewrap the remaining dough. Push it into a flat disk and roll it out into a 10-inch circle, resembling a flour tortilla, about ⅛ inch thick. Cut the circle into 8 triangles.

HEAT 2 INCHES OF OIL in a high-sided pan over medium heat to about 375°F. Fry 1 triangle at a time, constantly spooning hot oil over the top. The rush of hot fat encourages the dough to separate and puff into a cloud. Fry the palilli until it is golden on both sides, turning it over once. Drain on paper towels, blotting with more paper towels. Continue to roll out and fry the rest of the dough.

SERVE THE PALILLIS SPRINKLED with powdered sugar or with regular sugar. Some people like to eat them like the sopaipillas of New Mexico by biting off a corner and drizzling honey inside.

Makes about 24 palillis (my sons, Ian and O'Reilly, can eat them all)

NOTE: If you do not spoon the hot oil over the top, some palillis will puff and some will not. Until I figured out this secret, I always suffered some flat ones.

picnics

MERIENDAS DEL CAMPO

since the Californios had celebración down to a fine art, when they picnicked, they brought the whole show on the road. Without a thought about effort, they loaded the entire household into carts, or later, cars. Baskets of food, fine dishes, linens, blankets, musical instruments, children and old ladies, all were packed for traveling, whether it was down The Lane or across the Bay. The

Picnics were a favorite way to dine, especially when you got to wear your high-top button shoes and boater hats decorated with leaves, cherries, and birds.

picnic was simply an extension of the early pastoral life the Californios had become comfortable with. Anything eaten al fresco tasted better to them.

The *ambiente*, or atmosphere, of where you chose to have a picnic was as important as the picnic itself. In his book *Iberia*, James Michener told one of my favorite stories about choosing the perfect picnic spot. After inviting a Spanish friend's family for a day in the country, he was forced to drive the motorcar to a dozen spots before the grandmother gave her seal of approval. For their picnic, she insisted that there must be "ambiente," even if it took all day to find it. The scene was right out of nineteenth-century California—or a present-day excursion with my own grandmother.

Ambiente is not necessarily beauty. It is place, time, and everything you bring to the moment. Every year when Grandmama took me to see *Gone With the Wind*, she carried a huge purse to hide our picnic from the theater manager. The goodies were individually wrapped in old Christmas paper. Throughout the movie, Grandmama snapped open her purse and I could reach in and pull out a package. There was no order to it. I remember my excitement at untying ribbons in the dark to find, say, little deviled ham sandwiches with the crusts cut off. By the time we finished everything in Grandmama's purse, it was time to cry into our hankies when Rhett told Scarlett, "Frankly my dear, I don't give a damn."

The experience mildly built up my romantic backbone but even more made me appreciate the fun of taking a picnic wherever you might go. Some ambiente points can be given for picnics in unlikely places or almost spontaneous picnics, like when you picked a bouquet of watercress and just happened to have brought a loaf of bread with you for watercress sandwiches.

Our family picnics were carried from the beach at Santa Cruz to the banks of San Lorenzo River that ran through our mountain lot. There was always some form of potato salad, maybe roasted or spicy barbecued chickens, steamed crawdads from the river, *albóndigon*, sourdough bread, and there had to be one of my mother's homemade cakes or pies. For old-fashioned California picnics, tortillas were cooked over a campfire. For birthdays and saint's days, there were barbecued meats, marinated vegetable salads, artichokes, empanadas with various fillings, Devil's Food Cake, pies, and Biscochitos.

layered spanish potato salad

✕✕✕

This salad was called Spanish because anything that contained olive oil and olives was called Spanish by the Californios. Warm potatoes were always marinated with wine vinegar and olive oil to bring up the flavor in the salad.

Once, when upon arriving at our picnic spot it was discovered that the silverware had been left at home, Grandpa took us searching in the woods for perfect little willow branches. Using his pocket knife, he pared twig forks for everyone to use for eating their potato salad. I was probably about seven, and I remember nothing else about that day except the twig forks that provided the ultimate in ambiente!

    4 red-skinned potatoes, scrubbed
    2 tablespoons wine vinegar
    1 tablespoon olive oil
    Salt

Dressing
    ⅓ cup wine vinegar
    1½ teaspoons salt
    ½ teaspoon freshly ground black pepper

    2 green onions, minced

    ½ cup olive oil

Assembly

    ½ cup minced Italian parsley

    6 hard-boiled eggs, sliced

    ¼ cup blotted and minced pimiento

    ¾ cup pitted black olives, sliced

BOIL THE POTATOES IN THEIR JACKETS for about 25 to 30 minutes in salted water to cover over medium heat. Pierce with a thin paring knife to check tenderness.

WHEN THE POTATOES ARE TENDER, drain in a colander and let cool until you can remove the skins, about 10 minutes. Peel and slice the potatoes into a bowl. Give the potatoes a drink of vinegar and olive oil while warm. Add a sprinkle of salt. Let the potatoes marinate at room temperature for 30 minutes.

TO PREPARE THE DRESSING, whisk the vinegar, salt, pepper, green onions, and olive oil together.

SPREAD A LAYER OF POTATOES in a shallow serving dish, and drizzle with a little dressing. Add a couple of tablespoons of the parsley, a layer of sliced egg, a layer of pimiento, and scattered olives. Repeat the layering, adding more dressing over the potatoes as you go. Cover the salad and keep at room temperature for 1 hour before serving time.

Serves 8

NOTE: Sometimes a layer of little shrimp, about 1 cup, was added. First about ¼ cup of mayonnaise, thinned with a couple of tablespoons of the dressing and a shot of hot sauce, was poured over the shrimp.

marie's potato salad

xxx

Marie, my mother, made this potato salad for us frequently when we had our own picnics at our lot in the Santa Cruz Mountains. She preferred mealy russet potatoes, which she partially mashed, but she was loyal to Grandmama's old marinating technique, combined with her own mayonnaise dressing. The vinegar juice from pickled jalapeños was a secret seasoning of hers for a lot of things.

4 medium russet potatoes, scrubbed

Salt

2 tablespoons wine vinegar

2 tablespoons olive oil

1 cup mayonnaise

¼ cup old-fashioned yellow mustard

Freshly ground black pepper

¼ cup minced sweet onion

3 tablespoons sweet pickle relish

Salt to taste

1 teaspoon sugar

2 tablespoons jalapeño vinegar juice from pickled jalapeños

3 hard-boiled eggs, minced

2 tablespoons minced parsley, for garnish

Paprika, for garnish

CUT THE POTATOES INTO THIRDS, put in a saucepan, cover with water, and add 2 teaspoons of salt. Simmer, covered, over low heat for about 30 minutes, or until cracks form in the potato skins. The potatoes are meant to be slightly overcooked. Drain and place in a bowl. Pull off the skins. Use a large fork to break up the potatoes, partially mashing them. Pour the vinegar and olive oil over the potatoes while warm. Season with 1 teaspoon salt. Let marinate for 30 minutes.

BLEND THE MAYONNAISE WITH MUSTARD, pepper, onion, pickle relish, salt to taste, sugar, and vinegar juice. After the potatoes have marinated, stir in the mayonnaise mixture until well-blended. Taste to see if you want to add more of any of the seasonings. Stir in the eggs. Sprinkle with parsley and paprika. This potato salad should be served the day it is made, preferably while still slightly warm.

Serves 6

marie's spicy chicken

✕✕✕

One of the rules followed in the rancho kitchen was to mash garlic with salt to take away the sting yet leave the flavor. My mother added more spices to the salt and garlic than anyone except me. This chicken is great when finished on a barbecue grill so that it caramelizes, thanks to the brown sugar and chile. Mama often cooked this in her mountain kitchen, a huge barbecue grill of river stones with an iron rack laid on top. This chicken goes extremely well with my mother's potato salad (see page 184)

2 chickens (3 pounds each), cut into pieces
1 lemon, halved
2 tablespoons olive oil
5 cloves garlic
1 tablespoon kosher salt
3 tablespoons brown sugar
1 teaspoon dried oregano
¼ cup red chile powder, preferably Dixon
¼ cup minced cilantro

RUB THE CHICKENS WITH THE CUT LEMON, squeezing the juice under the skin. Rub with olive oil, which will help the seasoning paste stick better. Put the garlic and salt in a mortar and mash together, or put into the bowl of a food processor and blend. Add the brown sugar, oregano, chile powder, and cilantro. Purée into a paste.

USE HALF OF THE SEASONING PASTE for each chicken. Rub generously over all the surfaces and under parts of the skin that are easy to reach. Refrigerate the chickens for at least 1 to 2 hours, uncovered, so the seasoning penetrates. Remove and place in an oiled roasting pan. Let the chickens sit at room temperature while the oven heats up.

PREHEAT THE OVEN to 350°F. Bake for 30 minutes. Then, either place the chicken about 8 inches under a broiler to sear for 15 minutes, turning frequently, or place it on a medium-hot grill. Turn the chicken every couple of minutes so the seasoning paste doesn't burn.

Serves 8

albóndigon
[meat roll]

✕✕✕

This dish was a popular one for a picnic since it traveled easily and made great sandwiches with Green Chiles en Escabeche (page 123) or Escabeche de Cebollas Rojas (page 188).

In the old days the meat roll was wrapped in cheesecloth and the roll was poached, but I have found roasting to be much more flavorful. Sarsa always accompanied Albóndigon.

Meatloaf Mixture

> 2 pounds ground sirloin
>
> 8 ounces ground chicken or turkey
>
> I cup minced onion
>
> 2 jalapeño chiles, seeded and minced
>
> I tablespoon chile powder
>
> 2 teaspoons salt
>
> ½ teaspoon freshly ground black pepper
>
> 3 teaspoons dried oregano
>
> 2 eggs, beaten
>
> 8 ounces Homemade Chorizo (page 52) or store-bought chorizo
>
> I cup coarse bread crumbs, for coating

Filling

> I cup pitted olives, halved
>
> ½ cup minced parsley
>
> 2 cloves garlic, minced
>
> ¼ cup grated Parmesan cheese
>
> 2 carrots, cooked and sliced lengthwise into thin pieces
>
> 3 hard-boiled eggs, quartered
>
> 2 tablespoons olive oil

TO PREPARE THE MEATLOAF MIXTURE, put the ground sirloin, ground chicken, onion, jalapeños, chile powder, salt, pepper, oregano, and eggs in a large bowl. Crumble the chorizo (remove sausage casings if necessary) on top. Use your hands to lightly blend. Don't overwork or you will toughen the meat.

LAY OUT A DOUBLED SHEET OF WAX PAPER and sprinkle with bread crumbs. Lightly press half of the meat mixture on top of the crumbs in a 14 x 6-inch rectangle about 1 inch thick. Press the olives into the meat. Stir together the parsley, garlic, and cheese and sprinkle over the olives. Make a layer with the carrot slices and the egg quarters. Form the remaining meat mixture over the top. Pull up the sides of the wax paper to form the meat into a long roll and to distribute bread crumbs along the sides. Place in an oiled roasting pan. Gently ease out the wax paper once the albóndigon is in place. Brush olive oil over the top of the albóndigon to help it brown.

PREHEAT THE OVEN to 375°F. Bake for 45 minutes. Brush with olive oil a couple of more times during baking. Remove from the oven and let cool for at least 30 minutes. The meat will firm up and be easier to slice. Use wide spatulas to lift the meat roll to a platter. The slices, a mosaic of colors, look pretty on a bed of cilantro.

SLICE JUST BEFORE SERVING. Wrap in foil to carry to a picnic.

Serves 10 as picnic food or lunch

agua fresca de sandía

✕✕✕

The name of this recipe literally translates to "fresh water of watermelon," but other fruits such as mango, cantaloupe, and strawberry can very successfully be substituted for the watermelon, although it is our favorite. For a rancho-style summer barbecue, we make a big glass barrel of agua fresca, and sometimes it's more popular than the beer or wine if the day is particularly hot. Also, we like to think that the old-fashioned watermelon, with seeds, has more sweetness and flavor than the new seedless varieties. For larger parties we triple this amount and keep it in the traditional glass barrel, which can be purchased at restaurant supply houses or in Mexico.

6 to 8 cups diced watermelon, seeds removed and 1 tablespoon
    seeds reserved
2 cups cold water
¼ to ½ cup granulated sugar, depending on the sweetness
    of the melon
Juice of 1 lime
Lime wedges, for garnish

BLEND THE WATERMELON IN A BLENDER in batches, adding a little water and sugar to each batch. Purée into juice and pour into a glass pitcher. Flavor the last batch with lime juice, and stir in the tablespoon of black seeds. Serve agua fresca over ice and garnish with lime wedges.

Makes about 2½ quarts

escabeche de cebollas rojas
[marinated pink onions]

✕✕✕

The rancho cooks pickled almost everything or at least poured olive oil and vinegar over it. Perhaps this practice was a holdover of escabeche as a way of preserving. These pickled onions are delicious on top of slices of Albóndigon (page 186) for a sandwich. Choose flat red onions for this; they are the sweetest and mildest, and are typically available from summer to autumn.

4 cups red wine vinegar
I cup water
½ cup sugar
I ½ tablespoons sea salt or kosher salt
I tablespoon dried oregano
I bay leaf
2 large flat red onions, peeled and thinly sliced
2 tablespoons olive oil

COMBINE THE VINEGAR, water, sugar, and salt in a 2-quart saucepan. Bring to a simmer, stirring to dissolve sugar and salt, and immediately remove from the heat.

POUR INTO A BOWL AND ADD THE OREGANO, bay leaf, and onion slices. Marinate for at least 2 hours. When serving, remove the pink onions from the marinade and drizzle with a little of the olive oil. Store in the refrigerator for 1 to 2 weeks. If you add the olive oil to the marinade and then refrigerate, the oil will harden and rise to the top.

Makes about 1 quart

ensalada de nopalitos

xxx

Nopales, a type of prickly pear cactus, has remained very much a part of the California, Southwestern, and Mexican landscapes. Many old-timers insist on keeping at least one plant in the backyard for spring harvesting, when the young, tender paddles are newly sprouted. During the last decade, there has been a renewed interest in cactus because of its nutritional value and its taste when prepared properly. It is amazing how old foods die off and than resurface a few years later. You can serve this dish as a salad or use it as a filling for tacos.

I had always been unhappy with simply boiling cactus as has been done traditionally. In mentioning this to my Mexican vegetable man, he told me that sometimes we have to forget the old ways. He roasts his cactus paddles to retain the flavor, just as Rick Bayless, the famous chef of Frontera Grill, recommends.

I pound of nopalito (about 4 small and tender paddles)
I tablespoon olive oil
Sea salt or kosher salt
2 cloves garlic
I to 2 jalapeño chiles, seeded and minced
¼ cup minced onion
¼ cup minced cilantro
I lime
Olive oil (optional)
½ cup diced queso fresco

BUY DESPINED CACTUS PADDLES in a Latino market or prepare cactus according to instructions given on page 33. Rinse well under cold water.

PREHEAT THE OVEN to 375°F.

CUT THE CACTUS INTO THIN STRIPS resembling string beans. Place on a baking sheet, toss with the olive oil, and sprinkle with salt. Place the garlic and jalapeños on the edge of the baking sheet. Roast for about 20 minutes, stirring the strips at least twice while roasting. The juices will be released and then evaporate in that time. Remove from the oven and transfer the nopalito strips to a bowl to cool. (Alternatively, you can quickly poach the nopalito. See directions on page 33.) Chop the roasted garlic and jalapeños and sprinkle with salt.

COMBINE THE ONION AND CILANTRO in a small bowl. Stir in the garlic and jalapeños.

SQUEEZE LIME JUICE OVER THE NOPALITOS and stir in the roasted garlic mixture. Add a few teaspoons of olive oil, if you like. Sprinkle the queso fresco over the top.

Serves 6

piazza's roman artichokes

✕✕✕

On Rancho Los Tularcitos, the huge artichoke bush grew near one of the nopal plants. Someone would cut off an artichoke thistle and use it to clean the needles off the prickly pear before peeling with a pocket knife.

Steamed artichokes were relished with the leaves dipped in salt and olive oil or in this favorite recipe from Grandmama's Italian friend, Mrs. Piazza. These artichokes make good picnic food, even if the picnic is just in your own backyard or treehouse. You can also cut the artichokes in half to serve as an appetizer.

6 artichokes

1 lemon, halved

1 tablespoon olive oil

2 cups bread crumbs

2 cloves garlic, minced

¼ cup minced Italian parsley

1 tablespoon minced basil

1 teaspoon minced mint

1 teaspoon salt

Freshly ground black pepper

1 egg, beaten

3 tablespoons olive oil

2 to 3 tablespoons milk

¼ cup grated Parmesan cheese

TRIM OFF THE ARTICHOKE STEMS. Cut off the sharp points of the leaves and push them open. Rinse well. Rub the cut surfaces with lemon.

PLACE THE ARTICHOKES IN A STEAMER over a couple of inches of boiling water. Squeeze lemon juice over the tops and drizzle with olive oil. Steam until tender, about 35 minutes. Test by seeing if you can easily pull a leaf from the bottom. Remove and let cool.

WHILE THE ARTICHOKES ARE STEAMING, prepare the stuffing. Put the bread crumbs in a bowl. Add the garlic, parsley, basil, mint, salt, and pepper to taste. Stir in the egg, olive oil, milk, and cheese.

PREHEAT THE OVEN to 350°F.

WHEN THE COOKED ARTICHOKES ARE COOL enough to handle, pack a little of the stuffing between all of the leaves. Place in an oiled casserole dish and bake for 20 to 25 minutes.

Serves 6

VARIATION: When Grandmama could not obtain fresh artichokes, she packed this same stuffing into a pan with diced, canned artichoke hearts and baked it for 25 minutes at 350°F.

watercress sandwiches

⋊⋉

This is for one of those picnic times when you find a clear stream, fresh from spring rains, to pick watercress. Once, when we had some cold chicken from the night before and a loaf of bread with us, we found just a place. The cress was no bigger than the tip of a finger. It had a little bite but not overly so. We made the sandwiches and played in the stream while we chilled a couple of bottles of wine and juice for the children in the cold water.

Fresh nasturtium flowers work as well as watercress with buttered bread.

Thin slices of soft homemade-style bread, white or whole wheat,
   or Grandmama's Potato Pan Rolls (page 95)
1 stick unsalted butter, softened slightly in the sun
1 large bunch of tiny watercress, preferably from a stream bank,
   rinsed and stemmed
1 cold roasted chicken or just the breast
Mustard
Salt and pepper

SLICE THE BREAD THINLY and cut each slice into quarters. Spread lavishly with butter and press in the watercress leaves. Add tiny pieces of chicken, dabbed with mustard and lightly seasoned with salt and pepper. Lay on another piece of buttered bread. Cover the little sandwiches with a damp towel until ready to eat.

Makes as many as you have cress and bread for

NOTE: Richer, softer bread, like an old-fashioned potato bread or whole wheat, seems to work best for these sandwiches. The flavor of the cress melts right into the bread. These sandwiches are also good without the cold chicken.

terra cotta eggs

✕✕✕

These eggs, cooked in big pots with brown onion skins, were not just prepared every year for Easter, although they are ideal for Easter egg hunts (they're harder to find because of the natural color). They can also be brought in a basket to a picnic. The natural dye produced from the onion skins colors the eggs a beautiful terra cotta or radobe color. Some people even went to the trouble of wrapping soggy onion skins around each egg so they became more of a marbleized color. These eggs taste better than regular hard-boiled eggs. Don't even ask why.

About a month before you plan to cook the eggs, ask your produce manager for dry onion skins. They are usually peeled off every day and thrown away. Collect enough skins to fill your pot halfway. The day before cooking the eggs, make the natural dye.

Dry golden-brown onion skins
2 yellow onions, quartered
1 tablespoon salt
12 eggs

PUT THE ONION SKINS IN A LARGE POT with water to cover. They should be completely submerged. Add the onions and salt. Simmer over low heat for 1 hour. Turn off the heat and let the skins steep overnight. In the morning, you will have a pot of orangish dye. Using tongs, pull out most of the skins and discard.

ADD THE EGGS TO THE POT, bring to a boil, and cook over medium heat for 12 minutes. Turn off the heat and let the eggs steep for 10 minutes more. Remove, reserving the dye (you can reuse it for another batch) and let cool.

Makes 12

VARIATION: To flavor the eggs more, lift them out after 10 minutes of cooking, using a small strainer. Crack the shell all over using a table knife. (Don't worry, the whites are already set.) Place the cracked eggs back into the pot. Turn off the heat and let them steep for 10 minutes. They will absorb some of the onion flavor and, if you have done a good job of cracking, will be streaked with terra cotta. You cannot reuse this dye.

grandmama's oyster loaf

———————— ✕✕✕ ————————

While Grandpa's brothers ran Rancho Los Tularcitos, he busied himself with his fashionable haberdashery in downtown San Jose. He knew everyone and dressed some of the most important men in town. It was not unusual for him to get home late because he stopped off for a whiskey and a chat with his cronies at his favorite saloon. Following this refreshment, he would buy a traditional oyster loaf for Grandmama, who grew quite fond of oyster loaf but silently furious at Grandpa's dalliances.

Almost within minutes of finally having that very modern convenience, the telephone, installed, Grandmama received a call from Aunt Alice that Grandpa was at the saloon with another woman.

When Grandpa finally came home that night with the oyster loaf, Grandmama accused him of infidelity. He asked her where she got her information, and she pointed to the telephone. He ripped the newfangled instrument off the wall, loudly proclaiming, "If that's what you use it for, you won't have it." She never answered me when I asked if she ate the oyster loaf that night.

Life returned to normal in a few weeks. The telephone was reinstalled, the "other woman" never mentioned again, the whiskey stop resumed, and the oyster loaves came back. Grandmama even learned how to make the loaves when Grandpa was too old to go to the saloon.

Oyster loaves make good picnic food, especially if you don't have far to travel.

I long loaf of crusty French or Italian bread

4 tablespoons (½ stick) butter, melted

12 oysters

2 eggs, beaten with I tablespoon water

2 cups finely crushed soda crackers

¼ cup pure olive oil

2 tablespoons butter

Finely ground black pepper

2 tablespoons finely minced parsley

PREHEAT THE OVEN to 325°F.

CUT THE LOAF IN HALF LENGTHWISE and scoop out the insides, leaving 2 shells. Reserve the crumbs for another use. Brush the inside of the bread shells with melted butter. Warm the shells for 5 minutes, or until toasty. Set aside. Turn the oven up to 350°F.

DIP THE OYSTERS IN THE EGGS, letting the excess drip off, and then roll in the cracker crumbs. Heat the oil and 2 tablespoons butter in a skillet over medium heat until foamy. Add the oysters in batches and sauté until golden, turning over once, about 1½ minutes per side. Add more oil if necessary and remove any burnt cracker crumbs from pan. Sprinkle the oysters with pepper and drain on paper towels.

WHEN ALL OF THE OYSTERS ARE FRIED, heap them into the bottom shell, sprinkle with parsley, and cover with the top shell. Press together. Bake for 10 minutes, just to heat the loaf. Remove and serve immediately by cutting in slices. The oysters will fall out of the slices. Or wrap in brown paper or parchment paper, tie up with a string (which is what the saloon did), and carry to your picnic.

Serves 4 as a main course or 6 as an appetizer

NOTE: It is not traditional but a garlicky mayonnaise is quite delicious for dipping the bread and oysters into.

marie's devil's food cake

⋊⋉⋊⋉

Mama made this cake for so many birthday picnics that when anyone asked for birthday cake, it was expected to be this Devil's Food. The cake was iced with Divinity Frosting and was always placed on the glass cake dish covered with a shiny silver cover. Use Whipped Cream Frosting if you are pressed for time.

¾ cup unsweetened cocoa, not Dutch process

1 cup boiling water

2 cups cake flour, sifted

1 teaspoon baking soda

½ teaspoon baking powder

½ teaspoon salt

8 tablespoons (1 stick) butter, slightly softened

¾ cup (packed) brown sugar

¾ cup granulated sugar

1 tablespoon vanilla extract

2 eggs, at room temperature

½ cup buttermilk, at room temperature

1 recipe Divinity Frosting or Whipped Cream Frosting (recipes follow)

PREHEAT THE OVEN to 350°F. Grease two 8-inch cake pans with shortening and line with parchment paper or wax paper. Grease the paper or spray with baker's spray.

STIR THE COCOA POWDER into the water, blending well. Set aside to cool.

MEASURE OUT 2 CUPS OF SIFTED FLOUR by spooning it into the measuring cup and leveling with a knife. Resift the flour together with the baking soda, baking powder, and salt. Set aside.

WHIP THE BUTTER WITH AN ELECTRIC MIXER until fluffy. Slowly add the brown sugar and granulated sugar. Beat until very fluffy, almost 5 minutes. Add the vanilla. Whisk the 2 eggs together until well combined and drizzle into the butter-sugar mixture.

WITH THE MIXER ON LOW SPEED, add a fourth of the flour mixture. Add half of the buttermilk and then a portion of the cocoa mixture. After each addition, beat for just a few seconds. Stop the mixer each time you add ingredients and you will have less spattering and overmixing. Continue adding the dry ingredients, the buttermilk, and the cocoa in 2 more additions ending with the dry ingredients. Remove the bowl from the mixer and use a wide spatula to scrape down the sides. Give 3 or 4 turns with a whisk.

POUR THE BATTER INTO THE PREPARED PANS and place in the middle of the oven. Bake for 24 to 26 minutes or until cake springs back but is not dry when touched. A tester should come out clean, without a chocolate film. Cool cakes on rack for 10 minutes, then run a thin-bladed knife around the edges. Unmold the cakes. Peel off parchment paper.

FROST WITH DIVINITY FROSTING or Whipped Cream Frosting.

Serves 8 to 10

divinity frosting

3 egg whites
I teaspoon vanilla extract
1¾ cups sugar
I teaspoon corn syrup
⅛ teaspoon salt
½ cup water
8 marshmallows, cut into pieces with scissors
Fresh garden flowers, for decoration (optional)

USING AN ELECTRIC MIXER, beat the egg whites to stiff peaks. Add the vanilla toward the end of mixing. Set aside while you prepare the syrup.

COMBINE THE SUGAR, corn syrup, salt, and water in a saucepan over medium heat, stirring until the mixture comes to a boil. Cover the pan and simmer for 1 minute. This will help dissolve the sugar crystals. Uncover and continue to cook over low to medium heat until when you drop a teaspoon of syrup into a glass of cold water it forms a soft ball (about 238°F), about 8 to 10 minutes.

WITH THE ELECTRIC MIXER ON HIGH SPEED, pour the syrup in a thin stream over the beaten egg whites. Add the marshmallows while the egg whites are still hot so they melt easily. Beat until frosting is of good spreading consistency and cooled down, about 5 minutes longer.

SPREAD THE FROSTING BETWEEN THE LAYERS and over the entire cake, swirling the cloudlike frosting. Decorate the cake with fresh flowers, if you like.

Makes 4 cups, enough to frost an 8-inch layer cake (you will have some left over)

whipped cream frosting

I cup heavy cream, very cold
½ cup powdered sugar
1½ teaspoons vanilla extract
Fresh strawberries or raspberries, for decoration (optional)

USING THE WHISK ATTACHMENT on your mixer, whip the cream until very thick. Add the powdered sugar and vanilla. Continue whipping until fluffy. Spread it between the layers and over the entire cake. At the last minute, decorate with fresh strawberries or raspberries, if you like.

Makes about 2½ cups, enough to frost an 8-inch layer cake

coyotas de manzana

xxx

Coyotas, or flat empanadas or turnovers, were considered more of a traveling food or picnic food than a dessert. They were also filled with pieces of Cajeta de Membrillo (page 218) but we liked apple filling better.

Empanada Dough

> 2 cups unbleached all-purpose flour
>
> ½ teaspoon salt
>
> 1 tablespoon sugar
>
> ½ teaspoon baking powder
>
> ½ cup shortening
>
> ⅓ cup sour cream, thinned with 2 tablespoons milk

Apple Filling

> 3 apples, such as Granny Smith or Pippin, peeled, cored, and diced
>
> 1 tablespoon lemon juice
>
> 3 tablespoons sugar
>
> 2 teaspoons flour

Topping

> 2 tablespoons milk, for brushing pastry
>
> 2 tablespoons sugar, mixed with ½ teaspoon ground cinnamon

COMBINE THE FLOUR, salt, sugar, and baking powder in a mixing bowl or the bowl of a food processor and mix to blend. Add pieces of shortening, using a fork or pulsing the processor until you have crumbs. Stir in the sour cream and milk mixture. Blend or pulse to obtain a coarse mixture. Add 1 tablespoon more milk if there are any dry spots. Push the dough together into a flat disk. Wrap in plastic wrap and refrigerate for 20 minutes.

PLACE THE APPLES IN A BOWL and toss with lemon juice, sugar, and flour.

PREHEAT THE OVEN to 375°F.

DIVIDE THE DOUGH INTO 12 EQUAL PIECES and shape into flat circles. Roll each one out on a floured board until 5 to 6 inches across. Place ¼ cup apple filling on 6 of the circles. Moisten the edges with water. Place a second circle on top of the apple filling. Turn up the edges and pinch to seal. Brush the tops with milk and sprinkle with cinnamon sugar. Use a fork to prick rows of holes to release steam while baking.

PLACE THE COYOTAS ON A BAKING SHEET lined with parchment paper. Bake for 10 minutes. Turn the heat down to 350°F and bake for 20 minutes longer, until golden. Place on racks to cool. Eat while warm. To store, wrap in foil. They will keep for a day.

Makes 6 coyotas

postres

in the beginning, California ranchos were known more for their outdoor style of living and passion for barbecuing than for their desserts. The kitchens turned out hearty stews and soups, frijoles, and tortillas. Desserts were mostly fresh fruit, fruit paste like *Cajeta de Membrillo*, or quince paste, or fruit preserved in heavy syrup. The sophistication of Mexican baroque desserts was not

Who would have guessed that little Marie would grow up to be famous for her Lemon Meringue Pie and Devil's Food Cake?

found in the early backwater towns of San Francisco and Pueblo Los Angeles. Only when California opened up did cake arrive.

In the early years, Spain was so worried about covetous nations getting their foot in the door that they heavily restricted California's trade with other countries. A couple of ships a year were officially permitted to bring in supplies to California harbors. Once the missions developed the cottage industries that turned out native products, however, the padres needed buyers; hence, the fathers became very adept at smuggling. Still, certain luxuries like sugar and chocolate from Mexico were hard to obtain. When Mexico took over from Spain in 1821, it maintained trading restrictions along with imposing a heavy duty. It was still difficult to make a good cake.

With United States occupation in 1846, trade opened up and luxuries became available. To civilize their social life, the foreigners now free to stay in California introduced the joys of tea time. If given half a chance, Californios loved to adopt any custom, strange or not, that had to do with food. They embraced tea time as if it were their own, and that meant cakes, cookies, jams, curds, and biscuits were necessary. Most simple rancho kitchens, without any great knowledge of fine dessert-making, were hard-pressed. Many wealthy families brought cooks in from Boston, New York, or Paris. We had little wealth, but within the family we had someone with real dessert-making talent.

Nicolassa, one of the daughters of María Higuera, discovered her life's passion through tragedy. By some mysterious illness that even now no one can identify, she was struck blind at the age of sixteen. She had already shown a propensity for cooking and discovered the joys of pastry. Good pastry makers work by touch, and everyone said that Nicolassa had the hands of an angel. She never married but remained on the rancho with her two bachelor brothers. No one else could match her skill nor did they try until her niece, my mother Marie, showed interest even as a young girl. Under the tutelage of her aunt, Mama turned out scores of pies by the time she was fourteen, probably giving Aunt Nick a needed break. They made fruit pies all summer from the rancho's bountiful orchards of cherries, peaches, and apricots, and walnut pies in October. Lemon meringue pie was always in demand. Boysenberry and apple pies were baked when stone fruit was out of season.

Puddings were made as everyday comfort food and there was always a jar filled with cookies, the favorites being the soft molasses cookies and the Fig Empanaditas. When someone came to dinner, the first thing they started looking for—we laughed about their darting eyes—was one of Mama's desserts.

The Blending Fork

I was introduced to the wonders of a blending fork twenty-six years ago by the renowned cook Simca Beck, and I have never been without it ever since then. It has a thick aluminum handle and four pointed prongs about 2½ inches long. It gives me a certain pleasure to know that I could go anywhere with my fork and make tortillas or pie dough and not have to plug in something. The blending fork, far better for pastry than a pastry blender, can often be found in hardware stores or general cookware stores. Don't get me wrong—I still love my food processor, too.

aunt nicolassa's favorite pie crust

✕✕✕

I asked everyone in the family if they had this recipe, and no one did. Then, while working on this book, I received an omen. I was looking in an old notebook belonging to my mother, and a scribbled piece of paper fell out with exact instructions for this pie crust, written in my grandmother's hand. The technique is slightly different than usual recipes.

½ cup vegetable shortening, at room temperature

4 tablespoons (½ stick) butter, cold but not hard

1 teaspoon salt

1 teaspoon sugar

2 cups sifted all-purpose flour, or more as needed

5 to 6 tablespoons ice water

PUT THE SHORTENING AND BUTTER in a large mixing bowl and cream until fluffy, adding salt and sugar. The butter will remain in little bits. Add flour. Use a large blending fork or your fingertips to mix until the mixture looks crumbly. Add ice water by the tablespoonful, tossing with the fork or your fingers. Stop adding water when the pastry easily adheres together. Do not overmix. Press the dough together in a flat disk and refrigerate for 10 minutes.

DIVIDE THE DOUGH with one part a little larger than the other.

ROLL OUT THE LARGER PART OF DOUGH on a floured surface to fit a 9-inch pie pan. Use a spatula to keep lifting up the dough so it doesn't stick. Place it in the pan. Roll out the second half for the top crust.

Makes crust for one 9-inch double-crust pie

mama's apricot pie

———— ✕✕✕ ————

When apricots were at their peak in early July, Uncle John sent for his niece, Marie, to pay a long visit to the rancho—as long as the apricots lasted. It was understood that she would make all the pies he desired and since he ate one pie at a sitting, she baked four at a time.

>   1 recipe Aunt Nicolassa's Favorite Pie Crust (page 203)
>   6 cups ripe apricots, pitted and quartered
>   1 tablespoon lemon juice
>   ½ to ¾ cup sugar, depending on sweetness of fruit
>   2 tablespoons flour
>   ½ teaspoon almond extract

PREHEAT THE OVEN to 400°F.

ROLL OUT THE BOTTOM CRUST OF THE PIE and place in a 9-inch glass pie plate. Combine the apricots, lemon juice, sugar (using the lesser amount first and adding to taste), flour, and almond extract in a large bowl. Stir to mix well and pour the fruit into the pie shell. Roll out the second half of the dough and fit over the top of pie. Press together the edges and flute. Cut 3 slits in the top of the pie for steam to escape.

BAKE IN THE MIDDLE OF THE OVEN for 10 minutes. Turn the heat down to 375°F and bake for about 40 minutes more, or until the pie is golden brown. If apricot juices start to leak out of the pie, line a baking sheet with foil and place on the bottom of the oven to catch the juices.

Makes one 9-inch pie

NOTE: Mama liked naturally juicy pies, barely thickened. You can add 1 tablespoon more flour or quick-cooking tapioca for a thicker fruit filling.

sister's famous
walnut orchard pie

✕✕✕

Much of Rancho Los Tularcitos's income during the 1930s and '40s came from its abundant walnut orchards, but we also had five black walnut trees in our backyard in Los Altos when I was growing up. Mama used walnuts lavishly in everything, but she had been known for her pie since her growing-up days on the rancho. This pie is similar to pecan pie but more custardy and less sweet.

Flaky Pastry

 1 ⅓ cups bleached all-purpose flour

 2 teaspoons sugar

 ½ teaspoon salt

 8 tablespoons (1 stick) butter, chilled and cut into small pieces

 1 small egg or ¾ of a large egg, beaten

 3 teaspoons cold milk

Walnut Filling

 3 eggs

 ½ cup (packed) brown sugar

 ½ cup heavy cream

 1 scant cup light corn syrup

 2 teaspoons vanilla extract

 1 cup chopped walnuts

 8 whole walnuts, for garnish

TO PREPARE THE PASTRY, combine the flour, sugar, and salt in a mixing bowl or in the workbowl of a food processor and mix by stirring with a fork or pulsing. Add the butter and work it in with a fork or pulse with the processor until the mixture has the texture of coarse cornmeal. Beat the egg with the milk and drizzle all but 1 tablespoon into the flour mixture. Pinch the pastry together. If it easily sticks together, stop adding liquid; if still dry, add the rest of liquid. The pastry should not be wet or sticky.

DUMP THE PASTRY OUT ONTO A FLOURED BOARD and push it across the board with the heel of your hand. Scrape up and form into a 6-inch round. Wrap in plastic wrap and chill for 20 minutes. You can make the dough a couple of days in advance and freeze it, well wrapped. Thaw out at room temperature for 1½ hours. The dough is even flakier after freezing.

ROLL OUT THE DOUGH to fit a 9- or 10-inch pie pan. Flute the edges. Chill while you prepare the filling.

PREHEAT THE OVEN to 350°F.

TO PREPARE THE FILLING, beat the eggs in a bowl and add the brown sugar, cream, corn syrup, and vanilla. Stir in the chopped nuts. Pour the filling into the pastry shell and arrange the whole walnuts around the edge of the pie. Bake for 55 minutes. Do not overbake. The filling will continue to set up after the pie is removed from the oven.

Makes one 9- or 10-inch pie

great lemon meringue

✕✕✕

Mama's four brothers adored her pies, but the lemon meringue reigned supreme over all other pies and was the one they always begged her to make. There had to be several of these pies for any gathering attended by all of my uncles.

    1 recipe Flaky Pastry (page 207)
Lemon Filling
    1¾ cups sugar
    ½ teaspoon salt
    ½ cup plus 1 tablespoon cornstarch
    2 cups cold water
    4 egg yolks
    2 teaspoons grated lemon zest
    ⅓ cup lemon juice
    1 teaspoon pure vanilla extract
    1 tablespoon butter
Meringue
    4 egg whites
    ½ teaspoon cream of tartar
    ½ cup sugar
    ½ teaspoon vanilla extract

ROLL OUT THE PASTRY to fit a 10-inch glass pie pan. Trim off all but a 1-inch over-hang. Turn the edges of the pastry under and flute the edges. Prick the bottom of the pie shell with a fork and chill in the freezer for 20 minutes.

PREHEAT THE OVEN to 400°F.

REMOVE THE PIE SHELL from the freezer and line it with a piece of aluminum foil. Add 1 cup dry beans as weights to keep the shell from puffing. Bake for 8 minutes. Remove the beans and foil, reserving the beans for future use as pastry weights. Bake the shell for about 15 minutes more, or until golden. Remove and set aside.

TURN THE HEAT DOWN to 350°F.

TO PREPARE THE FILLING, whisk the sugar, salt, and cornstarch together in a saucepan. Slowly add cold water. Whisk to remove any lumps. Place the saucepan over medium heat and cook for 8 to 10 minutes. The filling will thicken rapidly. Remove from the heat. Drizzle a couple of tablespoons of the hot mixture into the egg yolks to temper them. Then whisk the egg mixture back to the custard. Return to low heat for 1 minute, whisking continually so lumps do not form. Remove from the heat and stir in the lemon zest, lemon juice, vanilla, and butter. Cover the pudding with a lid to keep it warm while you prepare the meringue.

TO PREPARE THE MERINGUE, beat the egg whites and cream of tartar with an electric mixer on high speed until foamy. Slowly add the sugar by tablespoons. Whisk until snowy, soft peaks form. Add the vanilla. Be careful not to beat the meringue into stiff peaks, or it will be difficult to swirl on top of the pie.

POUR THE WARM LEMON FILLING into the pie shell. Place huge dollops of meringue around the edges and in the center of the pie. Seal the meringue to the edges of the crust. This will help prevent weepy meringue. Bake for 12 to 15 minutes, or until the tips of the meringue are golden.

Serves 6 to 8

deep dish boysenberry pie

———— ✕✕✕ ————

My father had a huge boysenberry patch in our Los Altos backyard, and I hated picking the berries. By the time I had enough for a pie, my arms were covered in scratches, from reaching into the bushes. The pie made up for some of my injuries.

Boysenberry Filling

  8 cups boysenberries

  ¾ cup sugar

  3 tablespoons cornstarch

  I tablespoon lemon juice

Top Crust

  I ¼ cups all-purpose flour

  I teaspoon baking powder

  I tablespoon sugar

  ½ teaspoon salt

  8 tablespoons (I stick) butter, chilled and cut into small pieces

  I egg

  3 to 4 tablespoons cold milk

  I teaspoon vanilla extract

COMBINE THE BERRIES, sugar, cornstarch, and lemon juice in a bowl and set aside while you prepare the pastry. Oil a 2-quart glass or ceramic baking dish.

PREHEAT THE OVEN to 375°F.

TO PREPARE THE CRUST, combine the flour, baking powder, sugar, and salt. Work the butter into the flour mixture using a blending fork. Or combine the flour and add the butter in a food processor. Whisk the egg, milk, and vanilla together and add to the flour-butter mixture, stirring to distribute liquid. Wrap in plastic wrap and chill for 10 minutes.

FORM THE DOUGH INTO A FLAT DISK and roll it out on a floured board to fit the baking dish.

POUR THE BERRIES INTO THE DISH and place the pastry on top, fluting the edges against the sides of the dish. Bake for 30 minutes, or until crust is golden and berry juices are thickened and bubbling.

Makes 1 pie

the favorite apple pie

During the Gold Rush, a hungry homesick gentleman in distress was known to give up all of his gold nuggets for one apple pie. Pie bakers have been in demand ever since. This apple pie uses a variety of apples to add to the flavor, and they are cooked briefly before adding to the pie shell.

> 5 pounds apples, preferably a mixture of Granny Smith, Pippin,
>   Golden Delicious, or heirloom
> 2 tablespoons lemon juice
> 1 tablespoon butter
> 1 cup (packed) light brown sugar
> ¼ cup granulated sugar
> 1 teaspoon cinnamon
> 2 tablespoons flour
> 1 tablespoon cornstarch
> 1 recipe Aunt Nicolassa's Favorite Pie Crust (page 203)
> 1 egg plus 1 tablespoon milk, for glaze
> 2 teaspoons sugar

PEEL, CORE, AND SLICE THE APPLES ½ inch thick. Pour lemon juice over the apple slices and stir well to coat. Place the apples in a deep pot and add the butter, brown sugar, granulated sugar, and cinnamon. Set over medium heat and cook for 5 minutes. Add the flour and cornstarch and simmer for 5 minutes more. Transfer to a bowl and let the apple mixture cool.

PREHEAT THE OVEN to 375°F.

DIVIDE THE PIE CRUST DOUGH IN TWO, making one part larger. Roll out to fit into a 9-inch glass pie plate. Trim the overhang. Fill with the apples. Roll out the remaining pastry to a 10-inch circle and fit over top of pie. Press the edges together and flute. Cut several slits into the top pastry to allow for release of steam. Combine the eggs and milk and brush the glaze over the top crust and sprinkle with sugar. Place on the bottom shelf of the oven and bake for 1 hour 15 minutes or until golden on top and the juices are bubbling thickly. If the juices start to leak, line a baking sheet with foil and place on the bottom of the oven.

Serves 6

grandmama's prune cake

xxx

This cake was justifiably famous inside and outside the family. Grandmama's darkly rich cake, the same patina as her antique dining table, was served for Christmas like a fruit cake. For Easter it was baked in a lamb mold and covered in coconut icing.

1½ cups dried prunes

¾ cup water

8 ounces (1 stick) butter

½ cup (packed) brown sugar

1 cup granulated sugar

2 eggs

1½ cups all-purpose flour

½ teaspoon salt

1 teaspoon baking soda

1 teaspoon baking powder

2 tablespoons cocoa powder

1½ teaspoons ground cinnamon

½ teaspoon ground cloves

¼ teaspoon ground nutmeg

½ teaspoon ground allspice

1 cup chopped walnuts

Icing

2 tablespoons butter

1½ cups sifted powdered sugar

3 tablespoons hot milk, or more as needed

1 teaspoon vanilla extract

PREHEAT THE OVEN to 350°F. Grease a 12-cup Bundt mold.

SIMMER THE PRUNES in the water for 10 minutes to soften. Drain, reserving the liquid. Chop the prunes into very small pieces using a food processor.

CREAM THE BUTTER in a mixing bowl until fluffy, adding the brown sugar and the granulated sugar. Add the eggs, one at a time, beating after each one. Put the flour, salt, baking soda, baking powder, cocoa, cinnamon, cloves, nutmeg, and allspice in a bowl and whisk to combine. Set aside.

ADD THE PRUNES and ¼ cup of the reserved juice to the butter-egg mixture, blending well. Stir in the dry ingredients and walnuts. Pour immediately into the mold and bake for 40 to 45 minutes, or until a tester comes out clean. Cool the cake. If possible, wrap in foil for 1 day before serving. The flavors will deepen and become richer, as with fruitcake. Glaze with icing just before serving.

TO PREPARE THE ICING, blend the butter into the powdered sugar, adding hot milk and vanilla while whisking out lumps. Add more milk if necessary to get a good consistency. Spread over top and sides of cake.

Serves 8

angel pudding

———— ✕✕✕ ————

This pudding, true to the Spanish love of custards and puddings, was doled out to sick children like miracle medicine. This meant that all of the children in the family could get sick in a flash and then get miraculously well when the angel pudding arrived. We found out later that it was all part of the angel pudding test. If a child didn't want the pudding, he or she was seriously ill!

  1 cup sugar
  ½ cup all-purpose flour minus 1 tablespoon
  4 cups whole milk
  4 eggs, separated
  2 teaspoons vanilla extract
  Ground cinnamon, for dusting

WHISK TOGETHER THE SUGAR, flour, and milk in a 2-quart saucepan over medium heat. It will take about 5 minutes for the pudding to begin to thicken. While the milk is simmering, beat the egg yolks. Add about ¼ cup of the hot milk to the yolks to temper them, and then whisk back into the milk mixture. Reduce the heat to low. Keep stirring the pudding, cooking for a total of 10 minutes, until thickened. Remove from the heat and add the vanilla.

BEAT THE EGG WHITES TO SOFT PEAKS. Fold into the hot pudding, which will continue to cook the meringue. Pour the pudding into a glass bowl and sprinkle with a light dusting of cinnamon.

Serves 6 (or several bowls for a sick child)

crema de arroz
[rice cream]

Grandmama was known to have a sixth sense when angel pudding was needed but Mama's pudding of choice was rice cream.

1½ cups water
½ teaspoon salt
½ cup short-grain rice
3 cups whole milk
1 cinnamon stick
½ to ¾ cup sugar, to taste
3 egg yolks
1 teaspoon vanilla extract
1 tablespoon butter
Ground cinnamon, for dusting

BRING THE WATER AND SALT TO A BOIL in a 3-quart saucepan and stir in the rice. Cover and steam over low heat for 20 minutes. Stir in the milk, cinnamon stick, and sugar. Simmer, uncovered, over medium heat for 25 minutes or until the milk starts to coagulate around the edges and you have the beginnings of a pudding. Do not walk away—stir it frequently. The liquidy mixture will suddenly look creamier. Beat the egg yolks in a small bowl and drizzle in a few tablespoons of hot rice cream. Stir back into the rice pudding, keeping on low heat for just 2 or 3 minutes. Remove from the heat and add the vanilla and butter. Dust with ground cinnamon. The pudding will thicken more after chilling.

Serves 6

mama and br'er rabbit's best gingerbread

✕✕✕

Mama made the highest, lightest gingerbread I have ever tasted. This recipe appeared in my original *California Rancho Cooking* book, but I cannot leave it out here for it is too good. It was always served piled high with whipped cream as a treat on winter evenings. The original recipe was inspired by Br'er Rabbit molasses in the 1940s. I use this same molasses for the Puerquitos (page 214).

8 tablespoons (1 stick) butter
½ cup sugar
2 eggs
2 cups unbleached all-purpose flour
½ cup whole wheat flour
1 ½ teaspoons baking soda
1 teaspoon ground cinnamon
¾ teaspoon ground ginger
½ teaspoon ground cloves
½ teaspoon salt
1 cup molasses
1 cup hot water
3 teaspoons vanilla extract
1 cup heavy cream
2 to 3 tablespoons powdered sugar

PREHEAT THE OVEN to 350°F. Grease a 9-inch square pan.

CREAM THE BUTTER AND SUGAR in a mixing bowl until light and fluffy. Add the eggs, one at a time. In a large bowl, whisk together the all-purpose flour, whole wheat flour, baking soda, cinnamon, ginger, cloves, and salt. Combine the molasses, water, and 2 teaspoons of the vanilla and stir well.

ADD THE DRY INGREDIENTS to the butter-sugar mixture alternately with the liquid, ending with the dry mixture. Beat well after each addition. Pour into the pan. Bake for 45 minutes. Serve the gingerbread warm. Lightly whip the cream, flavoring it with powdered sugar and the remaining 1 teaspoon vanilla.

Serves 6 to 8

puerquitos
[piglet molasses cookies]

✕✕✕

In front of the grandiose post office in Querétaro, Mexico, a man appeared every afternoon with a tray of the fat molasses cookies known as Puerquitos. I never went to the post office in the morning because of this and, I never failed, every afternoon, to buy my Puerquito. It reminded me of my mother's soft molasses cookies. An old recipe gave me the clue that by stirring baking soda into molasses you can achieve the perfect soft texture. As my friend Beth Hensperger said, "Now pigs can fly."

8 tablespoons (1 stick) butter

¾ cup (packed) dark brown sugar

1 egg

2 teaspoons vanilla extract

3 tablespoons dark coffee

3½ cups unbleached all-purpose flour

1 teaspoon salt

1 teaspoon ground ginger

1 teaspoon ground cinnamon

1½ teaspoons baking soda

¾ cup molasses

1 egg beaten with 2 teaspoons water, for glaze

BEAT THE BUTTER IN A MIXING BOWL until fluffy, adding the brown sugar, egg, vanilla, and coffee. The mixture will look curdled.

STIR TOGETHER THE FLOUR, salt, ginger, and cinnamon until well-blended. Stir the baking soda into the molasses, which will become a bit foamy. This technique gives the cookies their distinctive texture.

USING AN ELECTRIC MIXER, beat the molasses into the sugar mixture. Add the flour mixture, 1 cup at a time, until the dough is well blended. Divide the dough in half, flatten into a disk, and wrap in plastic wrap. Chill for at least 2 hours to make dough easier to handle.

PREHEAT THE OVEN to 375°F 30 minutes before baking time.

ROLL OUT A PORTION OF THE DOUGH to ½ inch thick on a floured surface. Cut into piglets or use any large animal cutter, at least 4 x 3½-inches. (My Mexican puerquito mold looks as if it was constructed in an auto body shop!) Remove the dough scraps and chill before rerolling. Carefully place the cookies on a parchment paper–lined baking sheet. Brush with the egg glaze. Bake for 10 to 12 minutes. Do not overbake, as the puerquitos are meant to be soft. Cool on racks.

Makes about 18 large puerquitos

NOTE: The cookies will keep for 2 weeks in a tin.

VARIATION: Around the holidays these cookies are frosted with bright pink icing. To make the icing, combine 1 tablespoon soft butter, 1½ cups powdered sugar, and 2 tablespoons boiling water. Add a droplet of red food coloring. Frost the pigs after baking and cooling. Give each one a chocolate chip or raisin eye.

polenta dulce

✕✕✕

These creamy little squares taste similar to the *leche frita*, or fried custard, found in Spain, but better, because of the flavor added by the semolina. I watched a whole plate of these disappear at a dinner party—before dinner was served.

    4 cups whole milk
    1 cup sugar
    ½ cup finely ground semolina
    ½ cup regular Cream of Wheat
    Grated zest of 1 lemon
    2 tablespoons lemon juice
    1 teaspoon vanilla extract
    2 eggs, beaten
    2 cups corn flakes, finely crushed
    ½ to ¾ cup canola oil, for frying

BRING THE MILK TO A SIMMER in a 3-quart saucepan over medium heat. Stir in the sugar. Slowly add the semolina, Cream of Wheat, lemon zest, and juice. When thickened to a pudding consistency, remove from the heat and add the vanilla. Pour into a greased 13 x 9-inch dish and refrigerate until firm or chill, well wrapped, overnight. Cut into 1-inch squares.

BEAT THE EGGS. Finely crush the corn flakes. You can do this in a food processor but leave some texture. Dip the custard squares into the beaten egg, letting excess liquid drip off. Roll in cornflake crumbs.

HEAT THE OIL IN A SKILLET until hot and fry the squares until golden brown on both sides. Serve immediately or make several hours in advance.

Serves 8 to 10 as a sweet appetizer or 6 as dessert

biscochitos

✕✕✕

Biscochitos were the traditional sugar cookie served at Christmas. They were made with lard, which gives them their distinctive texture. You can substitute butter, which makes up for any of its shortcomings with flavor.

⅔ cup lard or unsalted butter

⅓ cup unsalted butter

I cup sugar

2 teaspoons vanilla extract

2 tablespoons brandy

I egg, beaten

I teaspoon anise seeds, crushed in a mortar or with a knife

I cup cake flour

I¾ cups all-purpose flour

½ teaspoon baking powder

½ teaspoon salt

¼ cup sugar, blended with ½ teaspoon ground cinnamon

BEAT THE LARD AND BUTTER (or use all butter) with an electric mixer until fluffy. Slowly add the sugar, vanilla, brandy, egg, and anise seeds. Whisk together the cake flour, all-purpose flour, baking powder, and salt and then add slowly to the egg-sugar mixture. The dough should be soft. Wrap in plastic wrap and chill for 2 hours.

PREHEAT THE OVEN to 350°F.

DIVIDE THE DOUGH INTO THIRDS. Roll out 1 portion on a floured board while you keep the remainder in the refrigerator. The dough should be about ¼ inch thick. Cut out shapes using a mold with a distinctive shape. (I use a cutter shaped like a little mission. In New Mexico, they prefer a fleur-de-lis shape.) Place the cookies on baking sheets lined with parchment paper.

SPRINKLE THE CINNAMON SUGAR over the tops of the cookies. Bake for 15 minutes, or until the cookies are golden around the edges. Cool on racks.

Makes 2 dozen large cookies

wedding cookies

✕✕✕

I learned how to make these meltingly good cookies while living in San Miguel de Allende, Mexico. They were also baked on some California ranchos for weddings, just as is still done in Mexico. Traditionally, the cookies are each wrapped in different colors of *papel de china*, or brightly colored tissue paper, and then piled in baskets.

2 cups all-purpose flour

1 cup pecans, lightly toasted

1 cup (2 sticks) unsalted butter, slightly softened but still cool

½ cup powdered sugar

1 teaspoon vanilla extract

½ teaspoon almond extract

1½ cups powdered sugar, for coating

Colored tissue paper, cut into 6-inch squares

GRIND THE FLOUR AND PECANS together in a food processor, pulsing until the nuts are finely ground. (The flour keeps the nuts from becoming pasty.) Cut the butter into pieces, drop into the workbowl, and process in short pulses. Add ½ cup of the powdered sugar, the vanilla, and almond extract. Transfer the cookie dough to a mixing bowl and work with a wooden spoon or your hands. Wrap the dough in plastic wrap and chill for 30 minutes.

PREHEAT THE OVEN to 350°F.

FORM THE COOKIES INTO WALNUT-SIZE BALLS. Bake on ungreased baking sheets for 14 minutes, or until golden around the edges. Cool the cookies briefly on racks and then place on wax paper. Sift powdered sugar on top, turning the cookies to entirely coat with sugar. The slight warmth of the cookie will make the coating adhere.

WHEN COOKIES ARE COOL, place each on in the center of a square of tissue paper. Bring up the corners of the tissue to the center and twist to close. I try to use at least 5 or 6 different colors of tissue. Place all of the wrapped cookies in a basket to show their colors to best advantage.

Makes about 35 wedding cookies

cajeta de membrillo
[quince paste]

xxx

Quince paste was one of the most popular sweets of Old California and to this day it remains popular in Mexico, South America, Spain, and Italy. It is even sold in gourmet food catalogs. The heady perfume of quince simmering is almost as good as its taste. Serve Cajeta de Membrillo after dinner with cheese and coffee or give some away as a gift.

These directions were given to be by Isabel Robles, a rancho descendant. Until I followed her directions to briefly bake the membrillo at low heat, I had runny paste. Isabel said that in the old days, the membrillo was dried out in the sun.

    4 pounds quince, washed
    2 Granny Smith apples, peeled
    8 cups sugar

QUINCE IS VERY HARD even when ripe, so be careful when cutting. Quarter and discard the seeds of the quince and apples. Place the fruit in a large pot and cover with water. Bring to a boil and gently simmer over low heat until completely tender, 40 to 45 minutes. Lift out the fruit and place in colander to drain and cool. Reserve the cooking water.

PURÉE THE FRUIT IN 4 OR 5 BATCHES using a blender, adding ¾ cup reserved cooking water to each batch. Pour each batch of purée into a very large pot (use a pot three times the volume of the purée). You should have about 2½ quarts of fruit purée. Add the sugar, stirring to blend. Bring to a simmer and cook over low heat for about 1 hour, stirring frequently. The purée will reduce in volume by one third as the water evaporates. Keep on the lowest possible heat and stir with a long spoon as the purée tends to sputter and spurt out of the pot. When you can push the spoon across the bottom of the pot, making a track, the fruit is cooked enough.

POUR THE FRUIT PURÉE into two 13 x 9-inch baking dishes lined with parchment paper. Let it air-dry for 2 days, covered with a towel. If the paste is still too soft to cut into squares, place in a 250-degree oven and bake for just 10 minutes. Turn off heat and leave the membrillo overnight in the oven so it will continue to dry out.

CUT THE PASTE INTO SQUARES. Place in wax paper–lined tins with tight lids. The membrillo becomes even more flavorful and moist with age. Store in the refrigerator for longer keeping.

Makes about 2 pounds

conserva de calabaza

✕✕✕

When the rare ingredient of sugar could be obtained in the late eighteenth and nine-teenth centuries, ranchero cooks made fruit pastes because they could be stored for months. A little piece of conserva might satisfy the sweet tooth.

This recipe, from the presidio days of Santa Barbara, was made every year by the Ortega family. It is still made on the rancho of Elizabeth Erro Hvolboll.

> 1 pumpkin, *chilacayote* or other thin-skinned squash variety (4 to 5 pounds)
> ½ cup slaked lime (see Note)
> 7 pounds (14 cups) brown sugar
> 1 teaspoon whole cloves
> 1 teaspoon ground ginger
> 1 teaspoon ground cinnamon

CUT THE PUMPKIN INTO QUARTERS and remove the seeds and excess fibers. Remove the skin. Cut into 3 x 1-inch pieces. Wash, place in a nonreactive container, cover with water, and sprinkle lime over all. Stir to mix well and let sit overnight.

WASH THE PUMPKIN CUBES WELL under running water to remove the lime.

MAKE A SYRUP by combining 5 pounds of the brown sugar and 2 quarts of water in a large saucepan. Add the spices and pumpkin. Bring to a boil and simmer over medium heat for 1 hour. Let sit overnight.

ADD 2 CUPS MORE SUGAR, bring to a boil and simmer for 1 hour. Let sit overnight again.

ADD THE REMAINING 2 CUPS BROWN SUGAR, bring to a boil, and simmer for 1 hour. Let sit overnight. The syrup will be concentrated by now.

PACK THE HOT PUMPKIN CANDY in sterilized jars and fill within a couple of inches of the top with hot syrup. You can seal the jars but it is not necessary due to the high concentration of sugar.

IF YOU WANT TO DRY THE CANDY, place it to dry on screens or parchment paper. In the past, this was done outdoors in the sun, which meant great visitations by ants and yellow jackets. I prefer to dry the candy in a 250-degree oven for 30 minutes. Then turn off the oven and leave the candy in it overnight. The candy should be crisp on the outside and soft in the center.

Makes enough for the whole rancho

NOTE: Slaked lime, or calcium hydroxide, is known as *cal* and can be purchased at a tortilla factory.

chocolate velvet

xxx

A rich cup of foamy chocolate was the first way the Old World was introduced to chocolate. The Aztecs took their chocolate in liquid form, unsweetened. Desserts and chocolate candy came much later. Chocolate was included in pack rations so the sustaining drink could be taken as *soldados de cuera*, or soldiers, made their way up the Anza trail. Later, all the enrichments were added, including an egg to help create more foam when the chocolate was whipped and also to make it thicker.

For weddings, chocolate beaters were kept busy. If chocolate foam remained in the bottom of the cup after it was drained, the marriage would last.

    2 tablespoons sugar
    Pinch of ground cinnamon
    2 teaspoons maizena or cornstarch
    4 cups whole milk
    3 ounces semisweet chocolate, chopped
    I egg, beaten
    I teaspoon vanilla extract

BLEND THE SUGAR, CINNAMON, AND MAIZENA into ½ cup of the milk in a saucepan. Add the remaining milk and chocolate. Bring to a gentle simmer over medium heat. When hot, stir a little of the milk mixture into the beaten egg to temper it, then whisk back into the pot of chocolate. Continue to whisk to slightly thicken. Remove from the heat and add the vanilla. Pour the hot chocolate into a tall pitcher so you can beat the chocolate to make it foamy. Twirl a whisk or *molinillo* between your palms as if you were rubbing them together. You can build up a couple of inches of foam doing this. Pour chocolate into wide cups and serve.

Serves 6

El Fin

California gatherings could not end until
everyone sang "Adios, Adios, Amores " The true meaning
of the song was widely interpreted until it just came to signify a
goodbye, an end of the day, an end to the fiesta, an ending.

Adíos, adíos, amores
Adíos, adíos, amores, Adíos porque me ausento
Por tanto sentimiento
Que tu me has dado a mi
Por eso ya no quiero
Amar más en la vida, A mi patria querida
Me voy a retirar.

xxx

Farewell, farewell love,
Farewell, farewell, for now I must part
From all the pain
That you have given me
For that reason, I choose not to love you more.
To my beloved country
I am returning.

Resources for Rancho Ingredients

The Baker's Catalogue
(King Arthur Flour)
P.O. Box 876
Norwich, VT 05055
(800) 827-6836
www.KingArthurFlour.com

Source for a variety of flours, grains, and semolina.

The Chile Shop
109 E. Water St.
Santa Fe, NM 87501
(505) 983-6080
www.thechileshop.com

For dried chile pods and chile powder, namely the great Dixon chile powder (medium hot).

Hobson Gardens
3656 East Hobson Rd.
Roswell, NM 88303
(800) 488-7298
www.hobsongardens.com

For fresh green chiles in season (August through September / October). From mild to very hot. Sun-dried chiles at end of season starting in November.

Pendery's of Texas
1221 Manufacturing St.
Dallas, TX 75207
(800) 533-1870
www.penderys.com

For chile powders and great whole chile pods and dried pods. The best source for real fideos.

Penzey's Spices
P.O. Box 933
Muskego, WI 53150
(800) 741-7787
www.penzeys.com

For chile powders, dried pods, and fresh spices such as cumin, Ceylon or Mexican cinnamon, and oregano. Excellent vanilla and cinnamon sugar.

Santa Cruz Chili and Spice Co.
P.O. Box 177
Tumacacori, AZ 85640
(520) 398-2591
www.santacruzchili.com

For red chile purée made from fresh red chiles every autumn; dried chile powders.

Santa Fe School of Cooking
116 W. San Francisco St.
Santa Fe, NM 87501
(505) 983-4511
www.santafeschoolofcooking
.com

For excellent stoneground masa harina and dried chiles.

Tierra Vegetable Farms
13684 Chalk Hill Rd.
Healdsburg, CA 95448
(888) 7-TIERRA
www.tierravegetables.com

Wonderful freshly smoked chipotles; other dried chiles and Roma tomatoes. At the Marin Farmers' Market on Sundays.

Windrose Farm
5750 El Pharo Rd.
Paso Robles, CA 93446
(805) 239-3757
windrose@tcsh.net

For chipotles smoked in a brick oven using fruit-tree woods; excellent heirloom tomatoes, chiles, and beans; smoked plum tomatoes; chile jams for glazes. At the Santa Barbara Farmers' Market on Saturdays.

All the cheeses required for Mexican and rancho cooking can be found in most supermarkets in California and the Southwest. Queso cotija is a more aged, crumblier cheese which can be substituted with feta cheese. Queso fresco is a fresh cheese with a soft texture and mild flavor. It can be substituted with farmer's cheese or queso blanco. Neither of these cheeses is a melting cheese such as Monterey Jack, Cheddar, or Italian Fontina which are best used for the enchilada fillings.

The Mozzarella Company
2944 Elm St.
Dallas, TX 75226
(800) 798-2954
www.mozzco.com

Carries queso blanco, similar to queso fresco. The version seasoned with epazote and serrano chile is especially good.

Bibliography

Aranda, Antonio Garrido, compilador. *Cultura Alimentaria: Andalucía-América.* Universidad Nacional Autónoma de México, México: 1996.

Bayless, Rick, with Deann Groen Bayless. *Authenic Mexican.* William Morrow and Company, Inc.: New York, 1987.

Bolton, Herbert Eugene. *Outpost of Empire: The Story of The Founding of San Francisco.* Alfred A. Knopf: New York, 1939.

Brown, Helen Evans. *West Coast Cookbook.* Little, Brown, and Company: Boston, 1952.

Cleveland, Bess A. *California Mission Recipes.* Charles E. Tuttle Company: Tokyo, 1965.

Cross, Ralph Herbert. *The Early Inns of California.* Cross and Brandt: San Francisco, 1954.

DeNevi, Donald, editor. *Sketches of Early California: A Collection of Personal Adventures.* Chronicle Books: San Francisco, 1971.

Edwards, Clarence E. *Bohemian San Francisco.* Paul Elder and Company: San Francisco, 1914.

Field, Maria Antonia. *Copa de Oro: Festival Days in Old California.* Cloister Press: San Francisco, 1948.

Goldstone, Maurice. *Food in the Americas.* Northridge, 1977, tract.

Haro, Carlos Brokmann. *La Cocina Mexicana a Través de los Siglos.* D.R. Editorial Clío, Libros y Videos, S.A. de C.V.: México, 1996.

James, George Wharton. *In and Out of the Old Missions.* Little, Brown, and Company: Boston, 1918.

Klein, Maggie Blyth. *The Feast of the Olive.* Aris Books: Berkeley, 1983.

Novo, Salvador. *Cocina Mexicana (Historia Gastronomica).* Editorial Porrúa, S.A.: México, 1973.

Packman, Ana Bégué de. *Early California Hospitality.* Academy Library Guild: Fresno, 1952.

Packman, Ana Bégué de. *Leather Dollars.* The Times Mirror Press: Los Angeles, 1932.

Peyton, James W. *La Cocina de la Frontera.* Red Crane Books: Santa Fe, 1994.

Tannahill, Real. *Food in History.* Three Rivers Press: New York, 1988.

Vega, Luis Antonio de. *Viaje Por La Cocina Española.* Salvat Editores, S.A.: Spain, 1969.

Weber, David J. *The Spanish Frontier in North America.* Yale University Press: New Haven, 1992.

Index

About the Author

Jacqueline Higuera McMahan was born in San Francisco and grew up in Los Altos when it was nothing but walnut and apricot orchards. She is an eighth-generation Californian whose family arrived in 1775 and lived on one of the last Spanish land grant ranchos. Rancho Los Tularcitos (nearly 4,000 acres along the southeastern shores of San Francicso Bay and up over the low-lying Diablo Mountains) was inhabited by the Higuera family and their *descendientes* for almost 130 years. While growing up, McMahan spent weekends on the rancho across the Bay. Over the years, the Higuera family upheld many traditions—the primary one being food. In the Higuera family, the cooks reigned supreme. McMahan began cooking at the age of 8 and took responsibility for family suppers by the age of 13.

After college McMahan lived in Mexico for a time, writing and cooking. Upon returning to the United States, she started a family, and a few years later established a cooking foundation. She studied with Simca Beck, co-author of *Mastering the Art of French Cooking*; Julie Dannenbaum; James Beard; and Paul Prudhomme. In 1983 McMahan, her husband, and two friends started their own publishing venture, The Olive Press, with which she has published six cookbooks, including *The Salsa Book, The Chipotle Chile Book,* and *The Red and Green Chile Book*. She writes a column for the *San Francisco Chronicle* ("South to North"), teaches cooking classes throughout the West, and lives with her husband in the San Gabriel Mountains in Southern California.